PRIME-TIME TELEVISION

Other books by
Fred Goldstein and Stan Goldstein

THE TV GUIDE QUIZ BOOK
STAR TREK SPACEFLIGHT CHRONOLOGY
DO YOU REMEMBER?
THE VIDEO PLAYER'S BACK-POCKET GUIDE SERIES

PRIME-TIME TELEVISION

A PICTORIAL HISTORY FROM MILTON BERLE TO "FALCON CREST"

FRED GOLDSTEIN & STAN GOLDSTEIN

An Opus Book
Crown Publishers,Inc.
New York

Published by Crown Publishers, Inc., One Park Avenue, New York, New York 10016 and simultaneously in Canada by General
Publishing Company Limited

Manufactured in the United States of America

Library of Congress Cataloging in Publication Data

Goldstein, Fred P.
   Prime-time television.

   Includes index.
   1. Television broadcasting—United States—Pictorial works. I. Goldstein, Stan.   II. Title.
PN1992.3.U5G65   1983   791.45′75′0973   83-7804
ISBN 0-517-55071-7

10 9 8 7 6 5 4 3 2 1

First Edition

DEDICATION

To Phyllis, Deb and Sher for their encouragement and love
and
To everyone who enjoys the magic of the picture box

ACKNOWLEDGMENTS

A book of this magnitude requires the cooperation of many people, and indeed many people have contributed. There are a few, however, who deserve to be particularly acknowledged: Sherri Goldstein for historical research, Mike Eisenberg for program data, Ira Golden, Steve Schwartz, and Bruce Block for photo research, Corinne Felder for art direction, Jill DiDomenico for typesetting, and Phyllis Goldstein for her dexterity with a typewriter. One other individual we would like to thank is our editor, Brandt Aymar, for his enthusiasm and cooperation.

CONTENTS

INTRODUCTION

This picture-book history of television will take you on a nostalgic journey that will show you how prime-time TV evolved in the more than three and a half decades since the picture box became a commercial reality.

These pages are brimming over with the best of television as well as the worst of television, the shows that made you laugh and those that made you cry, the series that made you wish TV was never invented and those that you wished would never go off the air.

With more than 2,000 photographs, this book is a comprehensive pictorial review (though not a complete one), starting with TV's beginnings in the late forties, through the Golden Age of programming of the fifties—with its emphasis on very high quality drama—to the conclusion of the 1981–82 season.

There are also photographs from programs which though not aired in the prime evening viewing hours certainly, because of their contribution, deserve to be in any book about television's history. These include "Broadway Open House," "Howdy Doody," "The Today Show," "The Tonight Show," "Omnibus," "The Merv Griffin Show," and "Saturday Night Live."

But more than merely being a scrapbook, *Prime-Time Television* contains a yearly historical overview of each television season that will entertain and enlighten TV fans young and old.

A television year in this book begins in September and ends the following August. All photographs are captioned with the show's name, the first and last telecast dates of its original run, the network(s) it was on and the names of the performers. One-of-a-kind programs, such as specials, spectaculars, and mini-series, are noted with their specific air dates.

Now it's time to sit back, enjoy, and revel in the many wonderful memories these photographs of shows we all grew up with will bring to mind.

1948-49

The Second World War had been over for three years when television's first real season began. During this period, the number of TV sets in use in the United States rose from approximately 7,000 to a little more than 1.1 million. While radio was still the No. 1 broadcast medium for entertainment, these figures did indicate that its influence and popularity were beginning to diminish. Although most Americans were aware of the new medium by this time, most had not yet had the opportunity to view the black picture box. And of those who had, their first experience with television was probably communal. They may have seen a sporting event on a set in a neighborhood bar, or watched a program on a set in the window of an appliance store, or even viewed TV in the lobby of a hotel or public building, where during those early years sets could be found. And, of course, another popular place where many had their first television experience was in the home of a pioneering neighbor. Needless to say, these adventurous souls of TV's early days were the most popular people on the block.

At the start of this season, four television networks existed: ABC, CBS, Dumont, and NBC. All four networks combined consisted of 37 stations, located in 22 cities. But although this was the medium's first year of full prime-time, seven-days-a-week, evening programming, it should be noted that some significant programming had taken place before this season.

Sporting events, particularly boxing, had already made an indelible impression on the medium. Programs like NBC's "The Gillette Cavalcade Of Sports," CBS's "Sports from Madison Square Garden," and Dumont's "Boxing from Jamaica Arena" each had a loyal following.

Quiz and audience-participation shows like "Cash and Carry," with Dennis James; "Americana," with the medium's first moderator, John Mason Brown, followed by Ben Grauer; and "Charade Quiz," with Bill Slater, all had

sizable audiences, as did "You Are an Artist," an instructional learn-to-draw show with one of TV's earliest celebrities, artist Jon Gnagy.

Other shows that were already popular included two cooking shows: "To the Queen's Taste," with Dione Lucas on CBS, and "In the Kelvinator Kitchen," with Alma Kitchell on NBC. Ted Mack's "The Original Amateur Hour," a descendant of the popular radio talent program, began a sporadic run of 22 years before this season and was to appear on all four networks. And contemporary television's oldest continuously running program, "Meet the Press," also began before this season. In its more than 35 years on the air, the show has been seen approximately half the time in the evening and the other half on Sunday mornings.

But the most significant programming before this season were two shows on NBC. "Kraft Television Theater" was the first sponsored major dramatic-anthology series. It also was the original program that launched television's Golden Age. "Kraft Theater" remained a fixture in the NBC lineup for more than 11 years. And the short-lived "Hour Glass," the first hour-long entertainment/variety series, was the pioneer for many of the top variety shows in the years to come.

Just before the fall television season, two programs debuted that were to have a considerable and long-range effect on the new medium. On June 6, 1948, the "Texaco Star Theater" premiered on NBC. Until that time, this show had been a long-running variety and dramatic radio program. The sponsor decided it wanted to change the format to a vaudevillian type of show with good talent and a strong host—and, most important, to enter the burgeoning televised world. The decision was made to stage a series of tryouts during June and July to select the right host from a list of well-known entertainment personalities. Milton Berle was hosting Texaco's radio program at the time, so it was only natural that he be asked to do the first televised "Texaco Star Theater." Berle was followed by

Henny Youngman, Morey Amsterdam, George Price, Jack Carter, Peter Donald, and Harry Richman in the role as tryout host. Then Berle was asked to do two more shows, after which he was selected to be the permanent host of the new show—which was to begin on September 21, 1948.

On that evening, television history was made. The show became an instant smash. And Milton Berle was on his way to becoming "Mr. Television"—a title he still wears proudly—so named because of the motivating factor he and his show had on the tremendous increase in the number of TV sets sold. This in turn helped the new medium blossom. As a result of his popularity, TV-set sales doubled after Berle's first year on the air. And Tuesday night became Berle's night. This meant that movie theaters, nightclubs, and restaurants were to experience a significant drop in business on Tuesday nights for the next few years.

The other important show to debut immediately before the start of the season was CBS's "Toast of the Town," with news columnist Ed Sullivan as host. At the time it was impossible to assess the landmark program the show would become. It went on to enjoy 23 years as a Sunday-night fixture, the longest-running variety show in television history.

The Sullivan show, though, was not an instant success like Berle's show. "Toast of the Town" gradually built an audience using a format that was more in keeping with the traditional vaudeville show than was "Texaco Star Theater." Ed Sullivan introduced the acts and stepped aside; he was not a performer (Berle, on the other hand, was—and he usually got his crazy antics into most of the skits). Sullivan brought to television exciting new acts as well as established talent, and that was where his talent lay. He had the innate ability to know what would go over well with the home viewer. From circus acts to opera, stand-up comedy to legitimate theater, popular music to classical dance, "Toast of the Town" gave many performers their television debut. A partial list includes: Jackie

Gleason, Bob Hope, Fred Astaire, Lena Horne, Dean Martin and Jerry Lewis, Eddie Fisher, Rosemary Clooney, Victor Borge, Fay Emerson, Larry Storch, Vaughn Monroe, and many, many more. The success of this show and the Berle show was very early evidence that television was not some trendy amusement, but rather that it would flourish and become the major entertainment medium in the country.

The Dumont Television Network, consisting of only two stations, New York and Washington, D.C., introduced before this season a number of TV firsts including the first regular network soap-opera series, "Faraway Hill," starring Flora Campbell. The series lasted only 12 weeks, but this type of program went on to develop legions of devoted fans. It also gave us the first nightly network news program as well as the first weekly family situation-comedy series, "Mary Kay and Johnny," starring the husband-and-wife team of Mary Kay and Johnny Stearns. This show eventually went on to NBC and CBS during its tenure of nearly three years. And "Small Fry Club," with Bob Emery, was network television's first successful children's program. Dumont aired the show every weekday night during most of its four-year run.

This season offered many notable pro-grams, particularly in the genre of dramatic anthology. "Ford Theatre," one of CBS's earliest sponsored series, was the vehicle many stars, and soon-to-be stars, used to play their first major television roles. They included Judy Holliday, Robert Young, Ernest Borgnine, Donna Reed, and Barry Sullivan. "Philco Television Playhouse," produced by Fred Coe, and later to be considered a Golden Age program, began a seven-year, Sunday-night run on NBC. Among those who made their first major TV appearance on the show were stars Lillian Gish, Dorothy Gish, and Paul Muni, and future star Walter Matthau.

"Studio One," another of the pro-grams that made up TV's Golden Age, was produced by Worthington Miner in its early years on CBS. The program began without a sponsor but Westing-house soon picked up the sponsorship. The company featured Betty Furness as its commercial spokesperson and "You can be sure if it's Westinghouse" as its advertising theme. Soon both became very recognizable to the American public. Actors who made their first major television appearance on "Studio One" included Jason Robards, Jr., Lorne Greene, and Inger Stevens. In addition, such unlikely dramatic performers at the time as Jackie Gleason, Art Carney, and newsman Mike Wallace each made a rare appearance. There were many name performers-to-be who played a half-dozen or more starring roles during the program's tenure: John Forsythe, James Daly, Leslie Nielsen, and Richard Kiley, to name a few. Charlton Heston had the lead in more than a dozen presentations, and some actors, James Dean and Warren Beatty, for example, made rare TV appearances on this show.

"Actor's Studio" was ABC's drama anthology for the season. Although it was only a short-run series, it is notable because it provided viewers with Marlon Brando's only dramatic television appearance before the one he gave in "Roots: The Next Generations" in 1979. Two other drama series that debuted late in the season were "Suspense" on CBS and "Fireside Theater" on NBC. "Suspense" was a longtime radio program that made the successful transition to television and ran on the network for more than five years. "Fireside Theater" was a fixture at 9:00 on Tuesday nights and became one of the 1950s' most durable dramas.

In the variety-show category, both musical and comedy, several programs debuted this season. The "Admiral Broadway Revue" had the distinction of being broadcast simultaneously on two

YOU ARE AN ARTIST: November 1, 1946–January 17, 1950, NBC.
Jon Gnagy (host)

PARTY LINE: June 8, 1947–August 31, 1947, NBC

WINNER TAKE ALL: July 6, 1948–October 3, 1950, CBS. *(Right)*
Bud Collyer (host)

networks, NBC and Dumont. This was Sid Caesar's first regular starring role and enabled him, and his comic genius, to team up with another gifted comic, Imogene Coca. "Cavalcade of Stars" was Dumont's answer to CBS's "Toast of the Town" and NBC's "Texaco Star Theater." The show was initially hosted by comedian Jack Carter, then Jerry Lester became host for a short time. Eventually, Lester would go on to make TV history by becoming the star of the first successful late-night program, "Broadway Open House." "Cavalcade of Stars," however, had its greatest success when Jackie Gleason took over as host. This was because many of Gleason's great characters—Reginald Van Gleason, the Poor Soul, Joe the Bartender, among others—were revealed for the first time. And this show was the forum he used to present his greatest work of all, the classic "The Honeymooners."

"Garroway At Large" and "The Fred Waring Show" were the other variety programs of merit that commenced this season. The Garroway show was noted for its meager sets, because of the low production budget, and for its host's straightforward style. Fred Waring had a longtime radio program that he transformed into a TV variety show. It was quite popular and during its five-year run on CBS it followed Ed Sullivan's "Toast of the Town."

Other notable programs that began this season were "Arthur Godfrey's Talent Scouts," "Kukla, Fran and Ollie" and "The Goldbergs." Arthur Godfrey, already a big star in the radio realm, quickly became one of television's outstanding personalities. His first TV show, "Talent Scouts," was an immediate hit, finding a home on CBS at 8:30 on Monday nights for nearly 10 years. Future stars who made their humble beginnings as winners on the show included Pat Boone, the McGuire Sisters, June Vali, the Chordettes, Carmel Quinn, and Shari Lewis. After "Talent Scouts" became an established hit, Godfrey went on to achieve a unique place in television history as the only star to have two top-rated shows on the air simultaneously, his second being "Arthur Godfrey and His Friends," which also began this season.

"Kukla, Fran and Ollie" was an evening children's show that was equally popular with adults. The program was first broadcast locally in Chicago before coming on the NBC network this season. Eventually, it went to ABC and then to educational television via PBS. Except for special productions, the show was done without a script.

Gertrude Berg created the role of Molly Goldberg on radio as early as 1929 and played the character for 20 years before she brought "The Goldbergs" to television. Molly Goldberg was a typical lovable Jewish mother who lived with her family in the Bronx, New York. The program became one of TV's early popular situation comedies, in major part because Berg exercised tight control over the program. Besides starring in it, she wrote and produced the series that was first on CBS, then NBC, followed by a short run on Dumont before going into syndication.

HOWDY DOODY: December 27, 1947–September 30, 1960, NBC; 1975, syndicated. Howdy Doody and "Buffalo Bob" Smith

MEET THE PRESS: Larry Spivak

JUVENILE JURY: April 3, 1947–September 14, 1954, NBC, CBS. Jack Barry (host) and the panel

TO THE QUEEN'S TASTE/THE DIONE LUCAS SHOW: February 25, 1948–December 29, 1949, CBS. Dione Lucas (chef/hostess)

MEET THE PRESS: November 6, 1947—, NBC. *(Second from right)* Martha Rountree, moderator and co-creator; *(second from left)* Larry Spivak, co-creator, with panel and guest

SMALL FRY CLUB: March 11, 1947–June 15, 1951, Dumont. Bob Emery (host)

HOUR GLASS: May 9, 1946–March 6, 1947, NBC. Doodles Weaver (guest)

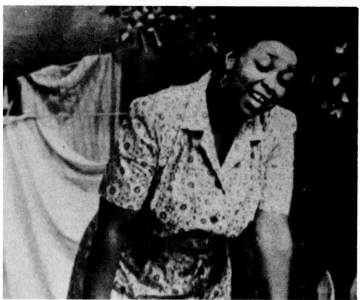

THE BORDEN SHOW: July 6, 1947–September 28, 1947, NBC. Ethel Waters (guest) in a scene from a drama presentation

MISSUS GOES A-SHOPPING: November 19, 1947–January 12, 1949, CBS

SEE WHAT YOU KNOW: February 19, 1946–October 24, 1946, CBS. Tex McCrary, Bennett Cerf, S. J. Perelman

CANDID CAMERA: August 10, 1948–September 3, 1967, ABC, NBC, CBS; 1974-78, syndicated. Allen Funt (creator and host)

CANDID CAMERA: Allen Funt filming a beauty contest for cats

WE THE PEOPLE: Celeste Holm (guest) and Dan Seymour

WE THE PEOPLE: June 1, 1948–September 26, 1952, CBS, NBC. *(Right)* Dan Seymour (host)

KRAFT TELEVISION THEATER: May 7, 1947–October 1, 1958, NBC, ABC. Ed Begley, Everett Sloane, and Richard Kiley in "Patterns"

KRAFT TELEVISION THEATER: Tommy Sands and Victor Jory in "Blood and Flesh"

KRAFT TELEVISION THEATER: Leo G. Carrol, Reynolds Evans, Margaret Phillips, and Janet Beecher in "The Late George Apley"

KRAFT TELEVISION THEATER: Ozzie Davis in "The Emperor Jones"

KRAFT TELEVISION THEATER: A scene from "A Night to Remember"

KRAFT TELEVISION THEATER: Sal Mineo in "Drummer Man"

THE BOB HOWARD SHOW: August 7, 1948–December 7, 1950, CBS. Bob Howard (host)

ACTOR'S STUDIO: September 26, 1948–January 31, 1950, ABC, CBS. Russell Collins, Butch Cavell, and unknown actor in an early drama presentation

BELIEVE IT OR NOT: March 1, 1949–September 28, 1950, NBC. Robert L. Ripley (host)

GIRL ABOUT TOWN (FOR YOUR PLEASURE) April 15, 1948–September 10, 1949, NBC. Earl Wrightson and Kyle MacDonnell (hostess)

THEY STAND ACCUSED: January 18, 1949–December 30, 1954, CBS, Dumont

MUSICAL MINIATURES: May 10, 1948–January 12, 1949, NBC. Helen Ryan and Max Showalter (guests)

THE ORIGINAL AMATEUR HOUR: January 18, 1948–September 27, 1970, Dumont, NBC, ABC, CBS. Ted Mack (host)

HOLLYWOOD SCREEN TEST: August 15, 1948–May 18, 1953, ABC. *(Right)* Neil Hamilton (host)

TOAST OF THE TOWN/THE ED SULLIVAN SHOW: Elvis Presley (guest)

TOAST OF THE TOWN/THE ED SULLIVAN SHOW: Jerry Lewis and Dean Martin (guests)

TOAST OF THE TOWN/THE ED SULLIVAN SHOW: Ed Sullivan with the Beatles

THE TOAST OF THE TOWN/THE ED SULLIVAN SHOW: June 20, 1948–June 6, 1971, CBS. Ed Sullivan

TOAST OF THE TOWN/THE ED SULLIVAN SHOW: Ed Sullivan and one of the many animal acts that appeared on the show

TOAST OF THE TOWN/THE ED SULLIVAN SHOW: Moiseyev Dancers (guests)

TOAST OF THE TOWN/THE ED SULLIVAN SHOW: The premiere show

TOAST OF THE TOWN/THE ED SULLIVAN SHOW: Ed Sullivan and commercial spokesperson Julia Meade

17

IT PAYS TO BE IGNORANT: June 6, 1949–September 27, 1951, CBS, NBC. Tom Howard (host), contestant, George Shelton, Lulu McConnell, and Harry McNaughton

ARTHUR GODFREY'S TALENT SCOUTS: Talent Scouts applause meter used to select weekly winners

THE ADMIRAL BROADWAY REVUE: January 28, 1949–June 3, 1949, NBC, Dumont. Sid Caesar and Imogene Coca

ARTHUR GODFREY'S TALENT SCOUTS: December 6, 1948–July 21, 1958, CBS. Arthur Godfrey (host)

LEAVE IT TO THE GIRLS: April 27, 1949–March 27, 1954, NBC, ABC. Maggi McNellis (hostess) and Eloise McElhone

THIS IS SHOW BUSINESS: July 15, 1949–September 11, 1956, CBS, NBC. George S. Kaufman, Clifton Fadiman (host), and Sam Levenson

THE MILTON BERLE SHOW (TEXACO STAR THEATER): Sid Stone

THE MILTON BERLE SHOW (TEXACO STAR THEATER): Danny O'Day and Jimmy Nelson

THE MILTON BERLE SHOW (TEXACO STAR THEATER): Milton Berle

THE MILTON BERLE SHOW (TEXACO STAR THEATER): Milton Berle

THE MILTON BERLE SHOW (TEXACO STAR THEATER): Milton Berle and Ruth Gilbert

THE MILTON BERLE SHOW (TEXACO STAR THEATER): September 21, 1948–June 9, 1953, NBC. Milton Berle (Mr. Television)

THE MILTON BERLE SHOW (TEXACO STAR THEATER): Milton Berle

STUDIO ONE: Mary Sinclair in "The Scarlet Letter"

STUDIO ONE: Grace Kelly in "The Kill"

STUDIO ONE: Eugenie Leontovich in "Image of Fear" (the series' last telecast)

STUDIO ONE: Leo Coleman and Marie Powers in "The Medium"

STUDIO ONE: Margaret O'Brien and James MacArthur in "Tongues of Angels"

STUDIO ONE: E. G. Marshall and Valerie Cossart in "Mary Poppins"

STUDIO ONE: Yul Brynner and Felicia Montealegre in "Flowers from a Stranger"

STUDIO ONE: Charlton Heston and Judith Evelyn in "Macbeth"

STUDIO ONE: Richard Webb and Patricia Collins in "The River Garden"

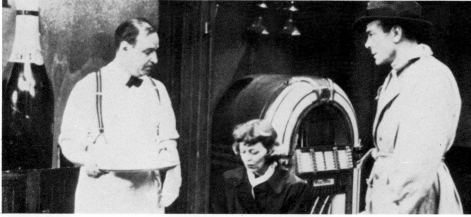
STUDIO ONE: November 7, 1948–September 29, 1958, CBS. Scene from "The Storm," starring Margaret Sullavan (the series' premiere telecast)

STUDIO ONE: Janet Swanson and Gracie Fields in "Mrs. Harris Goes to Paris"

FIREBALL FUN-FOR-ALL: June 26, 1949–October 27, 1949, NBC. Ole Olsen and Chick Johnson (hosts)

CAVALCADE OF STARS: June 4, 1949–January 28, 1950, Dumont. Jack Carter (host)

THE CLIFF EDWARDS SHOW: May 23, 1949–September 19, 1949, CBS. Cliff Edwards (host)

FIREBALL FUN-FOR-ALL: Ole Olsen and Chick Johnson

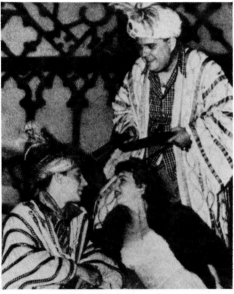

CAVALCADE OF STARS: Jack Carter with guests Janet Blair and Zero Mostel

CELEBRITY TIME: January 23, 1949–September 21, 1952, CBS, ABC. Conrad Nagel (host)

THE ROBERTA QUINLAN SHOW: May 3, 1949–November 23, 1951, NBC. Roberta Quinlan (hostess)

GARROWAY AT LARGE: April 16, 1949–June 25, 1954, NBC. Jack Haskell, Cliff Norton, Connie Russell, Dave Garroway (host), and dancers

THE VINCENT LOPEZ SHOW: March 7, 1949–July 11, 1951, Dumont. Vincent Lopez (host)

QUIZ KIDS: Clifton Fadiman (second host) and later "Quiz Kids" panel

QUIZ KIDS: March 1, 1949–September 27, 1956, NBC, CBS. Joe Kelly (original host) and early "Quiz Kids" panel

CAPTAIN VIDEO AND HIS VIDEO RANGERS: Al Hodge and Don Hastings

VERSATILE VARIETIES: August 28, 1949–December 14, 1951, NBC, CBS, ABC. "The Bonnie Maids" with host Harold Barry and Anne Francis *(right)*

ARTHUR GODFREY AND HIS FRIENDS: January 12, 1949–April 28, 1959, CBS. *(Front row)* Tony Marvin, Haleloke, Marion Marlowe, and two of the McGuire Sisters

ARTHUR GODFREY AND HIS FRIENDS: *(Second from right)* Frank Parker and the Mariners

CAPTAIN VIDEO AND HIS VIDEO RANGERS: June 27, 1949–April 1, 1955, Dumont; 1955–56, syndicated. Al Hodge (Captain Video)

PAUL WHITEMAN'S TV TEEN CLUB: April 2, 1949–March 28, 1954, ABC. Paul Whiteman (host) and Andrea McLaughlin

ARTHUR GODFREY AND HIS FRIENDS: Two of the McGuire Sisters and Arthur Godfrey (host)

THE WENDY BARRIE SHOW: November 10, 1948–September 27, 1950, NBC, Dumont, ABC. Juan Carlos Thorenz (guest) and Wendy Barrie (hostess)

WHO SAID THAT?: December 9, 1948–July 26, 1955, NBC, ABC. Bill Henry, H. V. Kaltenborn, Joy Hodges, and Morey Amsterdam

THE FRED WARING SHOW: April 17, 1949–May 30, 1954, CBS. Fred Waring (host)

THE PERRY COMO SHOW: December 24, 1948–June 12, 1963, NBC, CBS. Perry Como (host)

THE PERRY COMO SHOW: Perry Como and Ginger Rogers (guest)

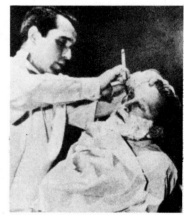

THE PERRY COMO SHOW: Perry Como and Kirk Douglas (guest)

THE PERRY COMO SHOW: Perry Como and Bob Hope (guest)

BREAK THE BANK: October 22, 1948–January 15, 1957, ABC, NBC, CBS. Contestants with Bert Parks (host)

KUKLA, FRAN AND OLLIE: November 29, 1948–August 31, 1957, NBC, ABC. Kukla, Burr Tillstrom, Ollie, and Fran Allison

PHILCO TELEVISION PLAYHOUSE: Jose Ferrer in "Cyrano de Bergerac"

PHILCO TELEVISION PLAYHOUSE: Bert Lytell, Oscar Karlweiss, and Richard Derr in "I Like It Here"

PHILCO TELEVISION PLAYHOUSE: Joanne Woodward and Kim Stanley in "Young Lady of Property"

PHILCO TELEVISION PLAYHOUSE: John Alberts and Judith Evelyn in "Camille"

PHILCO TELEVISION PLAYHOUSE: Martin Balsam, Don Murray, and Sidney Poitier in "A Man Ten Feet Tall"

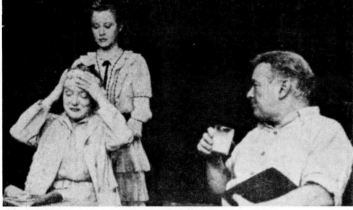

PHILCO TELEVISION PLAYHOUSE: Peggy Wood, Mary Orr, and Sidney Blackmer in "Dark Hammock"

PHILCO TELEVISION PLAYHOUSE: Perry Wilson, Lillian Gish, Helen Carew, and Bert Lytell in "The Late Christopher Bean"

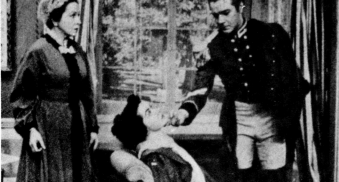

PHILCO TELEVISION PLAYHOUSE: October 3, 1948–October 22, 1955, NBC. Muriel Kirkland, Marsha Hunt, and Alfred Drake in "Quality Street"

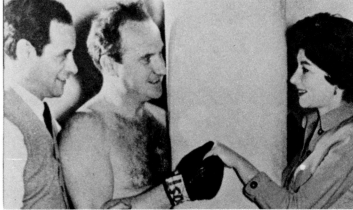

PHILCO TELEVISION PLAYHOUSE: Eli Wallach, Jack Warden, and Lee Grant in "Shadow of the Champ"

HOPALONG CASSIDY: William Boyd
(Hopalong Cassidy) and Topper

HOPALONG CASSIDY: June 24, 1949–December 23, 1951, NBC; 1952–54, syndicated. William Boyd

MAMA: Peggy Wood ("Mama" Marta Hansen) and Judson Laire

THE GOLDBERGS: Gertrude Berg (Molly Goldberg)

MAMA: July 1, 1949–July 27, 1956, CBS. Kevin Coughlin, Judson Laire, Peggy Wood, Dick Van Patten

THE GOLDBERGS: January 10, 1949–October 19, 1954, CBS, NBC, Dumont. Harold J. Stone, Eli Mintz, and Gertrude Berg

THE GOLDBERGS: *(Seated)* Arlene McQuade and Gertrude Berg *(Standing)* Philip Loeb and Larry Robinson

1949-50

As the fifties were about to begin, television was far from being a national viewing medium. The coast-to-coast coaxial cable, permitting television transmission over great distances, had not yet been completed. There were 107 stations operating in 65 cities and about 4 million TV sets to receive broadcasts. The networks were still operating at a loss, which was not unexpected considering the short amount of time they had been in existence. They were, however, well along in their development of a color system for broadcast and, for this season, began participating in a rating system to determine the most popular programs. All in all, the momentum and expectations were high regarding the ultimate success of this budding communication and entertainment medium.

This season, shows debuted in a variety of categories—including police/detective, quiz panel/audience participation, Westerns for children, and drama anthology—that would go on to achieve durable network runs.

NBC, television's leading network in these early years, continued its innovative style and began to explore the potential of expanded viewing time, particularly in the after-11:00 P.M. time period, and brought forth TV's first regularly scheduled late-night show, "Broadway Open House." In prime time, it introduced three outstanding programs that were to become part of television's Golden Age: "Robert Montgomery Presents," "Armstrong Circle Theater," and "Your Show of Shows."

"Robert Montgomery Presents" was a big-budget, live drama-anthology series produced and hosted by the distinguished Hollywood actor for whom the show was named. Performers including Joanne Woodward, Peter Falk, Zachary Scott, and Elizabeth Montgomery (Robert's daughter) either made their TV debut or were given the opportunity for their first major television role on this program. And established film star Claudette Colbert made one of her rare television appearances in this series.

The program was a Monday night staple on NBC for seven and a half years. As with the Montgomery show, "Armstrong Circle Theater" afforded many stars-to-be their first major TV drama roles. Anne Jackson, Telly Savalas, John Cassavetes, and Robert Duvall were just a few. The program had a 13-year life span, appearing first on NBC (7 years) and then on CBS (6 years).

"Your Show of Shows," starring Sid Caesar and Imogene Coca, was one of the most ambitious undertakings in the history of television. It was a live, 90-minute, weekly original-comedy show. This incredible feat was of consistent excellent quality and was seen on NBC at 9:00 each Saturday night for four years. Producer Max Liebman was responsible for putting together the show. During the previous season, he had worked with Caesar and Coca on the successful, but short-run (17 weeks), "Admiral Broadway Revue," so he knew his stars' talents well. The reason the popular "Revue" went off the air so quickly is unusual, to say the least. It seems that the show's success stimulated such high demand for Admiral-brand television sets that the sponsor, Admiral, could not keep up with the demand and decided to stop advertising. And when it stopped advertising, the show stopped. This was probably the only time in the history of the medium that this ever happened.

But it was on the Admiral show that the seeds began to sprout in Liebman's mind for "Your Show of Shows." This time he teamed up the incredibly funny duo of Caesar and Coca with two very funny men, Carl Reiner and Howard Morris. Backing up this quartet were an equally talented group of staff writers who went on to extraordinary careers in their own right: Mel Brooks, Neil Simon, Woody Allen, and Larry Gelbart. This marvelous variety show could probably have gone on for many years (the ratings were good), but the principals decided to pursue separate careers. And so, after just four years, one of TV's most outstanding programs ended.

On CBS, two notable programs began this season. "Mama" (actual start just prior to the new season), starring theatrical actress Peggy Wood as Marta Hansen in the title role, was one of the best of the early situation-comedy series. The story centered around the Hansens, a Norwegian family living in San Francisco during the early part of the twentieth century. The other cast principals were Judson Laire as carpenter Lars Hansen, otherwise known as Papa; Rosemary Rice as elder daughter Katrin, whose offscreen voice introduced each episode as she leafed through the family album; Dick Van Patten, who eventually starred in several sitcoms, the most recent being "Eight Is Enough," as son Nels; and first Iris Mann and then Robin Morgan, who today is a writer and feminist, as the Hansens' youngest child, Dagmar. The series enjoyed a long run (7 years) at 8:00 P.M. on Fridays.

CBS also debuted what was to become television's longest running prime-time game show, "What's My Line?" John Daly, who hosted the show during most of its tenure, was joined by panelists Dorothy Kilgallen, Arlene Francis, and Bennett Cerf. In addition, guest panelists who frequently appeared in the early years were Fred Allen, Herb Block, and Steve Allen. The show's success could probably be attributed to its very simple format; the panel of four tried to guess the occupation of the contestant, asking questions that could only be answered with a simple "yes" or "no." Further, a mystery contestant was featured each week. For this segment of the program the panelists were blindfolded as they attempted to guess not the guest's line but the guest's name. Many celebrities appeared on the show. A few include: Carl Sandburg, Salvador Dali, Ty Cobb, Frank Lloyd Wright, Eleanor Roosevelt, and Earl Warren. The first guest on the premiere show was New York Yankee Phil Rizzuto, while the last on the network finale was moderator John Daly. After its long network run, "What's My Line?" was seen in syndication for seven years, concluding in 1975.

"Martin Kane, Private Eye," starring William Gargan in the title role, was one of four police/detective programs worthy of mention. This series, and its star, were one of several that made the successful transition from radio to television during these early years. Over the course of its initial network run, four actors played Kane. Gargan was followed by Lloyd Nolan, Lee Tracy, and Mark Stevens. An interesting note about William Gargan is that he was a real-life private detective before his show-business days. "Man Against Crime" starred Ralph Bellamy as Mike Barnett, a tough, no-nonsense, hard-boiled New York private eye who used his brains and fists—not guns—to solve crimes! The program first aired on CBS, then went over to Dumont before ending its run on NBC.

An unusual cops-and-robbers show was the Dumont Network's "The Plainclothesman," starring Ken Lynch as a police lieutenant. This successful series employed the interesting feature of Lynch's face never being seen on screen. The viewer saw the action only from the lieutenant's point of view. That is, whatever he saw those at home saw. If he lit a cigarette, a hand would come up toward the camera with a light. If he was knocked down, the viewer looked up from floor level. And so on. This effect proved particularly fascinating to the viewers, and they responded favorably week after week, allowing the show to become one of the network's longest-lasting programs. Dumont cranked out another popular police show that enjoyed a long run: "Rocky King, Inside Detective," starring Roscoe Karns. Rocky King was a police detective on the New York City Homicide Squad. Interestingly, during the program's last season on the air, Karns's son, Todd, became a regular on the show, also in the role of a detective. It should be remembered that many shows on early television were performed live, these police/detective shows included. And, as with any live presentation, embarrassing snafus are bound to occur. These shows had their share.

Three quiz-panel/audience-participation programs became popular this television year. "Pantomime Quiz," with Mike Stokey as emcee, was originally a Los Angeles local program on station KTLA, where it was awarded the very first Emmy for most-popular television program before coming onto the networks. The show eventually appeared on all four networks before going into syndication in the late sixties. It was retired in 1970. "Twenty Questions" was originally a radio program that began in

1946. The point of the game was for a celebrity panel to identify an object that was hidden from their sight by asking no more than 20 questions. The only clue they were given was whether the thing in question was animal, mineral, or vegetable. Bill Slater hosted the show during the early years, followed by Jay Jackson. One of the earliest and most successful game shows created and produced by the team of Mark Goodson and Bill Todman was "Beat the Clock." During its entire network life of eight years, Bud Collyer, for a long time Superman on radio, was the host. He was ably assisted by a beautiful blonde named Roxanne, who became a celebrity in her own right. The show quickly became a hit because TV viewers really enjoyed the wild stunts and crazy feats contestants had to perform to win prizes. But before these stunts were used on the air, the producers hired unemployed actors to make sure the gags could actually be done. In the early fifties, an unknown, aspiring actor was given his first job in television testing stunts. His name was James Dean.

Cowboys and Indians started showing up all over the little screen in prime time this season. And the kids loved them. Four of the most popular of these programs were "The Lone Ranger," a

top-10 show within a year; "Hopalong Cassidy" (summer start), another top-10 show within a year; "The Cisco Kid," whose popularity would last for many years and would become one of the first series filmed in color; and "The Gene Autry Show," a series that enjoyed six years on CBS while cowboy Autry went from Western-film star to producer for the new medium.

In another genre, a children's show that was to become an all-time favorite was "Captain Video and His Video Rangers" (starting its first full season), which debuted on Dumont. For a short time, Richard Coogan, years later one of the stars of the Western series "The Californians," played the role of Captain Video. But career conflicts due to work on the legitimate stage forced the new TV hero to relinquish the role. Al Hodge, the Green Hornet for years on radio, was then selected to be the next, and last, Captain Video. Hodge was better suited to this kind of hero than Coogan. He had the voice, and, for TV, the look to make the new captain's twenty-second-century exploits more believable. The captain was assisted by the Video Ranger, played admirably by fifteen-year-old Don Hastings, who would go on to soap-opera fame in "As the World Turns." This show was the first and

THE KEN MURRAY SHOW: January 7, 1950–June 14, 1953, CBS. Ken Murray (host) and Laurie Anders

THE ILKA CHASE SHOW (GLAMOUR-GO-ROUND): February 16, 1950–August 10, 1950, CBS. Ilka Chase (hostess)

longest running of the early space adventures and it lasted until the Dumont network folded. Over the years, future stars including Jack Klugman, Tony Randall, and Ernest Borgnine appeared as guest villains.

In addition to those already mentioned, there were two other drama-anthology series of quality this season. ''The Big Story,'' a documentary drama based on actual case histories of events covered by journalists, appeared on NBC for almost eight years. There were several on-screen narrators affiliated with the program through the seasons, the two most well known being Ben Grauer and Burgess Meredith. ''The Web'' was a live drama series that ran from this season through the early fifties on CBS, and in the late fifties on NBC. Some of the many future stars seen early in their careers on this program were Grace Kelly, Jack Palance, Eva Marie Saint, and Paul Newman.

The season's most durable-to-be quality series was ''The Voice of Firestone,'' which commenced on NBC on September 5, 1949. This show, which originated on radio in 1928, devoted itself essentially to classical and semiclassical music, and on occasions featured popular music. The show's audience was generally small in terms of TV view-ing, but it remained on the air to become one of the most qualitative ever on a continuous basis. A loyal following enjoyed the show until its demise in 1963.

Finally, there were plenty of other things happening this season. Showbusiness personalities Garry Moore and Ken Murray each began hosting their own variety-show series. Bob Hope, one of radio's top comics, made his NBC debut in the special ''Star Spangled Revue.'' Singer Michael Douglas, later to achieve fame as Mike Douglas the talkshow host, received his first network exposure as a regular singing performer on ''Kay Kyser's Kollege of Musical Knowledge.'' And Ed McMahon, Johnny Carson's eventual sidekick, made his network debut as a ''red-nosed'' clown on CBS's popular Saturday circus program, ''The Big Top,'' with ringmaster Jack Sterling.

KAY KYSER'S KOLLEGE OF MUSICAL KNOWLEDGE: December 1, 1949–December 28, 1950; July 4, 1954–September 12, 1954, NBC. Kay Kyser (host) and Ish Kabbible

THE HERB SHRINER SHOW: November 7, 1949–April 3, 1952; October 2, 1956–December 4, 1956, NBC. Herb Shriner (host)

THE FAYE EMERSON SHOW: March 13, 1950–December 23, 1950, CBS, NBC. Faye Emerson (hostess)

THE STORK CLUB: July 7, 1950–October 31, 1953; September 11, 1954–July 24, 1955, CBS, ABC. Faye Emerson (guest) and Sherman Billingsley (host)

PANTOMIME QUIZ (STUMP THE STARS): October 4, 1949–September 21, 1959; September 17, 1962–September 16, 1963, CBS, Dumont, NBC, ABC; 1968–1970, syndicated

YOUR SHOW OF SHOWS: Carl Reiner, Sid Caesar, and Howard Morris

YOUR SHOW OF SHOWS: Howard Morris, Sid Caesar, and Carl Reiner as the Haircuts

YOUR SHOW OF SHOWS: Bill Hayes

YOUR SHOW OF SHOWS: Billy Williams Quartet

YOUR SHOW OF SHOWS: Final performance, June 5, 1954

YOUR SHOW OF SHOWS: Imogene Coca, Sid Caesar, and Carl Reiner

YOUR SHOW OF SHOWS: Imogene Coca and Sid Caesar

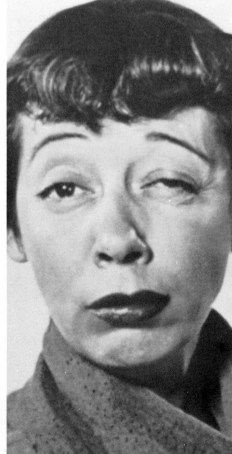

YOUR SHOW OF SHOWS: The Hamilton Trio

YOUR SHOW OF SHOWS: February 25, 1950–June 5, 1954, NBC. Sid Caesar

YOUR SHOW OF SHOWS: Imogene Coca

YOUR SHOW OF SHOWS: Sid Caesar and Imogene Coca

LIFE BEGINS AT EIGHTY: January 13, 1950–February 25, 1956, NBC, ABC, Dumont. Georgiana Carhart, "Doc" Bowers, Jack Barry (host), Isabelle Winlocke, and Rev. H. S. Hathaway

YOUR HIT PARADE: Cast includes Tommy Leonetti, Jill Corey, Alan Copeland, and Virginia Gibson (1957)

THE ARTHUR MURRAY PARTY: Kathryn Murray and the Arthur Murray Dancers

YOUR HIT PARADE: July 10, 1950–April 14, 1959; August 2, 1974–August 30, 1974, NBC, CBS. Cast includes Snooky Lanson, Gisele MacKenzie, Russell Arms, and Dorothy Collins (1953)

THE ARTHUR MURRAY PARTY: July 20, 1950–September 6, 1960, ABC, Dumont, CBS, NBC. Kathryn and Arthur Murray (host and hostess)

TWENTY QUESTIONS: November 26, 1949–May 3, 1955, ABC, Dumont, NBC. Johnny McPhee, Herb Polesie, Fred Vandeventer, Florence Renard, and Bill Slater (host)

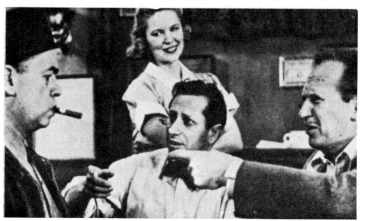

STUD'S PLACE: November 26, 1949–January 28, 1952, NBC, ABC. Win Stracke, Studs Terkel, Beverly Younger, and Chet Roble

THE ALAN YOUNG SHOW: *(Center)* Alan Young (host)

THE PAUL WHITEMAN REVUE: November 6, 1949–March 30, 1952, ABC. Paul Whiteman (host)

TALENT SEARCH: February 15, 1950–September 6, 1951, NBC. Skitch Henderson (host) and contestant

THE ALAN YOUNG SHOW: April 6, 1950–June 21, 1953, CBS. Alan Young and Candy McDowell

THE RUGGLES: November 3, 1949–June 19, 1952, ABC. Tommy Bernard, Judy Nugent, Charles Ruggles, and Margaret Kerry

SONGS FOR SALE: July 7, 1950–June 28, 1952, CBS. Contestant with Jan Murray (host)

THE GARRY MOORE SHOW: Durwood Kirby, Garry Moore (host), Denise Lor, and Ken Carson

THE GARRY MOORE SHOW: June 26, 1950–December 27, 1951, CBS. Garry Moore (host)

THE GARRY MOORE SHOW: Frank Simms, Garry Moore, Durward Kirby, Denise Lor, and Ken Carson

MAN AGAINST CRIME: October 7, 1949–July 4, 1954; July 1, 1956–August 26, 1956, CBS, Dumont, NBC. Ralph Bellamy and Gloria McGhee (guest)

NBC OPERA OF THE AIR: David Poleri and Leontyne Price in "Tosca"

NBC OPERA OF THE AIR: John Raitt and Susan Yager in "The Taming of the Shrew"

MAN AGAINST CRIME: Frank Lovejoy (1956)

NBC OPERA OF THE AIR: January 14, 1950–telecast sporadically during the 1950s. Kenneth Smith, William McGraw, and Marion Bell in "Down in the Valley"

ROBERT MONTGOMERY PRESENTS: June and Kathleen Lockhart in "The Burtons"

ROBERT MONTGOMERY PRESENTS: Darren McGavin and Mary Astor in "Sunset Boulevard"

ROBERT MONTGOMERY PRESENTS: Robert Montgomery in "The Lost Weekend"

ROBERT MONTGOMERY PRESENTS: January 30, 1950–June 24, 1957, NBC. Robert Montgomery (host)

ROBERT MONTGOMERY PRESENTS: Lee Bowman, Robert Montgomery, Phyllis Kirk, and John Newland in "The Great Gatsby"

ROBERT MONTGOMERY PRESENTS: Constance Bennett in "Onions in the Stew"

THE ALDRICH FAMILY: October 2, 1949–May 29, 1953, NBC. Bob Casey, House Jameson, and Barbara Robbins

THE JACK CARTER SHOW (THE SATURDAY NIGHT REVUE): February 25, 1950–June 2, 1951, NBC. Jack Carter (host)

THE JACK CARTER SHOW (THE SATURDAY NIGHT REVUE): Jackie Lockridge, Jack Carter, Donald Richards, and Susan Stewart

THE ALDRICH FAMILY: Bobby Ellis (the last Henry Aldrich), Barbara Robbins, House Jameson, and June Dayton (later cast)

ROCKY KING, INSIDE DETECTIVE: January 14, 1950–December 26, 1954, Dumont. Roscoe Karns (Rocky King)

THE ED WYNN SHOW: October 6, 1949–July 4, 1950, CBS. Ed Wynn (host)

FORD STAR REVUE: July 6, 1950–March 29, 1951, NBC. Paul and Grace Hartman

THE LITTLE SHOW: June 27, 1950–November 22, 1951, NBC; April 3, 1953–June 19, 1953, ABC. John Conti, host

THE ED WYNN SHOW: Ed Wynn and Dagmar

CAMEO THEATRE: May 16, 1950–August 21, 1955, NBC. Margaret O'Brien and Dean Stockwell in "Innocent Witness"

CAMEO THEATRE: Eric Fleming, Howard Richardson, Rita Gam, and Alfred Drake in "Dark of the Moon"

THE BIG STORY: September 16, 1949–June 26, 1957, NBC. Ben Grauer (narrator) and Victor Riesel (columnist)

THE PLAINCLOTHESMAN: October 12, 1949–December 30, 1954, Dumont. Ken Lynch

CALVALCADE OF STARS WITH JACKIE GLEASON: February 4, 1950–September 26, 1952, Dumont. Art Carney and Jackie Gleason as Charlie Bratten/the Loudmouth

CALVALCADE OF STARS WITH JACKIE GLEASON: Jackie Gleason as Fenwick Babbitt

CALVALCADE OF STARS WITH JACKIE GLEASON: Pert Kelton (the original Alice) and Jackie Gleason

CALVALCADE OF STARS WITH JACKIE GLEASON: Jackie Gleason as Reginald Van Gleason

CALVALCADE OF STARS WITH JACKIE GLEASON: Jackie Gleason as Joe the Bartender

CALVALCADE OF STARS WITH JACKIE GLEASON: Jackie Gleason as the Poor Soul

MARTIN KANE, PRIVATE EYE: September 1, 1949–June 17, 1954, NBC. William Gargan (the original Martin Kane)

MARTIN KANE, PRIVATE EYE: Lloyd Nolan (the second Martin Kane)

MARTIN KANE, PRIVATE EYE: Lee Tracy (the third Martin Kane) and Gene Lyons (guest)

MARTIN KANE, PRIVATE EYE: (Center) Mark Stevens (the fourth Martin Kane)

THE CISCO KID: Early 1950, syndicated. Duncan Renaldo (the Cisco Kid) and Leo Carillo

ARMSTRONG CIRCLE THEATER: Alexander Scourby and Marketa Kimbrell in "The Man Who Refused to Die"

THE VOICE OF FIRESTONE: Howard Barlow conducting Voice of Firestone Orchestra

THE WEB: Dan Barton and Robert Burton in an episode

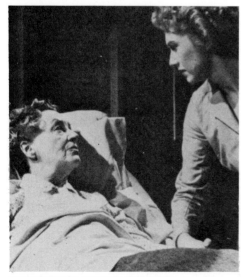

ARMSTRONG CIRCLE THEATER: June 6, 1950–August 28, 1963, NBC, CBS. Patricia Collinge and Mary Fickett in "Ward Three, 4 P.M. to Midnight"

THE VOICE OF FIRESTONE: September 5, 1949–June 16, 1963, NBC, ABC. Howard Barlow

THE WEB: July 4, 1950–September 26, 1954; July 7, 1957–October 6, 1957; March 27, 1961–September 11, 1961, CBS, NBC. Mary Alice Moore, Charles Nolte and unknown actor in "A Name for Death"

WHAT'S MY LINE?: February 2, 1950–September 3, 1967, CBS; 1968–1975, syndicated. Bennett Cerf, Arlene Francis, John Daly, Dorothy Kilgallen, and Fred Allen

WHAT'S MY LINE?: Dorothy Kilgallen, Bennett Cerf, Arlene Francis, Herb Block, and John Daly (host)

ANSWER YES OR NO: April 30, 1950–July 23, 1950, NBC. Arlene Francis and Moss Hart

THE ROBERT Q. LEWIS SHOW: July 16, 1950–January 7, 1951, CBS. Robert Q. Lewis (host) and Jane Wilson

EASY ACES: December 14, 1949–June 14, 1950, Dumont. Goodman and Jane Ace

BEAT THE CLOCK: March 23, 1950–September 12, 1958, CBS. Roxanne (assistant), Bud Collyer (host) and contestants

BROADWAY OPEN HOUSE: May 29 1950–August 24, 1951, NBC. Jerry Lester (host) surrounded by "Broadway Open House" regulars David Street, Wayne Howell, Dagmar, Ray Malone, and Milton DeLugg

THE GENE AUTRY SHOW: July 23, 1950–August 7, 1956, CBS. Gene Autry and his horse Champion

THE LIFE OF RILEY: October 4, 1949–March 28, 1950, NBC. Jackie Gleason (Chester A. Riley) and Rosemary DeCamp

THE BIG TOP: July 1, 1950–January 6, 1951, CBS. Jack Sterling (ringmaster) and clown (Ed McMahon)

THE LONE RANGER: September 15, 1949–September 12, 1957, ABC. The Lone Ranger (Clayton Moore/John Hart) and Tonto (Jay Silverheels)

1950-51

America, much to its disenchantment, found itself in another war shortly before this television season began. This time it was in far-off South Korea. American soldiers, along with United Nations troops, were sent to help the South Koreans fight off the invading communist North Korean forces. This troubling event, however, did not diminish TV viewers' high anticipation and expectations of the new season. The networks, particularly NBC, promoted their fall lineups heavily because for the first time many of radio's most popular stars were going to have their own shows. This group included Groucho Marx, George Burns and Gracie Allen, and Art Linkletter. Bob Hope and Fred Allen, two of radio's most luminous stars, appeared on a rotating basis along with other big names on NBC's "The Colgate Comedy Hour." Jack Benny, who had been a radio personality since 1932, cautiously made his television debut this season by doing four shows spread out over the entire TV year. Other familiar entertainers making the foray into television on a weekly basis were singer and film star Frank Sinatra, humorist Sam Levenson, and a different kind of radio veteran, the long-running show (since 1935) "Your Hit Parade."

The most popular new program of the season was "The Colgate Comedy Hour." This was NBC's Sunday-night answer to CBS's "Ed Sullivan Show," and it became the only new program to make the top-10 rating list. The "Comedy Hour" was a lavishly produced, big-budget comedy/variety extravaganza that featured numerous performers. In fact, during the first four years this show appeared opposite Sullivan it consistently garnered higher ratings. Among the funnymen who appeared as hosts this first season were the team of Dean Martin and Jerry Lewis, Eddie Cantor, and Donald O'Connor, as well as Hope and Allen. So confident was NBC in this entertainment format that it introduced another comedy/variety hour, this time on Wednesday nights. The "All Star Revue" was similar to the Sunday-night

show and had as rotating hosts this season such comic stars as Ed Wynn, Danny Thomas, Jack Carson, and Jimmy Durante. Needless to say, these two shows helped NBC corner the market on top comic talent this season.

The still-new medium was already giving strong indications that situation-comedy programming would become one of the pillars of each season's schedule. But while there were a number of sitcoms that debuted this fall, only two were noteworthy: "The George Burns and Gracie Allen Show" and "Amos 'n' Andy," both radio carry-overs. George Burns and Gracie Allen played themselves in a comedy about, naturally, a show-business couple. They brought their small supporting cast from their popular radio series. Bea Benaderet and Hal March played the Burns's neighbors, Blanche and Harry Morton; Bill Goodwin, who played himself, was the announcer and a friend of the Burns's; and Rolfe Sedan was the mailman, Mr. Beasley, who always gossiped with the chatty Gracie. In succeeding years the Harry Morton character was played by John Brown, Fred Clark, and Larry Keating, who is probably best remembered in the role. In the second year Bill Goodwin left to do his own show and Harry Von Zell was cast in the role of announcer. Burns and Allen enjoyed eight years with the show, building a heavy and loyal following. But in 1958 Gracie decided to retire, and thus so did the program. Burns made an attempt with another comedy series—but without his TV and real-life wife, it was not successful.

"Amos 'n' Andy" was a popular situation comedy that was the first TV series to feature an all-black cast. It began on radio in 1929, the brainchild of two white actors, Freeman Gosden and Charles Correll, who themselves played the principal characters. For television, though, the task of putting together just the right group of talented black actors resulted in nearly two years of preparation before the transition could be made. Approximately 800 actors auditioned for the several hilarious, outlandish roles on the

show before a cast was settled on. Alvin Childress was selected to play Amos Jones, an honest, straightforward, upstanding citizen who was the owner of, and driver for, the Fresh Air Cab Company of America. Spencer Williams, Jr., was chosen to be Andrew Brown, a gullible, lazy, good-natured soul who was usually an easy mark for his good friend George "Kingfish" Stevens. Tim Moore played to perfection the Kingfish, a slick con man always looking for a quick way to make a buck. Other characters included Sapphire Stevens, the Kingfish's nagging wife, who was always screaming for him to get a job, and Lightnin', the slow-moving janitor who cleaned up the Mystic Knights of the Sea lodge hall (of which Kingfish reigned as president). Ernestine Wade and Horace Stewart played these characters memorably. "Amos 'n' Andy's" popularity was high enough to assure a long network run, but because of opposition from black political groups, such as the NAACP, to the way blacks were portrayed, the sponsor withdrew from the program after only two seasons. This pressure kept other potential advertisers away too. Eventually, "Amos 'n' Andy" found its way back to television via syndication and was again embroiled in the same controversy. As a result, it went off the air for good in 1966.

As in previous seasons, drama anthologies were welcomed in a big way by the TV audience. And this season didn't disappoint, with three worthy newcomers. Many in this audience were already fans of the sixteen-year-old "Lux Radio Theatre"—so when the sponsor made the switch to television, there was an eager following. Numerous established stars and stars-to-be made their television debuts, or had their first major TV roles, on the "Lux Video Theatre." These included Edward G. Robinson, Peter Lorre, James Arness, Esther Williams, and Robert Stack. James Mason was the show's first host and was followed later by Otto Kruger and Gordon MacRae. This quality series ran for four years on CBS and then moved to NBC for three more years.

"Danger" was a suspense-filled weekly drama series on CBS for five years. The show maintained a consistent high quality of achievement through the efforts of some very talented directors, three of whom went on to become highly successful in later years. They are Hollywood directors Sidney Lumet and John Frankenheimer, and, interestingly, Yul Brynner. Multigifted Brynner worked frequently behind the camera in the early days of television before achieving fame in front of it. The third anthology of note was ABC's first hour-long drama series, "Pulitzer Prize Playhouse." The program featured a number of established performers including Melvyn Douglas, Raymond Massey, Edmond O'Brien, and Peggy Wood, and gave us the TV debut of Helen Hayes, one of the theater's most accomplished actresses, in "The Late Christopher Bean" by Emlyn Williams.

Two episodic drama series also became favorites with viewers. Bigtown, USA, the home of the Illustrated Press, a crusading daily newspaper, was the setting for the popular crime-drama show "Big Town." Patrick McVey starred as Steve Wilson, a hard-nosed reporter who teamed up with society columnist Lorelei Kilbourne, played by Mary K. Wells, to help fight crime and corruption in this metropolitan city. "Big Town" became one of the top-rated programs, not in this season but the next, and thereafter retained a loyal audience throughout its six years on the air. This series was another to originate on radio (in 1937) and for a time film star Edward G. Robinson played the Wilson character. On television, Mark Stevens eventually replaced McVey, and the character became the paper's managing editor. Lorelei also underwent casting changes as four more actresses played the character. One interesting highlight of the series was Grace Kelly's appearance as guest star on the premiere episode, October 5, 1950.

"Treasury Men in Action" was a 30-minute crime drama about the exploits of the U.S. Treasury Department and starred Walter Greaza as the "chief," the only regular cast member. The supporting cast changed from week to week over its five seasons and included such performers as Lee Marvin, Charles Bronson, Grace Kelly, Jack Klugman, and James Dean. The series first ran on ABC, then moved to NBC, and ended its network run back on ABC.

Even before this season, audience-participation shows were a staple of television programming. This TV year saw the debut of four that would have long life spans. "Truth or Consequences," with its creator, Ralph Edwards, as the program's first emcee, was an hilarious show in which contestants who didn't tell the truth had to pay the outrageous consequences. Other hosts over the years on the nighttime version (there was also a day show) were Jack Bailey, Steve Dunne, and Bob Barker. "You Asked For It," the show that went anywhere in the world to answer a viewer's question, was hosted by Art Baker, the show's creator, during most of its nine-year network life. Jack Smith became the emcee for the show's syndicated version. "Strike It Rich," the program in which viewers could aid contestants in desperate need through the "heartline," was hosted by Warren Hull throughout its full night and day CBS run.

That brings us to the fourth show, "You Bet Your Life" with Groucho Marx. Begun on radio in 1947, the show was completely centered around this Marx brother's quick-witted comic talent. Each week, George Fenneman, Groucho's sidekick, would start the proceedings by announcing, "And now, the one, the only, Groucho!" and laughter would abound for the next 30 minutes. Between the laughs, "You Bet Your Life" was a quiz show where contestants working in pairs had the opportunity to win money. But more often, the only opportunity they had was to be the brunt of Groucho's humor. This show was an immediate hit and stayed in the NBC lineup for the next 11 years.

ABC's expectations were very high when it brought one of the biggest names in music, Frank Sinatra, to television with a musical variety show this fall. Sinatra began a two-year run that was, unfortunately, doomed almost from the start. The network's programming strategy of placing him opposite big competition backfired. Instead of knocking off the competition, it knocked him off. In his first year, he was up against the high-rated "Your Show of Shows" on Saturday nights and did poorly in the ratings. For his second year, the network placed him against even stronger competition, the No. 2-rated "Texaco Star Theater" with Milton Berle. After this failure, Sinatra vowed he would not do a weekly series again, but in the latter part of the fifties he changed his mind and returned.

This season, well-known humorist Sam Levenson began hosting the first of three shows he would have during the fifties. This ex-schoolteacher based his homespun brand of humor on his observations of family life, both his own and others. During the time he did not have a show on the air, he made frequent appearances on Ed Sullivan's show and on various panel shows. He also substituted for Herb Shriner on "Two for the Money," and in 1959 filled in for five months for Arthur Godfrey, who was recuperating from a serious illness.

For years, radio listeners were familiar with this advertising pitch echoed by announcer Andre Baruch: "LSMFT — Lucky Strike Means Fine Tobacco." It also meant they were listening to "Your Hit Parade." But from now on, it would mean they were watching "Your Hit Parade," as the popular radio show of hit songs became a hit TV show. Each week the top songs that were determined by "Your Hit Parade survey checks, the best-sellers on sheet music and phonograph records, the songs most heard on the air and most played on the automatic coin machines . . ." were performed in elaborately produced settings. Among the early regulars on this show that was to become a Saturday-night staple for eight years were singers Eileen Wilson, Snooky Lanson, and Dorothy Collins, along with Raymond Scott and his orchestra. Later, other regulars included singers June Valli, Russell Arms, and Giselle MacKenzie.

THE FRANK SINATRA SHOW: October 7, 1950–April 1, 1952, CBS. Frank Sinatra (host)

THE SAM LEVENSON SHOW: January 27, 1951–June 10, 1952; April 27, 1959–September 25, 1959, CBS. Sam Levenson (host)

THE STU ERWIN SHOW: October 21, 1950–April 13, 1955, ABC. June Collyer and Stu Erwin

THE VAUGHN MONROE SHOW: October 10, 1950–July 3, 1951; August 31, 1954–September 6, 1955, CBS, NBC. Vaughn Monroe (host)

THE PRUDENTIAL FAMILY PLAYHOUSE: October 10, 1950–March 27, 1951, CBS. Logan Ramsey, Hazel Dawn, and Ruth Gordon in "Over 21"

SHOWTIME, U.S.A. October 1, 1950–June 24, 1951, ABC. Joey Faye, Phil Silvers, and chorus girls

I COVER TIMES SQUARE: October 5, 1950–January 11, 1951, ABC. Harold Huber

THE PAUL WINCHELL–JERRY MAHONEY SHOW: September 18, 1950–May 23, 1954, NBC. Jerry Mahoney and Paul Winchell

THE PETER LIND HAYES SHOW: November 23, 1950–March 29, 1951, NBC. Mary Healy and Peter Lind Hayes

YOU BET YOUR LIFE: October 5, 1950–September 21, 1961, NBC. George Fenneman and Groucho Marx (host)

DOWN YOU GO: May 30, 1951–September 8, 1956, ABC, CBS, Dumont, NBC. Dr. Bergan Evans (host), Francis Coughlin, and Toni Gilman

CAN YOU TOP THIS?: October 3, 1950–March 26, 1951, ABC. Peter Donald, Senator Ed Ford, Joe Laurie, Jr., Harry Hershfield, and Ward Wilson (host)

YOU BET YOUR LIFE: Stuffed duck that gave contestants extra money if they guessed the secret word, and Groucho Marx

IT'S NEWS TO ME: July 2, 1951–August 27, 1954, CBS. John Daly (host), Anna Lee, John Henry Faulk, Constance Bennett, and Quincy Howe

THE COLGATE COMEDY HOUR: Fred Allen

THE COLGATE COMEDY HOUR: Jimmy Durante

THE COLGATE COMEDY HOUR: Eddie Cantor

THE COLGATE COMEDY HOUR: Bob Hope

THE COLGATE COMEDY HOUR: Ben Blue

THE COLGATE COMEDY HOUR: September 10, 1950–December 25, 1955, NBC. Charlie McCarthy, Edgar Bergen, and Sue Carson

THE COLGATE COMEDY HOUR: Abbott and Costello

THE COLGATE COMEDY HOUR: Ethel Merman and Frank Sinatra

THE COLGATE COMEDY HOUR: Dean Martin and Jerry Lewis

ALL STAR REVUE (FOUR STAR REVUE):
Martha Raye

ALL STAR REVUE (FOUR STAR REVUE):
Jack Haley

ALL STAR REVUE (FOUR STAR REVUE):
Tallulah Bankhead

ALL STAR REVUE (FOUR STAR REVUE): October 4, 1950–April 18, 1953, NBC. Jimmy Durante, Helen Traubel, and Eddie Jackson

ALL STAR REVUE (FOUR STAR REVUE): Groucho Marx, Tallulah Bankhead, and Ethel Barrymore

AMOS 'N' ANDY: June 28, 1951–June 11, 1953, CBS. Alvin Childress, Tim Moore, and Spencer Williams, Jr. (Andy)

AMOS 'N' ANDY: Ernestine Wade and Tim Moore (Kingfish)

AMOS 'N' ANDY: Alvin Childress (Amos)

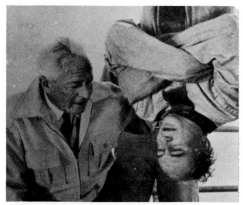

YOU ASKED FOR IT: December 29, 1950–September 27, 1959, Dumont, ABC; 1972, syndicated. Art Baker (first host)

YOU ASKED FOR IT: Jack Smith (second host) and Cleo (1958)

SOMERSET MAUGHAM THEATRE: October 18, 1950–December 10, 1951, CBS, NBC. Somerset Maugham (host)

THE GEORGE BURNS AND GRACIE ALLEN SHOW: Bea Benadaret, Larry Keating, George Burns, and Gracie Allen

BEULAH: Louise Beavers (the third Beulah) and Butterfly McQueen

BEULAH: Hattie McDaniel (the second Beulah)

THE GEORGE BURNS AND GRACIE ALLEN SHOW: October 12, 1950–September 22, 1958, CBS. Gracie Allen and George Burns

BEULAH: October 3, 1950–September 22, 1953, ABC. Ethel Waters (the original Beulah)

PULITZER PRIZE PLAYHOUSE: October 6, 1950–June 4, 1952, ABC. Helen Hayes and Charles Dingle in "The Late Christopher Bean"

BIG TOWN: Maxine Gates and Mark Stevens (1954–56)

PULITZER PRIZE PLAYHOUSE: Peggy Wood and Thomas Mitchell in "The Skin of Our Teeth"

FAYE EMERSON'S WONDERFUL TOWN: June 16, 1951–April 12, 1952, CBS. Faye Emerson (hostess)

BIG TOWN: October 5, 1950–October 2, 1956, CBS, Dumont, NBC. Jane Nigh and Patrick McVey (1950–54)

LUX VIDEO THEATER: October 2, 1950–September 12, 1957, CBS, NBC. *(Third from left)* Teresa Wright and Dan O'Herlihy in "The Enchanted Cottage"

LUX VIDEO THEATRE: J. Carrol Naish in "A Medal for Benny"

LUX VIDEO THEATRE: Dorothy Gish in "Miss Susie Slagle"

LUX VIDEO THEATRE: Mary Healy, Gordon MacRae, Sheila Stevens, and Peter Lind Hayes in "One Sunday Afternoon"

LUX VIDEO THEATRE: Diana Lynn and Ed Kemmer in "Princess O'Rourke"

LUX VIDEO THEATRE: Vivian Blaine and Richard Denning in "The Undesirable"

45

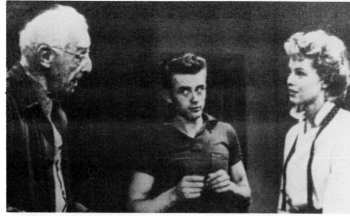

DANGER: September 19, 1950–May 31, 1955, CBS. Walter Hampden, James Dean, and Betsy Palmer in a drama presentation

FRONT PAGE DETECTIVE: July 6, 1951–November 13, 1953, Dumont. Edmund Lowe and John Davidson (guest)

RACKET SQUAD: 1950, syndicated; June 7, 1951–September 28, 1953, CBS. Reed Hadley and Ann Lee (guest)

THE CARMEL MYERS SHOW: June 26, 1951–February 21, 1952, ABC. Richard Rodgers (guest) and Carmel Myers (hostess)

THE FLORIAN ZABACH SHOW: March 10, 1951–June 9, 1951, CBS. Florian Zabach (host)

TREASURY MEN IN ACTION: September 11, 1950–September 30, 1955, ABC, NBC. Walter Greaza

STRIKE IT RICH: July 4, 1951–January 12, 1955, CBS. *(Right)* Warren Hull (host)

STAR OF THE FAMILY: Morton Downey (host) with guest

THE LILLI PALMER SHOW: March 29, 1951–June 28, 1951, CBS. Lilli Palmer (hostess)

TRUTH OR CONSEQUENCES: September 7, 1950–June 6, 1958, CBS, NBC. *(Second from left)* Ralph Edwards (host)

STAR OF THE FAMILY: September 22, 1950–June 26, 1952, CBS. Morton Downey

THE JACK BENNY PROGRAM: George Burns and Jack Benny as Gracie Allen

THE JACK BENNY PROGRAM: Eddie "Rochester" Anderson

THE JACK BENNY PROGRAM: Jack Benny and Bing Crosby

THE JACK BENNY PROGRAM: Jack Benny, Rochester, and Benny's car, "the Maxwell"

THE JACK BENNY PROGRAM: Mary Livingston

THE JACK BENNY PROGRAM: Don Wilson

THE JACK BENNY PROGRAM: October 28, 1950–September 10, 1965, CBS, NBC. Jack Benny

THE JACK BENNY PROGRAM: Jack Benny and Marilyn Monroe

ELLERY QUEEN: October 19, 1950– November 26, 1952, Dumont, ABC; 1954, syndicated. Lee Bowman (early Ellery Queen)

THE DOODLES WEAVER SHOW: June 9, 1951–September 1, 1951, NBC. Doodles Weaver (host)

THE STEVE ALLEN SHOW: December 25, 1950–September 11, 1952, CBS. Steve Allen (host)

ELLERY QUEEN: Hugh Marlowe (later Ellery Queen) and Joan Willes (guest)

MEET CORLISS ARCHER: July 12, 1951–March 29, 1952, CBS; 1954, syndicated. Lugena Sanders (Corliss Archer) and Bobby Ellis

A DATE WITH JUDY: June 2, 1951–September 30, 1953, ABC. Jimmie Sommers and Patricia Crowley (original Judy Foster)

WHO'S WHOSE: June 25, 1951 (one telecast), CBS. Robin Chandler and Phil Baker (co-hosts)

YOUNG MR. BOBBIN: August 26, 1951–May 18, 1952, NBC. Jane Seymour, Jackie Kelk (Mr. Bobbin), and Nydia Westman

THE HORACE HEIDT SHOW: October 2, 1950– September 24, 1951, CBS. *(Left, back)* Horace Heidt (host)

TV'S TOP TUNES: July 2, 1951–September 3, 1955, CBS. Peggy Lee and Mel Torme (the first hosts)

CRIME PHOTOGRAPHER: April 19, 1951– June 5, 1952, CBS. Darren McGavin

1951-52

This season television became a true national viewing medium. As the fall schedule was about to begin, the coast-to-coast coaxial cable was completed. This enabled 52 cities, totaling 94 stations, to be electronically linked—permitting viewers across the country to see a televised event or program simultaneously. Before this, less than 50 percent of the country's TV homes could be reached by live network television. Now 95 percent had the capability. And for the record, the first live coast-to-coast broadcast was President Harry Truman's address to the Japanese Peace Treaty Conference in San Francisco on September 4, 1951. This technological advance also enabled shows originating in Los Angeles to be broadcast live throughout the United States. It was a big boost to programming because many radio and film stars living and working on the West Coast were more receptive to the new medium, now that they no longer needed to go to New York to be involved with television.

Television's phenomenal growth was already significantly cutting into the audience of the other major entertainment mediums. Radio was way down in TV cities. Bob Hope's radio-show ratings dropped from approximately a 24 percent share in 1949 to a 13 percent share this year and was continuing downward. Movie theaters were closing across the country because attendance in cities with television was down from 20 percent to as much as 40 percent. By the end of 1951, ABC, NBC, and CBS (particularly the latter two) were for the first time making profits exceeding their radio-network operations. And television over all was profiting for the first time, with all but a few of the 108 operating stations finishing the year in the black. By the end of this season, more than 18 million sets would be in almost 30 percent of American homes.

While many familiar shows were back this season (giving TV a program lineup that was beginning to have the consistency radio had for years), there were several outstanding new series. "I Love Lucy," "Dragnet," "Goodyear Playhouse," "Hallmark Hall of Fame," and "See It Now" were all standouts. Also noteworthy were "Schlitz Playhouse of Stars" and "Mr. Peepers."

On Monday night, October 15, 1951, at 9:00 P.M., the curtain went up on a situation-comedy program that would become the most popular in the history of television. Red-haired film actress Lucille Ball and Cuban bandleader Desi Arnaz debuted as the uproarious stars of "I Love Lucy" on CBS, and the show became an overnight sensation. During the six years of this original network run, it ranked first four times, second once, and third once in the yearly ratings. But "I Love Lucy" has never been off the air, running consecutively for more than 30 years, and today its tens of millions of fans spread over several generations. The zany antics of Lucy and Desi and their close friends Fred and Ethel Mertz will probably go on making viewers laugh forever. More has been written and chronicled about this series than any other since the inception of television. Just a few tidbits: it was the first sitcom to be filmed before a live audience; Lucy and Ricky lived at 623 East 68th Street in Manhattan; the Mayer twins, Michael and Joseph, originally played little Ricky; and John Wayne made his TV debut on the show.

"The story you are about to see is true. The names have been changed to protect the innocent." This was the highly dramatic statement that preceded each episode of "Dragnet," a new police-drama series that began on NBC. Originating on radio in 1949, it easily made the shift to TV and remained one of the top programs during most of these initial network years. The show was created and directed by Jack Webb, who also starred as the taciturn Sgt. Joe Friday. This was the first series to depict police work for what it really is; mundane, tedious, and unglamorous. Certainly it was far from the romanticized image of crime fighting represented in countless earlier radio and television programs and in many films. Webb's original co-star from the radio series, Barton Yarborough, appeared in only one TV episode and then suddenly died of a heart attack. Subsequent co-stars, Barney Phillips, followed by Herb Ellis, were short term until Ben Alexander came along to play Friday's partner, Officer Frank Smith, for the remainder of the series. The show's title theme, composed by Walter Schumann and recorded by Ray Anthony and His Orchestra, became one of the top hits of 1953. After being off the air for most of the sixties, "Dragnet" made a network comeback in 1967 starring Webb with a new cast. It wasn't able to match the following of the original series but still managed a three-year run. And reruns can still be seen today.

"Goodyear Playhouse" was another quality program that today is considered part of TV's Golden Age. For six seasons, "Playhouse" presented full-hour, live, outstanding original plays. Three of these TV dramas, Paddy Chayefsky's "Marty," starring Rod Steiger, "The Catered Affair," with Thelma Ritter, and "The Bachelor Party," with Eddie Albert, were reshot for the big screen and became successful motion pictures. Among the future stars who gave their first major television performances were Rod Steiger, William Shatner, and Susan Strasberg. In its final three seasons on the air, though, the show changed its format to half-hour filmed dramas. Many stars appeared in these including Edward G. Robinson, Errol Flynn, Paul Douglas, and James Mason.

"When you care enough to send the very best," Hallmark Cards' perennial advertising theme, was first heard on "The Hallmark Hall of Fame" this season. Today, this show, after more than 30 years on the air, still is one of the most qualitative and respected anthology programs ever. It began as a half-hour weekly series hosted by Sarah Churchill. After a few years it evolved into a series of 90-minute to two-hour specials, three to six times a year, that have continued to this day. "Hall of Fame" was associated exclusively with NBC for years, but in the last few, their productions have been on both NBC and CBS. The series has presented classical and contemporary dramas, period plays, and musicals. A sampling of its many productions is a virtual hall of fame of famous works: "Hamlet," "Moby Dick," "Macbeth," "Alice in Wonderland," "The Taming of the Shrew," "Born Yesterday," "Cyrano de Bergerac," "The Fantasticks," "The Man Who Came to Dinner," "Brief Encounter," "Beauty and the Beast," and "Kiss Me Kate." And as good as the material were the stars. Julie Harris, Dame Judith Anderson, and Maurice Evans made frequent appearances. Mary Martin, Arthur Hill, George C. Scott, Hume Cronyn, Christopher Plummer, Richard Burton, Lee Remick, Robert Redford, Orson Welles, Sophia Loren, Martin Balsam, and Elizabeth Taylor, among others, appeared over the years.

"See It Now," with Edward R. Murrow live coast to coast, premiered on November 18, 1951, with a dramatic split-screen shot for viewers; for the first time, San Francisco's Golden Gate Bridge and New York's Brooklyn Bridge, 3,000 miles apart, were seen simultaneously. This show was the prototype for the in-depth, quality TV documentary; it was the impetus for television news to emerge from its infancy; and it provided the foundation for all future investigative reporting. Quite an accomplishment. And quite a show.

Two other shows of interest began this season. "Schlitz Playhouse of Stars," a fine anthology series, initially was an hour-long live show but gradually became a 30-minute filmed program over the course of its nearly eight years on CBS. Countless stars like David Niven and Rosalind Russell, and stars-to-be, like Lee Van Cleef, Janet Leigh, and Amanda Blake (the future Miss Kitty of "Gunsmoke"), made appearances on this show. Near the end of the TV year, NBC introduced a live situation comedy as a fill-in before the next season was to begin. The show, "Mr. Peepers," starred Wally Cox as a low-key junior high-school science teacher. Cox was supported by a talented cast that included Tony Randall, Marion Lorne, Patricia Benoit, and Ernest Truex. The show was supposed to run just eight weeks, but viewer response was so strong that NBC put it on its schedule for the forthcoming year. This replacement show lasted three years.

Entertainers with their own weekly evening shows were Ezio Pinza, Dennis Day, Kate Smith, Liberace, Bob (Elliott)

and Ray (Goulding), Herb Shriner, and country-and-Western singer Eddy Arnold. Two top personalities who would become regulars on the small screen for many years took the plunge: Red Skelton and Dinah Shore. And Jack Benny continued to enter the new medium cautiously, this time appearing on six occasions throughout the TV year.

NBC continued to expand viewing time and introduced the first daily early-morning network show, "Today." It began telecasting the World Series, an event it would exclusively cover for the next 25 years. And it also premiered the first opera written especially for television, "Amahl and the Night Visitors," on Christmas Eve. During this decade, the show became an annual holiday event.

On CBS, viewers had the opportunity to see one of the first adult science-fiction anthology series, "Out There," and one of the earliest medical shows, "City Hospital," starring Melville Ruick. And, late in the season, it hired a new anchorman to cover the forthcoming political conventions, Walter Cronkite.

Finally, two audience-participation shows began that were to be seen throughout the decade, "I've Got a Secret" and "Masquerade Party." The former's TV life span was far longer, and it remained on the CBS network until 1967. It then went off for several years, came back in syndication for a while, and returned to the network until its demise in 1976. Throughout most of the years, Garry Moore was its host. Subsequent hosts were Steve Allen and Bill Cullen. "Masquerade Party" debuted on NBC, then moved to CBS, and finally to ABC. Many of the best-known hosts of this programming genre worked on the show, including Bud Collyer, Robert Q. Lewis, Bert Parks, and Peter Donald.

SEE IT NOW: November 18, 1951–July 7, 1958, CBS. Edward R. Murrow (host)

SEE IT NOW: Grandma Moses

SEE IT NOW: Marion Anderson

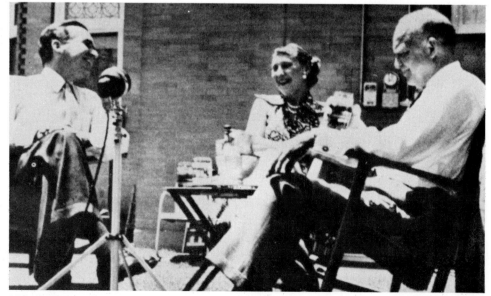

SEE IT NOW: Murrow with President and Mrs. Eisenhower

SKY KING: September 16, 1951–September 12, 1954, NBC, ABC. Kirby Grant (Sky King)

SKY KING: Gloria Winters

THE TODAY SHOW: January 14, 1952–present, NBC. Dave Garroway (original host)

SCHLITZ PLAYHOUSE OF STARS: October 5, 1951–March 27, 1959, CBS. James Dean and Pat Hardy in "The Unlighted Road"

SCHLITZ PLAYHOUSE OF STARS: CBS. Charles Nolte in "Billy Budd"

SCHLITZ PLAYHOUSE OF STARS: Scott Brady, Marie Windsor, and Ernie Kovacs in "The Salted Mine"

SCHLITZ PLAYHOUSE OF STARS: Madge Kennedy, Tom Moore, Francis X. Bushman, and Doris Kenyon in "The Secret"

SCHLITZ PLAYHOUSE OF STARS: Steve Forrest and James Gregory in "Policeman Faces a Bribe"

SCHLITZ PLAYHOUSE OF STARS: Guy Madison and Ronnie Know in "You Can't Win 'em All"

DOORWAY TO DANGER: July 4, 1952–August 28, 1953, NBC. Stacy Harris

CELANESE THEATER: October 3, 1951–June 25, 1952, ABC. Edna Best and Ruth Chatterton in "Old Acquaintance"

CELANESE THEATER: Richard Burton, June Havoc, and John Qualen in "Anna Christie"

WILD BILL HICKOK: Andy Devine and Guy Madison

THE DENNIS DAY SHOW: February 8, 1952–August 2, 1954, NBC. Dennis Day and Ann Blythe (guest)

THE DENNIS DAY SHOW: Dennis Day and Barbara Ruick

MR. DISTRICT ATTORNEY: October 1, 1951–June 23, 1952, ABC; 1954, syndicated. David Brian (Jay Jostyn was the original Mr. D.A.)

WILD BILL HICKOK: 1951–56, syndicated. Guy Madison (James Butler "Wild Bill" Hickok) and Andy Devine

THOSE TWO: November 26, 1951–April 24, 1953, NBC. Pinky Lee and Vivian Blaine

THOSE TWO: Martha Stewart and Pinky Lee

DRAGNET: Barney Phillips, Jack Webb, and Peggy Weber (guest)

THE RANGE RIDER: 1951–53, syndicated. Jock Mahoney

THE RANGE RIDER: Jock Mahoney and Dick West

DRAGNET: January 3, 1952–September 6, 1959, NBC. Jack Webb

DRAGNET: Jack Webb and Ben Alexander

GOODYEAR TELEVISION PLAYHOUSE: October 14, 1951–September 22, 1957, NBC. Julie Harris and Leslie Nielsen in "October Story" (the series' premiere telecast)

GOODYEAR TELEVISION PLAYHOUSE: Phyllis Newman and George Grizzard in "The Gene Austin Story"

GOODYEAR TELEVISION PLAYHOUSE: Thelma Ritter and Pat Henning in "The Catered Affair"

GOODYEAR TELEVISION PLAYHOUSE: Lillian Gish and Eva Marie Saint in "A Trip to Bountiful"

GOODYEAR TELEVISION PLAYHOUSE: Louis Edmonds, Cyril Ritchard, and Jill Kraft in "A Visit to a Small Planet"

GOODYEAR TELEVISION PLAYHOUSE: Rod Steiger and Nancy Marchand in "Marty"

GOODYEAR TELEVISION PLAYHOUSE: Gracie Fields, Roger Moore, and Jessica Tandy in "A Murder Is Announced"

HALLMARK HALL OF FAME: January 6, 1952–present, NBC, CBS. Lloyd Nolan, Helen Hayes, Burgess Meredith, Betty Field, and Lee Kinsolving in "Ah, Wilderness"

HALLMARK HALL OF FAME: Florence Reed, Mary Martin, and George Abbott in "The Skin of Our Teeth"

HALLMARK HALL OF FAME: Sarah Churchill, Barry Jones, Ruth Chatterton, and Maurice Evans in "Hamlet"

HALLMARK HALL OF FAME: Patricia Morrison, Alfred Drake, Julie Wilson, and Bill Hays in "Kiss Me Kate"

HALLMARK HALL OF FAME: Maurice Evans, Judith Anderson, Stants Cotsworth, and Richard Waring in "Macbeth"

HALLMARK HALL OF FAME: E. G. Marshall, Sidney Blackmer, Greer Garson, and Eileen Heckart in "The Little Foxes"

HALLMARK HALL OF FAME: Eli Wallach and Julie Harris in "The Lark"

HALLMARK HALL OF FAME: George Peppard and Julie Harris in "Little Moon of Alban"

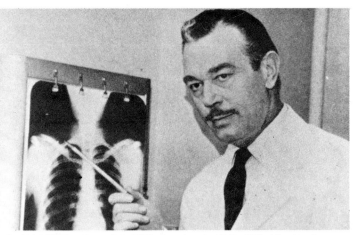

CITY HOSPITAL: March 25, 1952–October 1, 1953, CBS. Melville Ruick

THE NAME'S THE SAME: December 5, 1951–October 7, 1955, ABC. Abe Burrows, Joan Alexander, Meredith Wilson, and Robert Q. Lewis (host)

LIFE IS WORTH LIVING: February 12, 1952–April 8, 1957, Dumont, ABC. Bishop Fulton J. Sheen (host)

AMAHL AND THE NIGHT VISITORS: December 24, 1951, aired on Christmas Eve during most of the decade

FOREIGN INTRIGUE: 1951–55, syndicated. Ann Preville and James Daly

THE DOCTOR: August 24, 1952–June 28, 1953, NBC. Warner Anderson and Sandy Kenyon (guest)

MARK SABER: October 5, 1951– May 15, 1960, ABC, NBC. Tom Conway (original Mark Saber)

MARK SABER: Donald Gray (later Mark Saber)

I LOVE LUCY: October 15, 1951–September 24, 1961, CBS; 1967, syndicated. Lucille Ball, Vivian Vance, Desi Arnaz and William Frawley

I LOVE LUCY: Harry James (guest), Betty Grable (guest), William Frawley, Vivian Vance, Desi Arnaz, and Lucille Ball

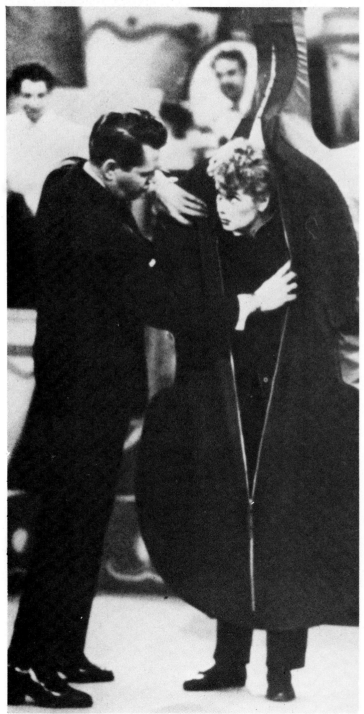

I LOVE LUCY: Desi Arnaz and Lucille Ball

I LOVE LUCY: Vivian Vance and William Frawley

I LOVE LUCY: Desi Arnaz and Lucille Ball

I LOVE LUCY: Vivian Vance, Lucille Ball, and William Frawley

I LOVE LUCY: Desi Arnaz and Lucille Ball (Lucy Ricardo)

THE DINAH SHORE SHOW: November 27, 1951–July 18, 1957, NBC. Dinah Shore (hostess)

THE ROY ROGERS SHOW: December 30, 1951–June 23, 1957, NBC. Roy Rogers and Dale Evans

THE DINAH SHORE SHOW: Louis Prima, Keely Smith, George Montgomery, Dinah Shore, Ernie Kovacs, and Edie Adams

I'VE GOT A SECRET: June 19, 1952–April 3, 1967, CBS; 1972, syndicated. Bill Cullen, Jayne Meadows, Garry Moore (host), Henry Morgan, and Faye Emerson

THE AL PEARCE SHOW: July 3, 1952–September 4, 1952, CBS. Al Pearce (host)

THE HUNTER: July 3, 1952–December 26, 1954, CBS, NBC. Rita Lynn and Barry Nelson (host)

MASQUERADE PARTY: July 14, 1952–September 16, 1960, NBC, CBS, ABC; 1972, syndicated. Phil Silvers, Buff Cobb, Ogden Nash, Ilka Chase, and Peter Donald (host)

MR. PEEPERS: July 3, 1952–June 12, 1955, NBC. Wally Cox (Robinson Peepers), Tony Randall, Marion Lorne, and Patricia Benoit

MR. PEEPERS: Patricia Benoit and Wally Cox (Mr. Peepers's wedding)

THE RED SKELTON SHOW: Red Skelton as Cookie the Sailor

THE RED SKELTON SHOW: Red Skelton as the Clown

THE RED SKELTON SHOW: September 30, 1951–August 29, 1971, NBC, CBS. Red Skelton as Clem Kaddidlehopper (the Yokel)

THE RED SKELTON SHOW: Red Skelton as Willy Lump Lump (the Drunk)

THE LIBERACE SHOW: July 1, 1952–August 28, 1952, NBC; 1953-55, syndicated; October 13, 1958–September 16, 1969, ABC, CBS. Liberace (host)

THE KATE SMITH EVENING HOUR: September 19, 1951–June 11, 1952, NBC. Kate Smith (hostess)

THE BIG PAYOFF: June 29, 1952–September 27, 1953, NBC. Contestants with Randy Merriman (host)

THE BIG PAYOFF: Bess Myerson (hostess)

MY FRIEND IRMA: January 8, 1952–June 25, 1954, CBS. Marie Wilson and Cathy Lewis

BOB AND RAY: November 26, 1951–September 28, 1953, NBC. Bob Elliott, Audrey Meadows, Ray Goulding

BOB AND RAY: Ray Goulding, Cloris Leachman, and Bob Elliott

MY FRIEND IRMA: Marie Wilson (Irma Peterson)

KIT CARSON: 1951, syndicated. Bill Williams (Kit Carson)

KIT CARSON: Bill Williams and Don Diamond

BOSTON BLACKIE: 1951, syndicated. Kent Taylor (Boston Blackie)

MY LITTLE MARGIE: June 16, 1952–August 24, 1955, CBS, NBC. Charles Farrell and Gale Storm (Margie Albright)

SUPERMAN: 1951–57, syndicated. George Reeves

1952-53

A generation of Democratic presidents, Roosevelt and Truman, was about to end shortly after the new television year began. Well-liked World War II military commander, and Republican, Dwight D. "Ike" Eisenhower would defeat Democratic nominee Adlai Stevenson for the White House. The war in faroff South Korea had been going on for more than two years and the new president, true to his campaign pledge, went there to use his influence to hasten its end. Ike's visit did not provide any significant progress in ending the conflict, but, through the magic of his TV coverage, it did provide Americans with a greater awareness of this distant land. Paralleling this was the general increase in war coverage by the networks, which were no longer willing to take a back seat to the print media on important events like this. They wanted to make their medium a prime source of news for the nation. In addition, as part of this increased news appetite, just prior to this season the networks had for the first time individually covered the presidential conventions. Previously, the coverage had been pooled.

The number of television stations by the end of this season would soar from 108 to nearly 200. Both CBS and NBC expanded their production facilities by opening West Coast studios, and thus enhanced their operations significantly. CBS located in Hollywood and NBC in Burbank, and thus began the anticipated Hollywood/television marriage. Another marriage that was already going well was the one between ordinary Americans and television. By this season, TV had really become an intricate part of many lives. Countless families began planning activities around the daily TV schedule. One event that indicated how much television was becoming part of the nation's everyday life occurred in midseason: Lucy and Ricky became the proud parents of a baby boy, Ricky, Jr., on "I Love Lucy" (January 19, 1953). The birth was seen by a record number of viewers (more than 70 percent of all sets were tuned into the program), further

evidence television had indeed become another member of the American family.

Other television events this season included the Ford Motor Company's extravagant 50th-anniversary show. Broadway's Mary Martin and Ethel Merman teamed up their abundant musical talent for this program, which was telecast simultaneously on NBC and CBS. The first national telecast of the Academy Awards presentation, in Hollywood, took place on March 19, 1953, with Bob Hope as emcee. British pomp and circumstance were brought into American homes when ABC, CBS, and NBC, in cooperation with the British Broadcasting Corporation (BBC), presented the coronation of Elizabeth II as the new queen of England. And ABC began bringing major-league baseball to the nation via its "Game of the Week" with Dizzy Dean doing the play-by-play.

Eight of the top-rated shows of the past season—"Arthur Godfrey's Talent Scouts," the "Texaco Star Theater," "Your Show of Shows," "I Love Lucy," "The Colgate Comedy Hour," "Arthur Godfrey and His Friends," "Fireside Theater," and "You Bet Your Life"—would again be among the top 10 shows this year. Also vying for a place on the list were Red Buttons, Ernie Kovacs, and Jackie Gleason. Comic Buttons, in his first season hosting his own variety show, was a smash. He opened each program with his "Ho-Ho" theme song, which remains his trademark. Buttons created several very funny characters, one of which always appeared each week. They were Rocky Buttons, a punch-drunk boxer; Keeglefarvan, a knuckleheaded German; Buttons the Bellboy; the Kupke Kid; and the Sad Sack.

Kovacs, already known to daytime viewers, got the opportunity to host his own prime-time variety show on CBS, opposite Milton Berle's "Texaco Star Theater." Kovacs's brilliant, innovative comedy style was excellently displayed on the program, but, unfortunately, up against Berle, the show had a short tenure.

CBS brought "The Great One," Gleason, to its network this fall to begin an association of nearly 20 years. Gleason was already one of the biggest stars on the Dumont network when CBS lured him away with a very lucrative (for that time) contract. Gleason was happy, his new network was happy, and he went on to become a Saturday-night fixture.

Three marvelous, qualitative programs debuted this season that would be rewarded with many honors over the next few years. "Omnibus," with host Alistair Cooke, was television drama and entertainment at its highest; "You Are There," hosted by newsman Walter Cronkite, was a historical drama that "covered" world-famous events; and the documentary series "Victory at Sea" used actual footage to tell the story of the Allies' triumph in World War II.

Two shows that were a little different from most programming began long runs this year. "Death Valley Days," the oldest, continuously broadcast Western on radio, made the jump to TV. Since 1930 it had been a favorite with millions, but when it got to television it didn't get on the networks. Rather, it found a home in syndication, where it ran for 18 years, cranking out almost 600 episodes. Stanley Andrews was the original host, followed by Ronald Reagan, Robert Taylor, and Dale Robertson. The other show was Ralph Edwards's unusual biographical show, "This Is Your Life." The program told the life story of a famous (or ordinary) person each week by surprising the guest of honor with long-lost friends and relatives from the past. It was a real tearjerker. Many celebrities were honored guests over its nine years on NBC, including Eddie Cantor, Lillian Roth, Lowell Thomas, and Stan Laurel and Oliver Hardy.

There was a proliferation of situation comedies this fall: "The Adventures of Ozzie and Harriet," "Our Miss Brooks," "Ethel and Albert," "Meet Millie," "I Married Joan," "My Hero," "Life with Luigi," "Doc Corkle," "Heaven for Betsy," "Leave It to Larry," "Private Secretary," "My Son Jeep," and for the second time, with a new cast, "The Life of Riley." Five of the shows in this large group were noteworthy.

"The Adventures of Ozzie and Harriet," on ABC, went on to become prime-time television's longest-running situation comedy (14 years). Like many sitcoms of this early era, it had its genesis on radio (1944). The program concerned itself with all the little adventures an active, middle-class family (in this case, real-life family Ozzie and Harriet Nelson and their sons, David and Ricky) might have. Ozzie Nelson not only created the show, he also produced, directed, and as head writer, wrote many of the episodes that basically centered around his growing boys. During the series' first five years on radio, child actors were used as the Nelsons' children. But in 1949 David and Ricky became part of the radio cast, and throughout the show's long TV tenure, viewers watched the boys grow up, start careers, marry, and have their real-life wives become part of the show. Ricky, while still on the show, became a big rock 'n' roll star while David got interested in the behind-the-camera activities of TV. The supporting cast over the years included Don DeFore as Thorny Thornberry, the Nelsons' neighbor; Lyle Talbot as Joe Randolph, a friend; Mary Jane Croft as Clara Randolph, Joe's wife; Frank Cady as Doc Williams; and Parley Baer as Darby, another friend.

"Our Miss Brooks" was another radio comedy, begun in 1948, that moved to television this fall. Eve Arden played the wisecracking Connie Brooks, Madison High's favorite teacher. During the series' stay on CBS, there were two settings for the show. The first was Madison High School, in the city of Madison; the second was Mrs. Nestor's Private Elementary School, in California's San Fernando Valley. Most of the original supporting cast from radio made the transition to television smoothly. These included Gale Gordon as Osgood Conklin, the school principal; Richard Crenna as Walter Denton, the student with the high-pitched voice; Jane Morgan as Mrs. Davis, Connie's landlady; and Gloria McMillan as Harriet Conklin, Osgood's daughter and Walter's girlfriend. Philip Boynton, Miss Brooks's heartthrob, played by Robert Rockwell, was the only regular cast member who had not been part of the radio cast. "Our Miss Brooks" became a top-15 show in its second year, on its way to a four-year run on Friday nights. In all, 127 episodes were aired.

"I Married Joan" starred Joan Davis and Jim Backus as Joan Stevens and Judge Bradley Stevens. The show was about the trials and tribulations of a prominent domestic-court judge and his well-meaning but scatterbrained wife. There were a number of performers in supporting roles, but the only one who appeared with any regularity was Beverly Wills, who played Joan's much-younger sister. Interestingly, off the set she was Davis's daughter. Ninety-eight episodes were aired in the three seasons it was on NBC.

Ann Sothern, the movies' popular Maisie, became Susie McNamara in "Private Secretary" on NBC. Susie worked for theatrical agent Peter Sands, played by Don Porter, who in later years would go on to become Gidget's father in the one-season sitcom of the same name. Violet Praskins—Vi to her friends—played by Ann Tyrrell, was Susie's confidante as well as the switchboard operator for the agency where they worked. The cast also included Jesse White, later of Maytag washer commercial fame, as Sands's rival agent Cagey Calhoun, and Joan Banks as Sylvia, who was always looking for a handsome man to woo.

The fifth situation comedy of special note was "The Life of Riley," which originated on radio for NBC in the early forties. Stage and film performer William Bendix took the title role in 1943 and the program developed a loyal following that, by the late forties, was a natural for television. But when the switch was made (the 1949–50 season) Bendix wasn't available because of film commitments, so Jackie Gleason got the opportunity and made it his first TV series. Unfortunately, Gleason's portrayal of the incompetent Riley didn't catch on and the show was canceled after one season. For this season, NBC decided to revive "Riley" with the popular Bendix in the role. They gave him a new TV cast and the show clicked almost immediately. The Riley family consisted of wife Peg, played by Marjorie Reynolds; Lugene Sanders as daughter Babs; and Wesley Morgan as son Junior. Neighbors Jim and Honeybee Gillis (Tom D'Andrea and Gloria Blondell) and friends Waldo Binney (Sterling Holloway) and Otto Schmidlap (Henry Kulky) were in most episodes. Riley was so popular because he was Mr. Average with the average American family. While he was a bumbler, he was a nice bumbler. When he got into a jam or was the victim of a problem, he would moan "What a revoltin' development this is!" Who could not like him? The show enjoyed five years on Friday nights.

In the genre of dramatic anthologies, prominent film stars Henry Fonda, Claude Rains, Janet Gaynor, and Joan Crawford made their TV debuts on various shows. "The Plymouth Playhouse," on ABC, was a short-run show responsible for launching three series in the subsequent season: "Jamie," on ABC, with child actor Brandon DeWilde; "Colonel Flack," with Alan Mowbray on Dumont; and "Justice," with Paul Douglas and Lee Grant on NBC. (Gary Merrill and Dane Clark were the stars of the weekly series.)

The best new anthology of this season was "General Electric Theater," seen throughout its CBS life on Sunday nights at 9:00. For the first two seasons, its well-made episodes were not hosted. Then, film star Ronald Reagan took on the role at the start of the 1954–55 season and continued until the show's conclusion in 1962, occasionally starring in some of the dramas himself. There were many famous faces who made their TV dramatic debuts in this series, including Alan Ladd, Joseph Cotten, Fred MacMurray, James Stewart, Bette Davis, Myrna Loy, Fred Astaire, and Sammy Davis, Jr. Reagan and his wife, Nancy Davis, starred in one episode, "Money and the Minister." This was one of the rare times the future president and first lady ever performed together. In the show's nine years, 200 dramas were produced.

I MARRIED JOAN: October 15, 1952–April 6, 1955, NBC. Jim Backus and Joan Davis (Joan Stevens)

DANGEROUS ASSIGNMENT: 1952, syndicated. Brian Donlevy.

THE LARRY STORCH SHOW: July 11, 1953–September 12, 1953, CBS. Larry Storch (host) and Dorothy Hart (guest)

LEAVE IT TO LARRY: October 14, 1952–December 23, 1952, CBS. Eddie Albert (Larry Tucker)

DEATH VALLEY DAYS: Nancy Hale and Fess Parker in "Kickapoo Run"

DEATH VALLEY DAYS: Gardner McKay and Laurie Carroll in "The Big Rendezvous"

PENTAGON U.S.A.: August 6, 1953–October 1, 1953, CBS. Addison Richards and Edward Binns

DEATH VALLEY DAYS: 1952–70, syndicated. Stanley Andrews, the first host of "Death Valley Days"

DEATH VALLEY DAYS: James Franciscus and Don Beddoe in "Lady of the Press"

JIMMY HUGHES, ROOKIE COP: May 8, 1953–July 3, 1953, Dumont. William Redfield (Jimmy Hughes)

OMNIBUS: Hermione Gingold and Darren McGavin in "The Virtuous Island"

OMNIBUS: Michael Redgrave in "She Stoops to Conquer"

OMNIBUS: Joanne Woodward and Royal Dano in "Abraham Lincoln: The Early Years"

OMNIBUS: Robert Goodier, William Shatner, and Christopher Plummer in "Oedipus the King"

OMNIBUS: November 9, 1952–May 10, 1959, ABC, CBS, NBC. Alistair Cooke (host)

OMNIBUS: Gene Kelly in "Dancing: A Man's Game"

OMNIBUS: Yul Brynner in "A Lodging for the Night"

THE FORD 50th ANNIVERSARY SHOW: June 15, 1953, CBS, NBC. Ethel Merman and Mary Martin

THE BILLY DANIELS SHOW: October 5, 1952–December 28, 1952, ABC. Billy Daniels (host)

FOUR STAR PLAYHOUSE: Ray Stricklyn and Ida Lupino in "That Woman"

CHINA SMITH: 1952–53, syndicated. Dan Duryea (China Smith)

WONDERFUL JOHN ACTION: July 12, 1953–October 6, 1953, NBC. Harry Holcombe (John Action), Virginia Dwyer, Ronnie Walken, and Ian Martin

FOUR STAR PLAYHOUSE: September 25, 1952–September 27, 1956, CBS. Charles Boyer, Dick Powell, Merle Oberon, and David Niven—several of the "Playhouse" stars

THE WALTER WINCHELL SHOW: October 5, 1952–December 28, 1956; October 2, 1960–November 6, 1960, ABC, NBC. Walter Winchell (reporter)

YOU ARE THERE: February 1, 1953–October 13, 1957, CBS. Walter Cronkite (host)

MEDALLION THEATRE: July 11, 1953–April 3, 1954, CBS. Charlton Heston in "A Day in Town"

NAME THAT TUNE: George de Witt with contestants Eddie Hodges and Marine Corps Maj. John Glenn

MEET MILLIE: Ross Ford and Elena Verdugo (Millie Bronson)

THE BUICK CIRCUS HOUR: John Raitt, Dolores Gray, and Joe E. Brown

NAME THAT TUNE: July 6, 1953–October 19, 1959, CBS, NBC; 1970, syndicated; July 29, 1974–January 3, 1975, NBC; 1974, syndicated; January 3, 1977–June 10, 1977, NBC. George de Witt (host)

MEET MILLIE: October 25, 1952–February 28, 1956, CBS. Elena Verdugo and Ross Ford

THE BUICK CIRCUS HOUR: October 7, 1952–June 16, 1953, NBC. Joe E. Brown (host)

PRIVATE SECRETARY: Ann Tyrrell, Ann Sothern, and Jesse White

PRIVATE SECRETARY: February 1, 1953–September 10, 1957, CBS, NBC. Ann Sothern and Don Porter

ETHEL AND ALBERT: April 25, 1953–July 6, 1956, NBC, CBS, ABC. Alan Bunch (Albert Arbuckle), Peg Lynch (Ethel Arbuckle)

LIFE WITH LUIGI: September 22, 1952–June 4, 1953, CBS. J. Carrol Naish (Luigi Basco), Alan Reed, and Jody Gilbert

THE SATURDAY NIGHT REVUE: June 6, 1953–September 5, 1953, NBC. Hoagy Carmichael (host)

THE LIFE OF RILEY: January 2, 1953–August 22, 1958, NBC. Marjorie Reynolds, Lugene Sanders, William Bendix (Chester A. Riley) and Wesley Morgan

VICTORY AT SEA: October 26, 1952–April 26, 1953, NBC.

THE ADVENTURES OF OZZIE AND HARRIET: Ricky, Harriet, Ozzie, and David Nelson (early)

THE ADVENTURES OF OZZIE AND HARRIET: October 10, 1952–September 3, 1966, ABC. Ricky, Ozzie, Harriet, and David Nelson

THE ACADEMY AWARDS: March 19, 1953, NBC. Bob Hope hosts the first national telecast of this event

BIFF BAKER, U.S.A.: November 13, 1952–March 25, 1953, CBS. Alan Hale, Jr. (Biff Baker) and Randy Stewart

COKE TIME WITH EDDIE FISHER: April 29, 1953–February 22, 1957, NBC. Eddie Fisher (host)

HEAVEN FOR BETSY: September 30, 1952–December 25, 1952, CBS. Cynthia Stone (Betsy) and Jack Lemmon

DOC CORKLE: October 5,1952–October 19, 1952, NBC. Hope Emerson, Chester Conklin, Eddie Mayehoff (Doc Corkle), Connie Marshall, Billie Burke, and Arnold Stang

MY SON JEEP: July 9, 1953–September 22, 1953, NBC. Anne Sargent, Martin Huston (Jeep), and Jeffrey Lynn

THE ERNIE KOVACS SHOW: December 30, 1952–April 14, 1953; July 2, 1956–September 10, 1956, CBS, NBC. Ernie Kovacs (host)

THE ERNIE KOVACS SHOW: Ernie Kovacs as lisping poet Percy Dovetonsils

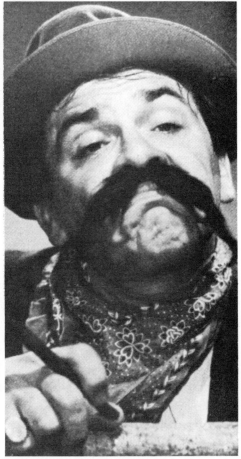

THE ERNIE KOVACS SHOW: Ernie Kovacs in character

THE RED BUTTONS SHOW: October 14, 1952–May 27, 1955, CBS, NBC. Red Buttons (host)

THE RED BUTTONS SHOW: Red Buttons as Rocky Buttons (a punch-drunk fighter)

THE RED BUTTONS SHOW: Red Buttons as Buttons the Bellboy

GENERAL ELECTRIC THEATER: Harpo and Chico Marx in "The Incredible Jewel Robbery"

GENERAL ELECTRIC THEATER: Ronald Reagan (host and occasional star) in "The Lord's Dollar"

GENERAL ELECTRIC THEATER: Bill Williams and Janet Gaynor in "Flying Wife"

GENERAL ELECTRIC THEATER: February 1, 1953–September 16, 1962; CBS. Charles Laughton and Eric Feldary in "The Last Lesson"

GENERAL ELECTRIC THEATER: Henry Fonda and Dorothy Malone in "Clown"

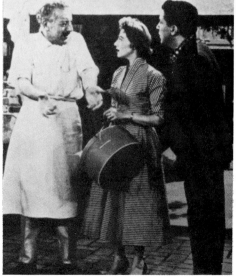

GENERAL ELECTRIC THEATER: Ezio Pinza, Joan Copland, and Mike Wallace in "The Half-Promised Land"

MY HERO: November 8, 1952–August 1, 1953, NBC. Gloria Winters and Robert Cummings

BALANCE YOUR BUDGET: October 18, 1952–May 2, 1953, CBS. Lynn Connor (assistant) and Bert Parks (host)

WHERE WAS I? September 2, 1952–October 6, 1953, Dumont. Peter Donald, Bill Cullen, and Nancy Guild

PLACE THE FACE: July 2, 1953–September 13, 1955, NBC, CBS. Bill Cullen (host) and contestants

JUDGE FOR YOURSELF: August 18, 1953–May 11, 1954, NBC. Kitty Kallen, Fred Allen (host), and the Skylarks

DOUBLE OR NOTHING: June 5, 1953–July 3, 1953, NBC. Bert Parks (host) and Joan Meinch

RAMAR OF THE JUNGLE: 1952–53, syndicated. Marjorie Lord and Jon Hall (Ramar)

ANNIE OAKLEY: 1952–56, syndicated. Brad Johnson, Gail Davis (Annie Oakley), and Jimmy Hawkins

OUR MISS BROOKS: October 3, 1952–September 21, 1956, CBS. Gale Gordon and Eve Arden (Connie Brooks)

THIS IS YOUR LIFE: October 1, 1952–September 10, 1961; 1970–71, syndicated. Ralph Edwards (host) and Lillian Roth (guest)

MR. AND MRS. NORTH: October 3, 1952–July 20, 1954, CBS, NBC. Barbara Britton and Richard Denning (Pamela and Jerry North)

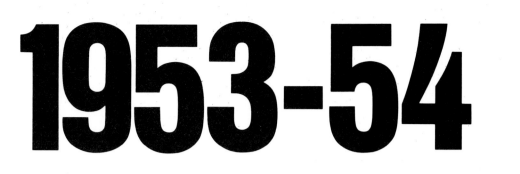

1953-54

Shortly before the season began, Americans were heartened by the end of the three-year-long Korean War. The truce was signed, prisoners of war were exchanged, and families eagerly anticipated having their loved ones home. President Eisenhower, however, cautioned the American people and the world that "an armistice had been won only on a single battlefield and peace had not yet been achieved in the world."

On the television battlefield, NBC had a new weapon in its arsenal: color. In August, just prior to the season, the network telecast its first color broadcast, which featured Kukla, Fran and Ollie with Arthur Fiedler and the Boston Pops Orchestra. NBC had a particular interest in color because its parent company, RCA, was one of the largest manufacturers of TV sets. For this reason, the network was more active in promoting color than its competitors.

Other NBC color-programming efforts this season were its annual "Amahl and the Night Visitors" for Christmas, a "Dragnet" episode with a Christmas story line, the "Tournament of Roses Parade" on New Year's day, and a few of "Your Hit Parade" shows. While this was quite small, it was a start. But a problem had also started. The cost of color sets was so high they weren't selling. Only 8,000 were built in the first six months of 1954. This resulted in only 68 hours of color broadcasting among all the networks in calendar year 1954. RCA and other manufacturers then decided to virtually stop production of these sets. Color-TV acceptance was still years away. And NBC's new weapon turned out to be a dud. On the brighter side, black-and-white-set sales were continuing to boom, with more than 6 million sold in 1953 and more than 7 million the following year.

The group of memorable or otherwise noteworthy shows were: "The U.S. Steel Hour," "The Kraft Television Theater" (ABC's version), "The Loretta Young Show" ("A Letter to Loretta"), Ed Murrow's interview series "Person to Person," and comedies "Make Room for Daddy" and "Topper."

ABC's "The U.S. Steel Hour" was on the air for 10 years (but on ABC only the first two seasons) and contributed richly to the history of live television drama. On this Golden Age program, performers such as Andy Griffith and Gene Hackman made their major TV debut, and even an unlikely dramatic actor, Johnny Carson, starred in two light dramas during the show's later years. "Kraft Television Theater," in addition to continuing on NBC, began appearing twice a week. Lee Remick, Tony Perkins, Anne Bancroft, George Peppard, Bradford Dillman, and Warren Beatty, among others, gave their first major TV performance on the series. The program's format allowed for such a variety of productions that even singers Gisele MacKenzie, Julius La Rosa, and Tommy Sands were found starring in music-related dramas. Both "Krafts" continued to give exposure to a multitude of actors and actresses early in their careers, including Paul Newman, Cloris Leachman, and Martin Milner. The exciting, compelling, original material on both programs was the result of efforts by the best writers in the business: Rod Serling, Paddy Chayefsky, Reginald Rose, and Tad Mosel, to name just a few.

Loretta Young's show began an eight-year stay on NBC Sunday nights. Her dramatic entrance at the beginning of each show, where she would come swirling through a doorway, dressed impeccably, and move to the center of a lavishly appointed setting to introduce the evening's episode, was memorable. In the early years she was not only the show's hostess but also its principal performer. Over the years many performers appeared several times, including Eddie Albert, Hugh O'Brian, James Daly, and Claude Akins. Ricardo Montalban and John Newland, who also directed many episodes, starred in nine or more shows.

Ed Murrow's second weekly television program, "Person to Person," remained a fixture on Friday nights at 10:30 for seven years. Murrow hosted as well as co-produced the show for almost six of the seven years. This was a program in which he interviewed celebrities and newsmakers live in their homes almost anywhere cameras could be taken in North America. From his TV studio, and with an inimitable style that included relaxing in a comfortable chair, cigarette in hand, Murrow (and thus the TV audience) would be shown around his guest's home. Some of the famous people who invited Murrow into their homes were the Duke and Duchess of Windsor, Leopold Stokowski, Roy Campanella, Marilyn Monroe, Fidel Castro, former New York Gov. Thomas Dewey, Sen. John F. Kennedy, and John Steinbeck. "Person to Person" was a fascinating, quality show. Each year it was nominated for, and many times received, various industry awards. And Murrow, himself, was also the recipient of many awards during the program's tenure. A heavy schedule, though, required him to relinquish his duty as host, and for a little more than the final season, Charles Collingwood took over.

Comedian Danny Thomas had been on and off television for a few years going nowhere. His nightclub-style comedy did not go over well on the small screen and at one point, in frustration, he condemned the medium as appealing "only to idiots"—and proclaimed that he would never get involved with it again. But things change. This season he brought to television a basically autobiographical situation comedy about a nightclub comic with a family. Its title: "Make Room for Daddy." The show was a quick winner and began an 11-year run, appearing the first four years on ABC and the next seven on CBS. Thomas had a strong supporting cast; Jean Hagen played his first wife, Margaret (ABC years); Sherry Jackson was his eleven-year-old daughter, Terry; Rusty Hamer was his seven-year-old son, Rusty; Marjorie Lord played his second wife (CBS years); and a second daughter, Linda, was played by Angela Cartwright (CBS years). The series' long success could be attributed to its believable handling of totally familiar domestic situations, the kind viewers experienced every day.

"Topper" was TV's first fantasy situation-comedy series. It was based on Thorne Smith's novel of the 1930s, which was made into a movie in 1937. "Topper" starred Leo G. Carroll as Cosmo Topper, a banker who, along with his wife, Henrietta (Lee Patrick), moved into a house haunted by the ghosts of the previous owners. Anne Jeffreys and Robert Sterling (husband and wife in real life) played the husband and wife ghosts Marion and George Kirby. The Kirbys mischievously, teasingly, and playfully befriended Topper. But as in other fantasies of this sort, only the principal character could see and hear them. This led to Topper's strange behavior, as seen by the people around him. Although it lasted only two seasons, this fun show was one of the best sitcoms this year.

But there was much more to this season than these half-dozen shows.

A onetime special was "General Foods 25th Anniversary Show." The company adopted Ford's formula of the previous season and celebrated its anniversary on TV. However, it went a little further than the carmaker and aired its show simultaneously on all four networks. Ford had used only CBS and NBC. Among the guests were Jack Benny, Mary Martin, Groucho Marx, John Raitt, Tony Martin, Rosemary Clooney, Yul Brynner, Ezio Pinza, Gordon MacRae, Ed Sullivan, and Rodgers and Hammerstein, whose music was featured throughout the show. Bob Hope, already on television as part of "The Colgate Comedy Hour," began to host his own monthly variety show. And Bing Crosby hosted and starred in his first telecast, but it would be almost a decade before he consented to do a weekly series.

There were a number of show-business performers who, for the first time, hosted their own prime-time programs.

Band leader Bob Crosby, brother of Bing, began a four-year stint on CBS with a variety show. Singer Jane Pickens and Tony Martin each had their own musical show. Spike Jones and his City Slicker band began on NBC, and in later years would be on CBS. The Dorsey Brothers, Jimmy and Tommy, hosted their musical program "Stage Show" on CBS. Elvis Presley made his national-television debut on the show at the tender age of twenty-one on January 28, 1956. In total, he made five appearances before his celebrated Ed Sullivan show appearance later that year in September. George Jessel, the "Toastmaster General of the United States," was signed by ABC to

host two shows this season, "The George Jessel Show" and "The Comeback Story," a drama-interview series. Both had short runs. Late in the TV year, a young Midwestern comedian from Nebraska who already was making a name for himself on local Los Angeles television began to host an audience-participation show on CBS. The program was "Earn Your Vacation," and the comedian was Johnny Carson.

And in programming, the medium's first series about a nurse starred Ella Raines in "Janet Dean, Registered Nurse." The longtime radio anthology "The Inner Sanctum" came to TV with its mysterious, creepy tales. Paul McGrath was the unseen host, Mr. Raymond. Comic hero "Joe Palooka," played by Jack Kirkwood, Jr., and literature's most famous sleuth, "Sherlock Holmes," starring Ronald Howard, ran for brief periods this season. An interesting counterspy series, "I Led Three Lives," debuted with Richard Carlson. The series was based on the true-life adventures of Herbert A. Philbrick, business executive, member of the American Communist Party, and undercover agent for the FBI. Though it never appeared on the networks, the 117 episodes shown in syndication developed a loyal following.

Unhappily, what also happened this season was the demise of "Your Show of Shows." Sid Caesar and company gave their last performance on June 5, 1954, as the season came to a close. The ratings were high, the viewers loyal, and the show could have gone on indefinitely, but Caesar and Imogene Coca felt it was time to go their separate ways and move on. Also another unhappy thing to happen was the difficulty Dumont had signing up strong network affiliates. It usually came in last in the competition to bring stations into the network lineup because it was continually losing money on its operations. By this season's end it was apparent that it would not be long before television would go from four networks to three.

PEPSI COLA PLAYHOUSE: October 2, 1953–June 26, 1955, ABC. Anita Colby (hostess)

THE TONY MARTIN SHOW: April 26, 1954–February 27, 1956, NBC. Tony Martin (host)

THE SPIKE JONES SHOW: January 2, 1954–September 25, 1961, NBC, CBS. Spike Jones and his band, the City Slickers

MAKE ROOM FOR DADDY (THE DANNY THOMAS SHOW): Sid Melton

MAKE ROOM FOR DADDY (THE DANNY THOMAS SHOW): September 29, 1953–September 14, 1964, ABC, CBS. Rusty Hamer, Angela Cartwright, Danny Thomas, Marjorie Lord, and *(standing)* Sherry Jackson (second family)

PUBLIC DEFENDER: March 11, 1954–June 23, 1955, CBS. Reed Hadley

BONINO: September 12, 1953–December 26, 1953, NBC. Mary Wickes and Ezio Pinza (Bonino)

MAKE ROOM FOR DADDY (THE DANNY THOMAS SHOW): *(Back)* Jean Hagen, Jessie White; *(front)* Rusty Hamer, Sherry Jackson, and Danny Thomas (first family)

MAKE ROOM FOR DADDY (THE DANNY THOMAS SHOW): Danny Thomas and Jean Hagen

THE MARRIAGE: July 1, 1954–August 19, 1954, NBC. Jessica Tandy, Larry Gates (guest), and Hume Cronyn

THAT'S MY BOY: April 10, 1954–January 1, 1955, CBS. Gil Stratton, Jr., and Eddie Mayehoff

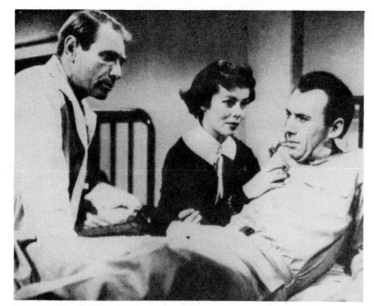

U.S. STEEL HOUR: October 27, 1953–June 12, 1963, ABC, CBS. Gary Merrill, Phyllis Kirk, and Richard Kiley in "P.O.W."

U.S. STEEL HOUR: Imogene Coca, Will Kulva, and Jack Klugman in "Funny Heart"

U.S. STEEL HOUR: Basil Rathbone, Jack Carson, Florence Henderson, and Jimmy Boyd in "Huck Finn"

U.S. STEEL HOUR: William Shatner, Kevin Coughlin, and Cameron Prud'Homme in "Old Marshalls Never Die"

U.S. STEEL HOUR: Patty Duke and Helen Hayes in "One Red Rose for Christmas"

U.S. STEEL HOUR: Wally Cox, Josephine Hyll, and Kenny Delmar in "The Meanest Man in the World"

U.S. STEEL HOUR: Paul Newman, George Peppard, and Albert Salmi in "Bang the Drum Slowly"

U.S. STEEL HOUR: Gloria Vanderbilt, Patty Duke, and Gene Coffin in "Family Happiness"

U.S. STEEL HOUR: Andy Griffith in "No Time for Sergeants"

THE JACK PAAR SHOW: July 17, 1954–September 4, 1954, CBS. Jack Paar (host)

THE MICKEY ROONEY SHOW: August 28, 1954–June 4, 1955, NBC. Mickey Rooney

THE MICKEY ROONEY SHOW: Mickey Rooney and Joan Jordan (guest)

THE BLUE ANGEL: July 6, 1954–October 12, 1954, CBS. Polly Bergen (hostess) and Orson Bean (host)

JUKEBOX JURY: September 13, 1953–March 28, 1954, ABC; 1959, syndicated. Page Cavanaugh, Lois Butler, Desi Arnaz, and Peter Potter (host)

DROODLES: June 21, 1954–September 24, 1954, NBC. Roger Price (host)

ON THE BOARDWALK: May 30, 1954–August 1, 1954, ABC. Paul Whiteman (host)

SHERLOCK HOLMES: Early 1954, syndicated. Ronald Howard (Sherlock Holmes)

MY FAVORITE STORY: 1953–54, syndicated. Adolphe Menjou (host)

I LED THREE LIVES: 1953–56, syndicated. Richard Carlson (foreground)

JAMIE: October 5, 1953–October 4, 1954, ABC. Ernest Truex and Brandon DeWilde (Jamie)

THE MOTOROLA TV HOUR: November 3, 1953–May 18, 1954, ABC. Maria Riva and Jack Palance in "The Brandenburg Gate"

BACK THAT FACT: October 22, 1953–November 26, 1953, ABC. Bob Hope (guest) and Joey Adams (host)

JAMIE: Polly Knowles, Ernest Truex, Brandon DeWilde, and Kathy Nolan

LIFE WITH ELIZABETH: 1953–54, syndicated. Del Moore and Betty White (Elizabeth)

STAGE SHOW: July 3, 1954–September 22, 1956, CBS. Jimmy and Tommy Dorsey (hosts)

THE RAY BOLGER SHOW (WHERE'S RAYMOND?): October 8, 1953–June 10, 1955, ABC. Marjie Millar and Ray Bolger

COLONEL HUMPHREY FLACK: October 7, 1953–July 2, 1954, Dumont. Frank Jenks and Alan Mowbray (Colonel Flack)

JUSTICE: April 8, 1954–March 25, 1956, NBC. Philip Abbott, Oscar Homolka, and Dane Clark in an episode

THE LORETTA YOUNG SHOW (A LETTER TO LORETTA): Donna Boyce, Loretta Young, and Malcolm Cassel in "Twenty-Cent Tip"

GENERAL FOODS 25TH ANNIVERSARY SHOW: Ezio Pinza and Mary Martin in a scene from "South Pacific"

THE LORETTA YOUNG SHOW (A LETTER TO LORETTA): September 20, 1953–September 10, 1961, NBC. Loretta Young (hostess)

THE LORETTA YOUNG SHOW (A LETTER TO LORETTA): Loretta Young in character-role costume between scenes

GENERAL FOODS 25TH ANNIVERSARY SHOW: March 28, 1954, ABC, CBS, Dumont, NBC. Yul Brynner and Patricia Morrison in a scene from "The King and I"

PERSON TO PERSON: October 2, 1953–September 15, 1961, CBS. Edward R. Murrow (host)

PERSON TO PERSON: Marlon Brando

PERSON TO PERSON: Maria Callas

PERSON TO PERSON: Jackie Robinson and family

PERSON TO PERSON: The Duke and Duchess of Windsor

LIFE WITH FATHER: November 22, 1953–July 5, 1955, CBS. Leon Ames and Lurene Tuttle

PRIDE OF THE FAMILY: October 2, 1953–September 24, 1954, ABC. Bobby Hyatt, Fay Wray, Paul Hartman, and Natalie Wood

ON YOUR WAY: September 9, 1953–April 17, 1954, Dumont, ABC. Hostess Kathy Godfrey (sister of Arthur Godfrey)

EARN YOUR VACATION: May 23, 1954–September 5, 1954, CBS. Jackie Loughery and Johnny Carson (host)

THE DUKE: July 2, 1954–September 10, 1954, NBC. Paul Gilbert (Duke London)

THE MAN BEHIND THE BADGE: October 11, 1953–October 3, 1954, CBS. Charles Bickford (host and narrator)

WHO'S THE BOSS?: February 19, 1954–August 20, 1954, ABC. *(Standing, far right)* host Walter Kiernan and guests, Johnny and Joe Louis

JANET DEAN, REGISTERED NURSE: Early 1954, syndicated. Ella Raines (Janet Dean)

DR. I.Q.: November 4, 1953–October 10, 1954; December 14, 1958–March 23, 1959, ABC. James McClain (Dr. I.Q.)

THE WORLD OF MR. SWEENEY: June 30, 1954–December 31, 1955, NBC. Charles Ruggles (Cicero P. Sweeney) and Glen Walker

THE BOB HOPE SHOW: Bob Hope, Lucille Ball, Dinah Shore, and Bob Crosby

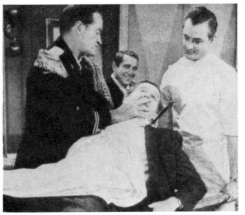

THE BOB HOPE SHOW: October 12, 1953–May 22, 1956, NBC. Bob Hope and Joan Crawford

THE BOB HOPE SHOW: Bob Hope, Perry Como, Milton Berle, and unknown actor

THE BOB HOPE SHOW: Bob Hope (host) and Jane Russell

MY FAVORITE HUSBAND: September 12, 1953–September 8, 1957, CBS. Joan Caulfield (first wife), Barry Nelson, and Steve Dunne (guest)

MY FAVORITE HUSBAND: Vanessa Brown (later wife), Barry Nelson, and Sarah Selby (guest)

SONG SNAPSHOTS ON A SUMMER HOLIDAY: June 24, 1954–September 9, 1954, CBS. Merv Griffin and Betty Ann Grove

THE RAY MILLAND SHOW (MEET MR. McNUTLEY): September 17, 1953–September 30, 1955, CBS. Ray Milland (Ray McNutley) and Phyllis Avery

THE RAY MILLAND SHOW (MEET MR. McNUTLEY): Ray Milland and Miriam Hopkins (guest)

DOUGLAS FAIRBANKS PRESENTS: Douglas Fairbanks, Jr., and Robin Wheeler in another of the series' productions

TOPPER: October 9, 1953–September 30, 1955, CBS. Leo G. Carroll (Cosmo Topper) and Lee Patrick

TOPPER: Buck, Robert Sterling, Leo G. Carroll, and Anne Jeffreys

DOUGLAS FAIRBANKS PRESENTS: 1953–56, syndicated. Douglas Fairbanks, Jr., and Eileen Moore in "Lochinvar"

1954-55

During the closing months of the 1953–54 season, the nation, and particularly television viewers, had become preoccupied with the activities and motivations of Sen. Joseph McCarthy of Wisconsin. McCarthy to this time had made a career as a relentless seeker of communists and subversives in the United States. He had a style of using half-truths and vague associations to inflame and badger congressional witnesses, and generally employed any means to stir up controversy. Viewers had already become aware of the vile, callous, and opportunistic individual he was from his attempted rebuttal to ''A Report on Senator Joseph McCarthy,'' presented on Ed Murrow's ''See It Now'' earlier in the year. Now McCarthy was in another controversial situation, this time with the U.S. Army regarding his attempt to receive preferential treatment for one of his staff members who had recently been drafted.

The Army/McCarthy public hearings began on April 22, 1954, and went on for two months. The full daily proceedings were telecast live by ABC and Dumont (CBS and NBC did nightly recaps). These smaller networks had little or no day network programming, and thus had available time to carry the contentious hearings. At first the viewing audience was less than ABC and Dumont had anticipated, but as the personalities and issues heated, viewing exceeded expectations—giving these networks impressive daytime ratings. The national exposure received by ABC gave it the impetus to approach national advertisers to buy network time during the day, so that it could challenge bigger NBC and CBS in daytime programming.

The hearings were Joseph McCarthy's downfall. Not long after this season began, he was condemned by the U.S. Senate. The networks and viewers were glad to get rid of him. Programming returned to normal and the new season began with significant increases in TV stations and homes with sets. More than 400 stations were in operation and close to 60 percent of all homes were tuning in.

As this season was about to start, an American tradition came to television. John Daly and Bess Myerson were co-hosts for the first telecast of the ''Miss America Pageant'' from Atlantic City, N.J., which was carried by ABC. Lee Ann Meriwether of California was the first TV winner and went on to pursue an acting career that, years later, led to her getting back on television. She was featured on ''Batman'' (as Cat Woman), ''The Time Tunnel,'' ''The New Andy Griffith Show,'' and, most recently, ''Barnaby Jones.''

Jack Benny, another American tradition, who in previous years did only a handful of shows, began doing his new show on an alternate-week basis. It was an instant hit and became a top-10 rated program for the year. There were other personalities already familiar to viewers who began their own regular prime-time shows as well. George Gobel (Lonesome George, as he was affectionately known), who was perennially a guest on other shows, began five years on CBS followed by a one-year stint on NBC. He made the top-10 rankings this year and was among the top 15 the next.

Jimmy Durante, previously one of the rotating hosts on ''The Colgate Comedy Hour,'' began a half-hour variety show on NBC. Jack Carson, who often hosted ''The All Star Revue'' and ''The Colgate Comedy Hour,'' commenced his own 30-minute series on NBC. Singer Julius La Rosa did the first of three musical variety shows he would host over the years. Johnny Carson had been writing for comic Red Skelton and already had hosted a short-lived prime-time audience-participation show, ''Earn Your Vacation,'' when fate called upon him. Skelton fell ill one night this season and Carson, at the last minute, was asked to fill in on his live comedy-variety show. His funny performance won him his own show later in the season on CBS.

Two musical programs began this season that were significant. Early in the TV year, Red Foley, a veteran of the Grand Ole Opry, kicked off ''Ozark Jubilee'' on ABC. This program went on to become a major national showcase for country-and-Western music and was on the network for more than five years. In the closing months of the season, ABC also presented ''The Lawrence Welk Show.'' A local Los Angeles program before coming to the network, the show, which didn't go over well with the critics, was intended to be a summer replacement. Instead, it simply became another in a very long list of hits that confounded the critics. The Welk show was one of the most tenacious of musical programs, or, for that matter, of any program in the history of the medium. Welk and his Champagne Music ran consecutively—network and first-run syndication—for 27 years and consistently achieved high ratings.

Among other news of note this season, Sid Caesar and Imogene Coca each began their own programs. Caesar's was the more successful, lasting three years, while Coca's was on only this one season. Steve Allen hosted the seventh annual Emmy Awards (NBC), which was nationally televised for the first time (March 7, 1955). Two famous dogs from the movies made their TV debuts. Rin Tin Tin, the German shepherd, starred in his own Western adventure series, and Lassie, the collie, in her own family adventure series. And finally, CBS came up with a public-affairs program, ''Face the Nation,'' to rival NBC's ''Meet the Press.'' The program, seen in prime time as well as on weekend days, concluded its run of many years during the summer of 1983.

The word ''spectacular'' became part of the programming jargon this season. Spectaculars were one-time, 90-minute shows that had big budgets and big stars. Programs making up this ambitious group were ''Producers' Showcase,'' ''Sunday on the Town,'' ''Max Liebman Spectaculars,'' ''The Best of Broadway,'' and ''Shower of Stars.'' On these shows, which were usually presented once every four weeks, some of the medium's all-time outstanding presentations appeared. Among them were ''Peter Pan,'' with Mary Martin and Cyril Ritchard, a smashing hit that received such acclaim that the entire live production was repeated the following season; and "The Petrified Forest," starring Humphrey Bogart, Henry Fonda, and Lauren Bacall. Both Bogart and Bacall made their dramatic TV debuts in the presentation. In re-creating his role of the criminal Duke Mantee, Bogart made his only dramatic appearance on television. Frank Sinatra, Paul Newman, and Eva Marie Saint appeared in the musical adaptation of Thornton Wilder's "Our Town," and Lee J. Cobb and Ruth Roman performed in "Darkness at Noon."

Other presentations included "A Christmas Carol," with Fredric March; "Caesar and Cleopatra," with Claire Bloom and Cedric Hardwicke; Ginger Rogers (her TV debut) and Martyn Green in Noel Coward's "Tonight at 8:30"; "The Man Who Came to Dinner," with Buster Keaton, Merle Oberon, Bert Lahr, Joan Bennett, and Monty Woolley; "Arsenic and Old Lace," with Peter Lorre, Helen Hayes, and Boris Karloff; and "The Great Sebastians," with Alfred Lunt and Lynn Fontanne in their television debut. This impressive list contains but a few of the substantial, enriching theatrical presentations that were aired on these spectaculars.

Weekly programming's most outstanding series this season was "Disneyland," Walt Disney's diversified adventure show. And the story of how it came to television is an adventure itself. From the beginning, the ABC television network was far behind NBC and CBS in the all-important ratings race. This was because it wasn't a strong network. It had only 40 stations in its nationwide lineup prior to this season, compared with 164 for NBC and 113 for CBS. So

ABC went to Hollywood for help. Previously it received financial support from movieland when it merged with United Paramount Theaters. Now it was seeking production and development help for its weak programming structure (in reality, all the networks were looking to affiliate themselves with the vast resources of the major film studios).

But Hollywood was not receptive to ABC's entreaty: the studios saw the new industry as a direct threat to their well-being. For the most part, they refused to produce programming and were unwilling to distribute recent theatrical films for television. But at this time, maverick Walt Disney and the Disney Studios were looking for an opportunity to do weekly television. What's more, Disney had already laid the foundation for his vast amusement park in Anaheim, California, and was seeking additional financial help. His discussions with NBC and CBS proved unsatisfactory, but ABC was receptive both to his series and to investing in the amusement park. This deal was a major coup for ABC. In this first season, "Disneyland" gave the network its first top-10 program in five years. For television in general, it was also important because the program's success brought down the walls of resistance by the major studios. Next season, Warner Brothers, MGM, and Twentieth Century-Fox would all get involved with their new allies.

Over the years, "Disneyland" went through several name changes. The next was "Walt Disney Presents," then "Walt Disney's Wonderful World," and finally, "Walt Disney." The popularity and durability of the show was such that in 1982–83 the program had been on for 29 consecutive television seasons and had

become the longest running prime-time series. Disney Studios then decided to leave commercial television and enter the burgeoning field of cable TV.

And now let's take a close-up look at two dramas, three sitcoms, and the biggest surprise of the year.

"Climax" was the best drama anthology to begin this fall. Hosted by William Lundigan (later to star in the "realistic" science-fiction series "Men into Space"), and later co-hosted with Mary Costa, the series initially presented live dramas but gradually switched over to film for most of its four years on CBS. Among the productions were "Casino Royale," with Barry Nelson as an American James Bond; "Fear Strikes Out," with Tab Hunter as baseball star Jimmy Piersall; and "Edge of Night," with Tom Laughlin, who in later years would star in the "Billy Jack" films.

"The Millionaire," another drama anthology, concerned itself with eccentric multibillionaire John Beresford Tipton's passion of giving away a million dollars to people he never met. Each week he would give his executive secretary, Michael Anthony, played by Marvin Miller, the huge tax-free cashier's check with instructions on who was to receive it. Viewers would then delight in watching how lives were changed by the windfall. Tipton's face was never seen on screen, only the back of his head or hand. And his voice was that of announcer Paul Frees. The show caught on quickly and was among the top-rated during most of its six-year run.

Lily Ruskin was the rare mother-in-law who was loved by, and lived with, her son-in-law and daughter in the very popular situation comedy "December Bride." Spring Byington starred as Lily,

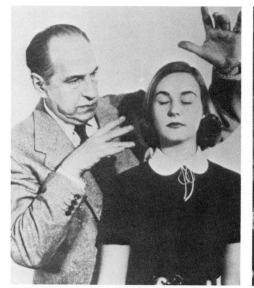

THE DUNNINGER SHOW: June 25, 1955–October 10, 1956, NBC, ABC. Joseph Dunninger (host)

LOVE THAT BOB (THE BOB CUMMINGS SHOW): January 2, 1955–September 15, 1959, NBC, CBS. Bob Cummings (Bob Collins)

MAKE THE CONNECTION: July 7, 1955–September 29, 1955, NBC. Gene Klavan, Jim McKay (host), Eddie Bracken, and Betty White

Jean Miller was her son-in-law, Matt Henshaw, and Frances Rafferty was daughter Ruth Henshaw. Others in the cast included Harry Morgan as next-door neighbor Pete Porter and Verna Felton as Lily's close friend Hilda Crocker. "December Bride" was a success from the start ranking 12th this season, moving up to 6th place next season and 5th place in its third year. In total, the show ran seven seasons on CBS: five seasons of original shows, totaling 159 episodes, and two years of network reruns.

"Father Knows Best" was another of the popular late-forties radio series that made it to television. Robert Young as Jim Anderson, the head of the ideal Anderson family, was the only member of the cast to make the transition to TV. This series was wholesome fifties situation comedy at its best, set in the model town of Springfield, at 607 South Maple Street. The family consisted of wife Margaret, eldest daughter Betty (also known as Princess), son Jim, Jr. (called Bud), and Kathy, the youngest (Kitten). They were played by Jane Wyatt, Elinor Donahue, Billy Gray, and Lauren Chapin, respectively. The series did not fare well during this season because it was on the air too late in the evening for the whole family to watch. As a result, it was canceled, but viewer protests demanded that the series be reinstated and positioned in an earlier time slot. This turned the program's ratings around as it moved steadily up to sixth place in the final year of its original run. In total, "Father Knows Best" was on for nine years, five seasons of original shows and four of network reruns—becoming one of TV's most popular family comedies.

This season's third sitcom of note was "The Bob Cummings Show," starring Bob Cummings in the role of Bob Collins, professional photographer. Collins photographed beautiful models by day and wined and dined them by night, while he lived with his widowed sister, Margaret, played by Rosemary DeCamp, who was always telling him to get married and settle down. Then there was Schultzy (Charmaine Schultz) played by Ann B. Davis, his hospitable assistant who was in love with him but felt she could not compete with all the exciting women in his life. And the other member of the clan was Chuck, his teenage nephew, who really loved his uncle and tried to emulate him in his own social life. Dwayne Hickman, the future Dobie Gillis, played Chuck. The series ran first on NBC, then CBS, and then on NBC again. In total, 173 episodes were telecast before the show went into syndication with the new title "Love That Bob."

And finally, the year's biggest surprise took place near the very end of the season when CBS introduced the first prime-time big-money game show, "The $64,000 Question," a truly instant success that would replace "I Love Lucy" next season as TV's No. 1 show. Hosted by Hal March, who was assisted by Lynn Dollar, the show employed the highly dramatic Isolation Booth, utilized so that contestants would not be distracted when answering the difficult, big-money questions. The questions themselves were compiled by Dr. Bergen Evans, who served as the judge in disputes. Revlon Cosmetics sponsored the program and would go on to sponsor the show's counterpart, "The $64,000 Challenge," the next season. Some of the successful contestants who would eventually become well known were Dr. Joyce Brothers, Barbara Feldon (later of "Get Smart" fame), and Geoffrey Holder. This program ushered in the whole era of big-money game shows.

HONESTLY, CELESTE: October 10, 1954– December 5, 1954, CBS. Scott McKay and Celeste Holm (Celeste Anders)

UPBEAT: July 5, 1955–September 22, 1955, CBS. Mindy Carson (guest)

SO THIS IS HOLLYWOOD: January 1, 1955– August 19, 1955, NBC. Mitzi Green

PASSPORT TO DANGER: 1954–55, syndicated. Cesar Romero

THE SOLDIERS: June 25, 1955–September 3, 1955, NBC. Hal March and Tom D'Andrea

THE FOLLIES OF SUZY: October 23, 1954, NBC. Jeanmaire and Dick Shawn

PROMENADE: May 22, 1955, NBC. Tyrone Power, Kay Starr, Judy Holliday, and Janet Blair

THE CHOCOLATE SOLDIER: June 4, 1955, NBC. Rise Stevens and Eddie Albert

SATINS AND SPURS: September 12, 1954, NBC. Betty Hutton

THE SWIFT SHOW WAGON (SHOW WAGON): January 8, 1955–October 1, 1955, NBC. Reita Green, Doreen Donley, Horace Heidt (host), and Charlene Lance

NAUGHTY MARIETTA: January 15, 1955, NBC. Alfred Drake, Patrice Munsel, and John Conti *(right)*

LADY IN THE DARK: September 25, 1954, NBC. Ann Sothern

WILLY: September 18, 1954–July 7, 1955, CBS. Whitfield Connor and June Havoc (Willy)

THE BEST OF BROADWAY: Peggy Ann Garner, Charles Drake, Diana Lynn, Rhonda Fleming, and Elsa Lanchester in "Stage Door"

THE BEST OF BROADWAY: Thelma Ritter, Russell Collins, Jackie Gleason, Cathy O'Donnell, Carleton Carpenter, and Alice Ghostley in "The Show Off"

THE BEST OF BROADWAY: Charles Coburn, Fredric March, Helen Hayes, Claudette Colbert, Kent Smith, and Nancy Olsen in "The Royal Family"

THE BEST OF BROADWAY: Buster Keaton, Merle Oberon, Joan Bennett, Bert Lahr, Monty Woolley, and ZaSu Pitts in "The Man Who Came to Dinner"

THE BEST OF BROADWAY: Art Carney, Ethel Merman, and Jack E. Leonard in "Panama Hatti"

THE BEST OF BROADWAY: Martha Hyer, Joseph Cotten, Piper Laurie, and Gene Nelson in "Broadway"

THE BEST OF BROADWAY: September 15, 1954–May 4, 1955, CBS. Peter Lorre, John Alexander, Helen Hayes, Boris Karloff, Orson Bean, and Billie Burke in "Arsenic and Old Lace"

THE BEST OF BROADWAY: John Payne, Dorothy McGuire, Herbert Marshall, and Richard Carlson in "The Philadelphia Story"

THE JOHNNY CARSON SHOW: June 30, 1955–September 28, 1956, CBS. Johnny Carson and Glenn Turnbull

SHOWER OF STARS: September 30, 1954–April 17, 1958, CBS. Gene Nelson, Beverly Tyler, Edgar Bergen, and Sheree North in "Lend an Ear"

SHOWER OF STARS: James Gleason, Dan Dailey, Marilyn Maxwell, Jack Oakie, and Helene Stanley in "Burlesque"

WATERFRONT: 1954–56, syndicated. Preston Foster and Pinky Tomlin

PROFESSIONAL FATHER: January 8, 1955–July 2, 1955, CBS. Steve Dunne and Barbara Billingsley

DUFFY'S TAVERN: 1954, syndicated. Pattee Chapman, Ed Gardner (Duffy), and Alan Reed

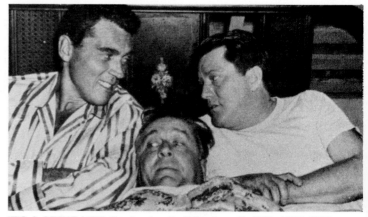

IT'S A GREAT LIFE: September 7, 1954–June 3, 1956, NBC. William Bishop, James Dunn, and Michael O'Shea

PRODUCER'S SHOWCASE: October 18, 1954–June 24, 1957, NBC. Nina Foch, Joseph Cotten, and Margaret Sullavan in "State of the Union"

PRODUCER'S SHOWCASE: Judith Evelyn, Mel Ferrer, and Audrey Hepburn in "Mayerling"

PRODUCER'S SHOWCASE: Broderick Crawford, Dennis O'Keefe, and Wally Cox in "Yellow Jack"

PRODUCER'S SHOWCASE: Jose Ferrer, Christopher Plummer, and Claire Bloom in "Cyrano de Bergerac"

PRODUCER'S SHOWCASE: Alfred Lunt and Lynn Fontanne in "The Great Sebastians"

PRODUCER'S SHOWCASE: Lee J. Cobb and Ruth Roman in "Darkness at Noon"

PRODUCER'S SHOWCASE: Ginger Rogers, Martyn Green, and Estelle Winwood in "Tonight at 8:30"

PRODUCER'S SHOWCASE: Humphrey Bogart in "The Petrified Forest"

STAGE 7: January 30, 1955–September 25, 1955, CBS. Dan Barton and Alexis Smith in "To Kill a Man"

NORBY: January 5, 1955–April 6, 1955, NBC. Joan Lorring and David Wayne (Norby)

COLONEL MARCH OF SCOTLAND YARD: 1954, syndicated. Boris Karloff (Colonel March)

THE HENNY AND ROCKY SHOW: June 1, 1955–August 31, 1955, ABC. Rocky Graziano (co-host), Marion Colby, and Henny Youngman (co-host)

THE PEE WEE KING SHOW: May 23, 1955–September 5, 1958, ABC. Pee Wee King (host) and Goldie Hill (guest)

APPOINTMENT WITH ADVENTURE: April 3, 1955–April 1, 1956, CBS. Louis Jourdan and Mala Powers (guest)

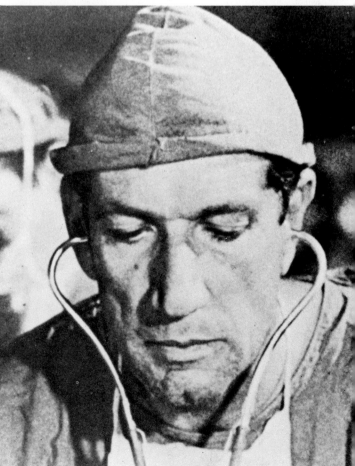

MEDIC: September 13, 1954–November 19, 1956, NBC. Richard Boone

FATHER KNOWS BEST: October 3, 1954–April 5, 1963, CBS, NBC, ABC. *(Front)* Lauren Chapin, Billy Gray *(back)*; Elinor Donahue, Robert Young, and Jane Wyatt

FATHER KNOWS BEST: Billy Gray, Lauren Chapin, Robert Young, Jane Wyatt, and Elinor Donahue

FATHER KNOWS BEST: Jane Wyatt, Billy Gray, Lauren Chapin, Elinor Donahue, and Robert Young

MUSICAL CHAIRS: July 9, 1955–September 17, 1955, NBC. Bobby Troup (panelist)

JANE WYMAN THEATER: August 30, 1955–May 29, 1958, NBC. Jane Wyman (hostess) and occasional star

THE FRANKIE LAINE SHOW: July 20, 1955–September 19, 1956, CBS; 1957, syndicated. Frankie Laine (host)

THE FRANKIE LAINE SHOW: Frankie Laine and Connie Russell (guest)

THE LINEUP: October 1, 1954–January 20, 1960, CBS. Warner Anderson and Ben Guthrie

THE HALLS OF IVY: October 19, 1954–September 29, 1955, CBS. Benita Hume and Ronald Colman

THE JIMMY DURANTE SHOW: October 2, 1954–September 21, 1957, NBC, CBS. Jimmy Durante (host)

WHAT'S GOING ON?: November 28, 1954–December 2, 1954, ABC. Lee Bowman (host), Kitty Carlisle, and Hy Gardner

THE INNER SANCTUM: 1954, syndicated. John Alexander and Paul Stewart in an early episode

THE LAWRENCE WELK SHOW: July 2, 1955–September 4, 1971, ABC; 1971–82, syndicated. Lawrence Welk

THE LAWRENCE WELK SHOW: Alice Lon (the original Champagne Lady) and Lawrence Welk

THE LAWRENCE WELK SHOW: Lawrence Welk (host)

PETER PAN: March 7, 1955, NBC. Mary Martin (Peter Pan) and cast

PETER PAN: Mary Martin

DISNEYLAND/WALT DISNEY: Walt Disney (host)

DISNEYLAND/WALT DISNEY: Fess Parker and Buddy Ebsen in "Davy Crockett"

DISNEYLAND/WALT DISNEY: October 27, 1954–February 15, 1983, ABC, NBC, CBS. Disneyland

DISNEYLAND/WALT DISNEY: *(Center)* Fess Parker and Buddy Ebsen in "Davy Crockett"

THOSE WHITING GIRLS: July 4, 1955–September 30, 1957, CBS. Mabel Albertson, Johnny Mercer (guest), and Margaret and Barbara Whiting

DAMON RUNYON THEATRE: April 16, 1955–June 30, 1956, CBS. Gene White, Robert Strauss, and Vivian Blaine in "Pick the Winner"

LASSIE: September 12, 1954–September 12, 1971, CBS; 1971–74, syndicated. George Cleveland, Jan Clayton, and *(seated)* Tommy Rettig (original "Lassie" family)

LASSIE: June Lockhart, Hugh Reilly, and *(seated)* Jon Provost (last "Lassie" family)

THE $64,000 QUESTION: June 7, 1955–November 2, 1958, CBS. Hal March (host) with contestant

THE LONE WOLF: 1955, syndicated. Louis Hayward (Mike Lanyard, the Lone Wolf)

THE GEORGE GOBEL SHOW: George Gobel and Jeff Donnell

THE GEORGE GOBEL SHOW: Eddie Fisher, Debbie Reynolds (guest), and George Gobel

DECEMBER BRIDE: *(Front)* Francis Rafferty, Spring Byington, Dean Miller; *(back)* Verna Felton and Harry Morgan

DECEMBER BRIDE: October 4, 1954–April 20, 1961, CBS. Spring Byington

THE GEORGE GOBEL SHOW: October 2, 1954–June 5, 1960, NBC, CBS. George Gobel (host

94

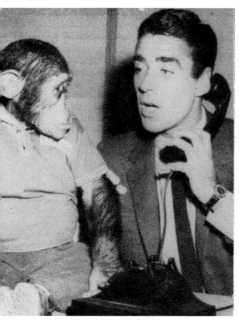

DEAR PHOEBE: Peter Lawford

DEAR PHOEBE: September 10, 1954–
September 2, 1955, NBC. Marcia Henderson
and Peter Lawford (Phoebe Goodheart)

TONIGHT—STEVE ALLEN: September 27, 1954–January 25, 1957, NBC. Steve Allen (host)

TONIGHT—STEVE ALLEN: Steve Allen with guests George
Montgomery and Dinah Shore

TONIGHT—STEVE ALLEN: "Tonight" regulars Skitch Henderson,
Gene Rayburn, Edie Gormé, and Steve Lawrence with Steve Allen

THE MILLIONAIRE: January 19, 1955–September 28, 1960, CBS. Marvin Miller

RIN TIN TIN: October 15, 1954–August 28, 1959, ABC. Jim Brown, Lee Aaker, and Rin Tin Tin

OZARK JUBILEE (JUBILEE U.S.A.): January 22, 1955–November 21, 1961, CBS. Red Foley (emcee) and Carla Rowe

1955-56

Making the news as the season began were President Eisenhower, who was in the hospital with a mild heart attack (he would soon recover); former President Truman, who just had his enlightening White House memoirs published; and television itself, which was about to become heavily involved with Hollywood after years of trying to get in the front door.

That front door was opened the previous season when ABC successfully negotiated with Disney for the film studio to provide it with programming. Following in the steps of this marriage, Warner Brothers and M-G-M Studios were receptive to ABC's suggestion to produce original shows for its network. As a result, Warners produced an hour-long rotating series based on three of its successful films titled ''Warner Brothers Presents.'' The individual series were ''Casablanca,'' ''Cheyenne,'' and ''King's Row,'' and actor Gig Young served as host/narrator for the one-season series.

M-G-M's series for ABC was ''M-G-M Parade,'' which was a documentary about the studio's films and stars with previews of upcoming movies and a behind-the-scenes look at the movie business in general. Actor, and eventual politician, George Murphy was initially the show's host, but Walter Pidgeon took over the role toward the end of this one-season series. Meanwhile on CBS, Twentieth Century-Fox commenced programming for TV this year with ''The 20th Century-Fox Hour,'' a drama-anthology series that lasted two seasons.

Although viewing patterns were firmly established and 10 of the previous season's 15 top shows were again in the top 15—''I Love Lucy,'' ''Ed Sullivan,'' ''Disneyland,'' ''Jack Benny,'' ''December Bride,'' ''You Bet Your Life,'' ''Dragnet,'' ''I've Got a Secret,'' ''Ford Theatre,'' and ''George Gobel,'' there were new trends emerging. In the industry over all, CBS surprised NBC and for the first time was the leader in top-rated programs. In programming, two things were happening. In the wake of

last season's (as well as this season's) smash, ''The $64,000 Question,'' an influx of big-money quiz shows debuted. NBC's ''The $100,000 Big Surprise,'' with Jack Barry as host, followed by Mike Wallace; ''The $64,000 Challenge'' (CBS), where only big winners from ''Question'' had the opportunity to compete. Among this show's winners who had also achieved a degree of fame on ''Question'' were Dr. Joyce Brothers, Myrt Powers, Gino Prato, and, best known of all, Teddy Nadler. Nadler's photographic memory allowed him to become the biggest game-show winner in the history of television. His combined winnings from the two shows was $264,000. ''High Finance,'' also on CBS, began as the season was coming to a close. Dennis James was host of this current-events quiz show in which contestants had the chance to win in excess of $50,000, though no one ever did. These kinds of shows would remain in vogue for the next two seasons.

The other programming trend, which would last much longer, was the advent of the ''adult'' Western. While it would be two years before viewer acceptance and respect would make it the dominating TV genre of the late fifties and early sixties, three such shows began this season. ABC introduced ''The Life and Legend of Wyatt Earp'' on Tuesday, September 6, 1955 from 8:30 to 9:00 P.M. Hugh O'Brian starred as Marshal Wyatt Earp, whose trademark was the long Buntline Special pistols he packed. The series was based somewhat on the life of the real Marshal Earp (1848–1929). O'Brian was a young actor who had appeared in many dramatic anthologies before winning the role. This six-year show catapulted him to fame.

In the same week, CBS premiered ''Gunsmoke.'' This series had originally been on CBS radio, where it began in 1952 with William Conrad (later to gain fame as ''Cannon'' and ''Nero Wolfe'') in the main role as Marshal Matt Dillon. For the TV version the network wanted John Wayne to star, but Wayne would not commit himself to the rigorous discipline

necessary for a weekly series. But he suggested they talk to a relatively unknown actor named James Arness, and the rest, as they say, is history. ''Gunsmoke,'' first as a half-hour, then an hour, show, was a CBS fixture for 20 years, becoming the longest continuously running Western in TV history.

ABC's second adult Western was the previously mentioned ''Cheyenne,'' starring Clint Walker as Cheyenne Bodie, a tough, laconic drifter in the years after the Civil War. Although originally part of the short-lived ''Warner Brothers Presents,'' this show had the right chemistry and remained on the air for eight years.

Aside from the debut of adult Westerns and the mania over big-money quiz shows, there were other program highlights this season.

''Alfred Hitchcock Presents'' began a decade of quality mystery and melodrama productions. Hollywood director Hitchcock hosted the half-hour program, which opened with his rotund silhouette filling a caricatured line drawing of his profile. During the later years, the program expanded to an hour format and the name changed to ''The Alfred Hitchcock Hour.'' Some of the stars who appeared over the years included Robert Redford, Peter Fonda, Katharine Ross, Dick Van Dyke, Judy Canova, Steve McQueen, Joanne Woodward, and Cloris Leachman. There were also a number of performers who made multiple appearances. These included Barbara Bel Geddes (four), Gena Rowlands (four), Paul Hartman (five), Robert Horton (five), Brian Keith (five), Gary Merrill (seven), and Phyllis Thaxter (eight). The series was well received by viewers and was among the top 30 programs during most of its original CBS and NBC network run.

''The Honeymooners'' was a situation comedy that Jackie Gleason first brought to television as part of his involvement with earlier shows. This season it became an original half-hour series of its own. The Great One, playing bus driver Ralph Kramden, created and starred in the show along with Art

Carney, as neighbor Ed Norton, Audrey Meadows, as Ralph's wife, Alice, and Joyce Randolph, as Ed's wife, Trixie. Gleason contracted with CBS to do 78 episodes, but after completing one year's worth, 39, he decided not to do more. The show was always performed before a live audience and used an advanced filming process known as Electronicam for syndication purposes. In later years, "The Honeymooners" appeared as a segment of "The Jackie Gleason Show" and ranged in length from 15 minutes to as long as an hour. Since its inception, Gleason as well as Carney starred in their same roles, but over the years there were four actresses who played the role of Alice: Pert Kelton, Audrey Meadows, Sue Ann Langdon, and Sheila MacRae. And there were four who played the role of Trixie: Elaine Stritch, Joyce Meadows, Patricia Wilson, and Jane Kean. Other tidbits: the Kramdens and Nortons lived at 328 Chauncy Street, in the Bensonhurst section of Brooklyn, and the show's theme song was "You're My Greatest Love." The 39 half-hour episodes have been seen over and over through the years and today are considered classic early television situation comedy.

Master Sgt. Ernie Bilko, a classic con man if there ever was one, was at the center of most scandalous things that were happening at Camp Fremont Army Base, which was part of the larger Fort Baxter in Roseville, Kansas. As star of the popular situation-comedy series "You'll Never Get Rich" ("The Phil Silvers Show"), Phil Silvers was brilliant as the loudmouthed, quick-witted Bilko. Through the seasons, there were many different regulars in the cast but the major members were Harvey Lembeck as Barbella, Allan Melvin as Henshaw, Paul Ford as Colonel Hall, Maurice Gosfield as Doberman, Herbie Faye as Fender, Billy Sands as Paparelli, Joe E. Ross as Ritzik, and Jimmy Little as Grover. During this decade, the series was one of the few to feature black performers, and, because Silvers loved sports, to use well-known figures in guest shots. These included baseball stars Yogi Berra, Whitey Ford, and Gil McDougald, as well as boxers Lou Nova, Maxie Shapiro, and Walter Cartier. The show was also a springboard for future stars like Fred Gwynne, Dick Van Dyke, and Alan Alda. Silvers and the show enjoyed four seasons on CBS, but when he tried another sitcom in the sixties, he lasted only one season. It seemed that the TV audience could not accept him as anyone but Sergeant Bilko.

Finally, there was "Ford Star Jubilee," a monthly series of one- to two-hour specials sponsored by the Ford Motor Company. Although it was short-lived (one season), it had an impressive list of productions. In the premiere show, Judy Garland made her TV debut in a musical variety special. Other outstanding presentations were "The Caine Mutiny," with Lloyd Nolan; Noel Coward's "Blithe Spirit," with Lauren Bacall and Noel Coward (making his TV debut); "Twentieth Century," with Betty Grable and Orson Welles; and "High Tor," a musical fantasy based on Maxwell Anderson's play, with Bing Crosby and Julie Andrews (in her TV debut). In addition, "Ford Star Jubilee" had the distinction of introducing to television the classic 1939 film *The Wizard of Oz*, which went on to become an annual TV event.

SERGEANT PRESTON OF THE YUKON: September 29, 1955–September 25, 1958, CBS. Richard Simmons (Sergeant Preston) and Yukon King (his faithful dog)

PLAYWRIGHTS '56: October 4, 1955–June 19, 1956, NBC. Kim Stanley in "Flight"

LONG JOHN SILVER: 1955, syndicated. Robert Newton (Long John)

THE $64,000 CHALLENGE: April 8, 1956–September 14, 1958, CBS. Sonny Fox (host) with contestants Vincent Price and Billy Pearson

THE BIG SURPRISE (THE $100,000 BIG SURPRISE): October 8, 1955–April 2, 1957, NBC. Mike Wallace (host) and assistants Sue Oakland and Mary Gardiner

BRAVE EAGLE: September 28, 1955–June 6, 1956, CBS. Keith Larsen (Brave Eagle)

THE ALCOA HOUR/ALCOA THEATRE: Eileen Heckart and Hume Cronyn in "No License to Kill"

THE ALCOA HOUR/ALCOA THEATRE: Eric Portman and Shelley Winters in "A Double Life"

THE ALCOA HOUR/ALCOA THEATRE: Cornelia Otis Skinner and Dennis King in "Merry Christmas, Mr. Baxter"

THE ALCOA HOUR/ALCOA THEATRE: October 14, 1955–September 19, 1960, NBC. Lee Meriwether, Ed Wynn, Evelyn Varden, and Betsy Palmer in "The Protege"

THE ALCOA HOUR/ALCOA THEATRE: Mickey Rooney in "Eddie"

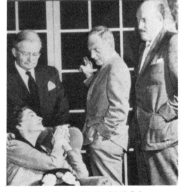

THE ALCOA HOUR/ALCOA THEATRE: Mildred Dunnock, Claude Rains, Everett Sloane, and Fred Clark in "President"

WANTED: October 20, 1955–January 12, 1956, CBS. Walter McGraw (host)

GUNSMOKE: James Arness, Burt Reynolds, Milburn Stone, Amanda Blake, and Ken Curtis

GUNSMOKE: Amanda Blake and James Arness

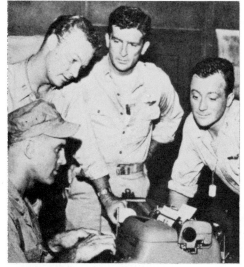

NAVY LOG: September 20, 1955–September 25, 1958, CBS, ABC. Mike Garrett *(seated)*, Morgan Jones, Robert Knapp, and Bill Allyn in an episode

FABIAN OF SCOTLAND YARD: 1955, syndicated. Bruce Seton (Inspector Fabian)

GUNSMOKE: September 10, 1955–September 1, 1975, CBS. Dennis Weaver and James Arness

SOLDIERS OF FORTUNE: 1955, syndicated. John Russell and Chick Chandler

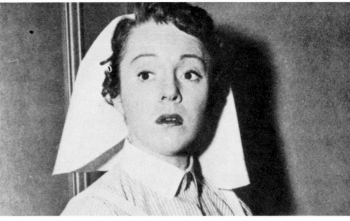

SCREEN DIRECTORS PLAYHOUSE: October 5, 1955–September 26, 1956, NBC. Pat Hitchcock (Alfred's daughter) in "White Corridors"

FORD STAR JUBILEE: David Wayne and Judy Garland

FORD STAR JUBILEE: Lauren Bacall and Noel Coward in "Blithe Spirit"

FORD STAR JUBILEE: Lloyd Nolan and Barry Sullivan in "Caine Mutiny Court Martial"

FORD STAR JUBILEE: Judy Garland

FORD STAR JUBILEE: September 24, 1955–November 3, 1956, CBS. Lillian Gish, Raymond Massey, and Jack Lemmon in "The Day Lincoln Was Shot"

FORD STAR JUBILEE: Noel Coward and Mary Martin in "Together with Music"

FORD STAR JUBILEE: Ray Collins, Betty Grable, Orson Welles, and Keenan Wynn in "Twentieth Century"

FORD STAR JUBILEE: Noel Coward and Edna Best in "This Happy Breed"

THE 20TH CENTURY-FOX HOUR: October 5, 1955–September 18, 1957, CBS. Dana Wynter and Robert Stack in "Laura"

THE 20TH CENTURY-FOX HOUR: Cameron Mitchell and Vera Miles in "Man on the Ledge"

THE 20TH CENTURY-FOX HOUR: Michael Wilding and Merle Oberon in "Cavalcade"

THE 20TH CENTURY-FOX HOUR: Arthur Franz and Joanne Woodward in "The Late George Apley"

FRONTIER: September 25, 1955–September 9, 1956, NBC. Walter Coy (*on horse*), narrator and occasional star, and Peter Votrian in an episode

THE VIC DAMONE SHOW: July 2, 1956–September 11, 1957; June 22, 1967–September 7, 1967, CBS, NBC. Vic Damone (host)

THE RUSS MORGAN SHOW: July 7, 1956–September 1, 1956, CBS. Russ Morgan (host) and Helen O'Connell

GUY LOMBARDO'S DIAMOND JUBILEE: March 6, 1956–June 12, 1956, CBS. Guy Lombardo (host)

THE HONEYMOONERS: Jackie Gleason, Art Carney, Audrey Meadows, and Joyce Randolph (early cast)

THE HONEYMOONERS: *(Front)* Sheila MacRae, Jane Kean; *(back)* Jackie Gleason, Art Carney (later cast)

THE HONEYMOONERS: October 1, 1955–September 26, 1956; January 5, 1971–May 9, 1971, CBS. Jackie Gleason (Ralph Kramden)

STAR STAGE: September 8, 1955–September 7, 1956, NBC. Greer Garson and Linda Bennett in "Career"

THE GRAND OLE OPRY: October 15, 1955–September 15, 1956, ABC. Minnie Pearl

YOU'LL NEVER GET RICH (THE PHIL SILVERS SHOW): September 20, 1955–September 11, 1959, CBS. Phil Silvers (Sgt. Ernie Bilko)

HIGHWAY PATROL: 1955–59, syndicated. Broderick Crawford *(left)*

YOU'LL NEVER GET RICH (THE PHIL SILVERS SHOW): Allan Melvin, Harvey Lembeck, Phil Silvers, Billy Sands, Eric Fleming, and Herbie Faye

THE CRUSADER: October 7, 1955–December 28, 1956, CBS. Brian Keith and Hildegarde Christian (guest)

YOU'LL NEVER GET RICH (THE PHIL SILVERS SHOW): Phil Silvers and Al Hodge (guest)

IT'S ALWAYS JAN: September 10, 1955–June 30, 1956, CBS. Jeri Lou James, Pat Bright, Bob Jellison, and Janis Paige (Jan Stewart)

THE LIFE AND LEGEND OF WYATT EARP: September 6, 1955–September 26, 1961, ABC. Hugh O'Brian (Wyatt Earp)

CAPTAIN DAVID GRIEF: 1955–56, syndicated. Maxwell Reed *(center, David Grief)*

ALFRED HITCHCOCK PRESENTS/THE ALFRED HITCHCOCK HOUR: October 2, 1955–September 6, 1965, CBS, NBC. Alfred Hitchcock (host)

THE STEVE ALLEN SHOW: June 24, 1956–December 27, 1961, NBC, ABC. Dayton Allen, Bill Dana, Louis Nye, Steve Allen, Don Knotts, Pat Harrington, Jr., and Gabe Dell

THE STEVE ALLEN SHOW: Steve Allen (host), with guests Andy Griffith, Imogene Coca, and Elvis Presley

THE KAISER ALUMINUM HOUR: Paul Newman in "The Rag Jungle"

CRUNCH AND DES: 1955, syndicated. Forrest Tucker (Crunch)

THE KAISER ALUMINUM HOUR: July 3, 1956–June 18, 1957, NBC. Claude Rains and Marisa Pavan in "Antigone"

THE FRANKIE CARLE SHOW (THE GOLDEN TOUCH OF FRANKIE CARLE): August 7, 1956–October 29, 1956, NBC. Frankie Carle (host) and Joanne Gilbert (guest)

NBC COMEDY HOUR: January 8, 1956–June 10, 1956, NBC. Pat Sheehan (guest)

CHEYENNE: September 20, 1955–September 13, 1963, ABC. Clint Walker (Cheyenne Bodie)

JUNGLE JIM: 1955, syndicated. Johnny Weissmuller with his chimpanzee Tamba

JUNGLE JIM: Johnny Weismuller (Jungle Jim), actress unidentified, and Tamba

THE JAYE P. MORGAN SHOW: June 13, 1956–August 24, 1956, NBC. Jaye P. Morgan (hostess)

THE ADVENTURES OF ROBIN HOOD: September 26, 1955–September 22, 1958, CBS. Richard Greene (Robin Hood)

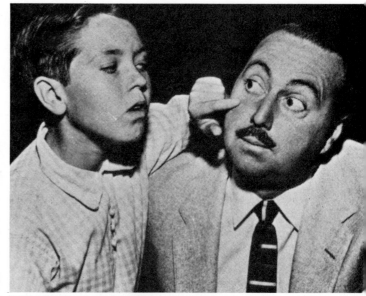

THE GREAT GILDERSLEEVE: 1955–56, syndicated. Ronald Keith and Willard Waterman (Throckmorton P. Gildersleeve)

THE GREAT GILDERSLEEVE: Willard Waterman and Stephanie Griffin

SCIENCE FICTION THEATER: 1955–56, syndicated. Truman Bradley (host)

SCIENCE FICTION THEATER: Zachary Scott examines a patient in an episode

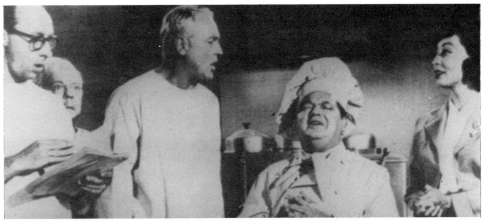

THE CHARLES FARRELL SHOW: July 2, 1956–September 24, 1956, CBS. Richard Deacon, Charles Winninger, Charles Farrell, Lem Askin, and Marie Windsor

THE CHARLES FARRELL SHOW: Ann Lee, Charles Farrell, and Marie Windsor

THE PEOPLE'S CHOICE: October 6, 1955–September 25, 1958, NBC. Jackie Cooper, Cleo the basset hound, and Patricia Breslin

JOE AND MABLE: September 20, 1955–September 25, 1956, CBS. Larry Blyden, Nina Talbot, and Luella Gear

JOE AND MABLE: Nina Talbot (Mable), Larry Blyden (Joe), and Shirl Conway

THE MARTHA RAYE SHOW: September 20, 1955–May 20, 1956, NBC. Rocky Graziano and Martha Raye (hostess)

HIGH TOR: March 10, 1956, CBS. Julie Andrews and Bing Crosby

ROSALINDA: July 23, 1956, NBC. Cyril Ritchard and Jean Fenn

BABES IN TOYLAND: December 24, 1955, NBC. Wally Cox

MARCO POLO: April 14, 1956, NBC. Doretta Morrow, Alfred Drake, and Beatrice Kraft

DEAREST ENEMY: November 26, 1955, NBC. Robert Sterling and Anne Jeffreys

1956-57

At the presidential nominating conventions, which concluded shortly before the start of the new fall television year, NBC viewers were introduced to two new anchormen, Chet Huntley and David Brinkley, who this season would begin "The Huntley-Brinkley Report," an early-evening newscast. All network convention viewers watched as the Democrats renominated Stevenson for president, this time with Estes Kefauver as his running mate, while the Republicans overwhelmingly renominated President Eisenhower and Vice-President Nixon for a second term. And, of course, just as overwhelmingly, Ike and Nixon won for a second time.

But the Eisenhower landslide was nothing compared with the winner television was becoming: TV sets were selling at the rate of more than 6½ million per year. More than 70 percent of American homes now were equipped with the black picture box. The cost of airing a 60-second commercial in prime time exceeded $18,000, and the networks were making more money more quickly than ever.

But interestingly, while the industry continued to boom, this season turned out to be somewhat of a bust. First, the new season began without the Dumont Television Network. Dumont in recent years suffered many setbacks, particularly in its ability to put together a competitive lineup of affiliate stations that contributed to financial problems over all. The network's demise was inevitable, considering these problems, and after less than a decade in operation, it ceased to exist. Second, for the first time in eight years, Milton Berle—who was Mr. Television—did not have a show of his own. And third, there was a long list of shows that debuted that were mediocre, at best.

Many of these programs lasted a season or less. These included situation comedies such as "Hey Jeannie," with Jeannie Carson; "The Brothers," featuring Gale Gordon and Bob Sweeney; "The Adventures of Hiram Holiday," starring Wally Cox; Buddy Hackett in

"Stanley"; "Blondie," with Pamela Britton and Arthur Lake; "A Date with the Angels," featuring Betty White and Bill Williams; and "The Marge and Gower Champion Show." In the adventure/crime/drama genre, there were series like "The Buccaneers," with Robert Shaw; "Sir Lancelot," featuring William Russell; "77th Bengal Lancers," featuring Warren Stevens; "Judge Roy Bean," starring Edgar Buchanan; "The Man Called X," with Barry Sullivan, and "N.O.P.D.," with Stacy Harris.

Series lasting no more than two seasons included these undistinguished programs: sitcom "Mr. Adams and Eve," starring Howard Duff and Ida Lupino; and adventures such as "Broken Arrow," starring Michael Ansara, "Jim Bowie," with Scott Forbes, "Sheriff of Cochise," and "West Point Story," which really was no better than the rest but did feature such performers as Clint Eastwood and future stars Barbara Eden and Leonard Nimoy in their first major TV roles.

But the season did have some highlights. Ironically, one of these was one of the greatest shows in television history. For this was the year "Playhouse 90" debuted.

Among the fine live dramatic anthologies of TV's Golden Age, "Playhouse 90," with its weekly 90-minute presentations, is regarded as the most ambitious. The series' big budget afforded the opportunity to employ the best actors, writers, directors, and producers in the business. More than 100 quality productions were mounted during its four years on CBS (a fifth season consisted of reruns). Rod Serling had the distinction of being the author of the first two of these productions. The premiere show, "Forbidden Area," featured Charlton Heston, Tab Hunter, Dianna Lynn, Vincent Price, and Jackie Coogan. The second week's drama was one of television's most unforgettable and widely acclaimed dramatic presentations, "Requiem for a Heavyweight." This story of a broken-down fighter starred Jack Palance as the boxer, Keenan Wynn as

his manager, along with Ed Wynn and Kim Hunter. Other excellent shows were: "Eloise," with Evelyn Rudie in the title role and Ethel Barrymore, Louis Jourdan, and Kay Thompson; "The Miracle Worker," with Patty McCormick, Teresa Wright, and Burl Ives, which eventually ran on Broadway and later as a film; "Charlie's Aunt," with Jeanette MacDonald in a rare TV appearance and Art Carney; "The Comedian," with Mickey Rooney; "Three Men on a Horse," with Carol Channing in a rare TV dramatic role and Johnny Carson in his dramatic debut; "Without Incident," with Errol Flynn; "The Plot to Kill Stalin," with Melvyn Douglas and Eli Wallach; "Judgment at Nuremberg," with Claude Rains and Maximilian Schell, which later became a movie; and "Face of the Hero," with Jack Lemmon. This is just a sampling of the outstanding shows viewers enjoyed on this outstanding series.

NBC's "Colgate Comedy Hour" was *the* program most people tuned into at 8:00 Sunday nights during the early fifties. In later years, though, Ed Sullivan's competing show had come on strong and taken over the time period. So this season, NBC was determined to recapture, or at least compete strongly for, the time slot. It selected late-night personality Steve Allen and "The Steve Allen Show" to battle Sullivan with a new comedy/variety program. Allen used Sullivan's vaudeville format plus performed his own comedy sketches with the already-familiar supporting cast he had developed on "The Tonight Show." This combination format made it a strong competitor to Sullivan, and for the succeeding three seasons there was a fierce ratings rivalry between the two personalities. NBC improved its Sunday-night standing, but in the end Sullivan endured, and Allen and company moved to Monday nights.

"Twenty-One" was NBC's next big-money quiz show. From the start, anticipation at the network was high that this show would match CBS's "Question" and "Challenge" in the ratings.

Jack Barry, in addition to being the host, co-created the show with his partner, Dan Enright. The program's concept was loosely based on the card game blackjack: the two contestants competed against each other, with the first to score 21 points the winner. And of course, to add to the drama, each player was put in the now-familiar individual isolation booths on stage. Some of the big winners were Elfrida Von Nardroff ($220,500), Charles Van Dooren ($129,000), and Hank Bloomgarden ($98,500) before the show was abruptly taken off the air after two seasons as a result of an ongoing investigation into several quiz shows that were involved in giving correct answers to contestants in advance. This cheating scandal brought to an end the era of big-money quiz shows. And it kept Jack Barry off the networks for the next decade.

The final highlight this season was "To Tell the Truth," another fine audience-participation show developed by the team of Mark Goodson and Bill Todman. To date, these prolific creators were responsible for "Winner Take All," "Beat the Clock," "What's My Line?" "I've Got a Secret," "The Name's the Same," and "It's News to Me." This year's entry debuted under the title "Nothing But the Truth," but it was quickly renamed after the premiere telecast. The program would go on to become one of TV's most popular game shows ever as CBS presented it many years in prime time and then continued its run during the day. In addition, after it left the network it spent a number of years in syndication—totaling 21 seasons in all. Bud Collyer hosted during all the network years, and, while there were many regular panelists, the ones most frequently seen, particularly during the early years, were Kitty Carlisle, Tom Poston, Polly Bergen, and Hy Gardner. After each panelist decided which of the three contestants was telling the truth, Collyer would end the round with a line that was to become famous: "Will the real (name of guest) please stand up!"

Among other things that happened this season, popular bandleader Ray Anthony hosted his own musical variety hour on ABC; comedian Jonathan Winters went on NBC with a 15-minute show; Andy Williams hosted a 15-minute music show (with June Valli) on NBC; singer Nat King Cole became the first major black entertainer with his own network show, a 15-minute music program on NBC; and Jerry Lewis had his first variety special since splitting up with Dean Martin.

Finally, contrary to the trend of short

lifespans among many new shows, "Oh Susanna," a situation comedy, began a four-year network run. Gale Storm, previously of the "My Little Margie" series and then for a short time the hostess of the "NBC Comedy Hour," played the title role of Susanna Pomeroy, the social director of the luxury liner SS *Ocean Queen*. Ably cast in the supporting role of her friend was ZaSu Pitts as Esmerelda "Nugey" Nugent. The program ran for three years on CBS followed by a year on ABC and then went into syndication.

THE WEST POINT STORY: October 5, 1956–July 1, 1958, CBS, ABC. Donald May (host of series, here appearing in role)

WIRE SERVICE: October 4, 1956–September 13, 1959, ABC. Dane Clark, Mercedes McCambridge, and George Brent

WASHINGTON SQUARE: October 21, 1956–June 13, 1957, NBC. Meta and Harry with Ray Bolger

NOAH'S ARK: September 18, 1956–October 5, 1958, NBC. May Wynn and Paul Burke (Noah McCann)

THE MARGE AND GOWER CHAMPION SHOW: March 31, 1957–June 9, 1957, CBS. Marge and Gower Champion and Jack Whiting

THE MARGE AND GOWER CHAMPION SHOW: Gower and Marge Champion

THE BROTHERS: October 2, 1956–March 26, 1957, CBS. Ann Morris, Nancy Hadley, Bob Sweeney, and Gale Gordon

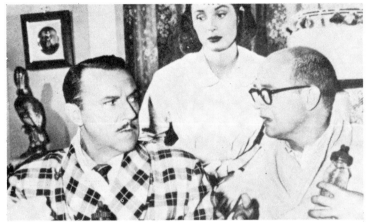

THE BROTHERS: Gale Gordon, Nancy Hadley, and Bob Sweeney

PANIC: March 5, 1957–September 17, 1957, NBC. Pamela and James Mason in an episode

CONFLICT: September 18, 1956–September 3, 1957, ABC. Virginia Mayo, Edmund Lowe, and Audrey Conti in an episode

RICHARD DIAMOND, PRIVATE DETECTIVE: July 1, 1957–September 6, 1960, CBS, NBC. Chris White (guest) and David Janssen (Richard Diamond)

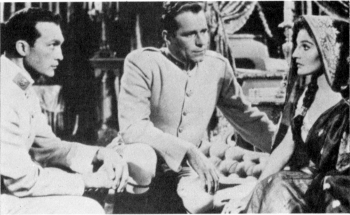

THE 77 BENGAL LANCERS: October 21, 1956–June 2, 1957, NBC. Warren Stevens, Phil Carey, and Lita Milan (guest)

DESTINY: July 5, 1957–September 26, 1958, CBS. Constance Towers and Mark Stevens in an episode

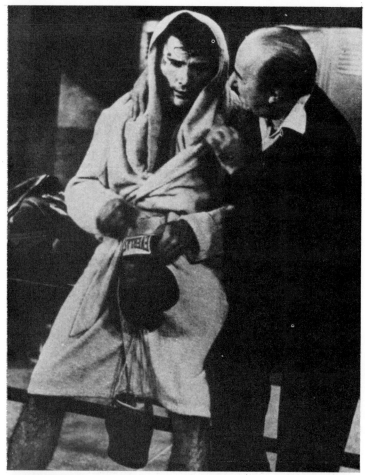

PLAYHOUSE 90: October 4, 1956–May 18, 1960, CBS. Jack Palance and Ed Wynn in "Requiem for a Heavyweight"

PLAYHOUSE 90: Eli Wallach and Melvyn Douglas in "The Plot to Kill Stalin"

PLAYHOUSE 90: Jason Robards, Jr., Maria Schell, Eli Wallach, Maureen Stapleton, Steven Hill, and Nehemiah Persoff in "For Whom the Bell Tolls"

PLAYHOUSE 90: Art Carney and Jeanette MacDonald in "Charley's Aunt"

PLAYHOUSE 90: Polly Bergen in "The Helen Morgan Story"

THE JIMMY DEAN SHOW: Jimmy Dean and the Noteworthies

GEORGE SANDERS MYSTERY THEATRE: John Archer and Mae Clark in an episode

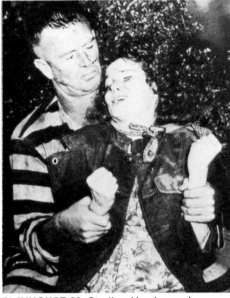

PLAYHOUSE 90: Sterling Hayden and Geraldine Page in "Old Man"

THE JIMMY DEAN SHOW: June 22, 1957– September 14, 1957, CBS. Jimmy Dean (host)

GEORGE SANDERS MYSTERY THEATRE: June 22, 1957–September 14, 1957, NBC. George Sanders (host)

PLAYHOUSE 90: Kay Thompson and Evelyn Rudie in "Eloise"

PLAYHOUSE 90: Betsy Palmer and Jackie Gleason in "The Time of Your Life"

TO TELL THE TRUTH: December 18, 1956–May 22, 1967, CBS. Bud Collyer (host), Polly Bergen, Ralph Bellamy, Kitty Carlisle, and Hy Gardner

THE WIZARD OF OZ: November 3, 1956 (first television showing presented on Ford Star Jubilee), CBS. Judy Garland and Ray Bolger

THE WIZARD OF OZ: Judy Garland, Jack Haley, and Ray Bolger

HOLIDAY ON ICE: December 22, 1956, NBC. Sonja Henie

BORN YESTERDAY: October 28, 1956, NBC. Paul Douglas and Mary Martin

RUGGLES OF RED GAP: February 3, 1957, NBC. Peter Lawford, Jane Powell, Imogene Coca, David Wayne, and Michael Redgrave

HIGH BUTTON SHOES: November 24, 1956, NBC. Nanette Fabray

TREASURE HUNT: September 7, 1956–June 17, 1958, ABC, NBC. Jan Murray (host) and assistant Marian Stafford

STANLEY: September 24, 1956–March 11, 1957, NBC. Buddy Hackett (Stanley Peck)

TWENTY-ONE: Jack Barry and contestant Vivienne Nearing

DICK POWELL'S ZANE GREY THEATER: October 5, 1956–September 20, 1962, CBS. Dick Powell (host)

SIR LANCELOT: September 24, 1956–June 24, 1957, NBC. Gary Thorne and William Russell (Sir Lancelot)

THE BUCCANEERS: September 23, 1956–September 14, 1957, CBS. Robert Shaw and unknown actors

TWENTY-ONE: September 12, 1956–October 16, 1958, NBC. Jack Barry (host)

I SPY: 1956, syndicated. Raymond Massey

THE TENNESSEE ERNIE FORD SHOW: October 4, 1956–June 29, 1961, NBC. Tennessee Ernie Ford surrounded by his cast

DR. HUDSON'S SECRET JOURNAL: 1956–57, syndicated. John Howard (Dr. Hudson)

THE DINAH SHORE CHEVY SHOW: October 5, 1956–May 12, 1963, NBC. Frank Sinatra (guest) and Dinah Shore

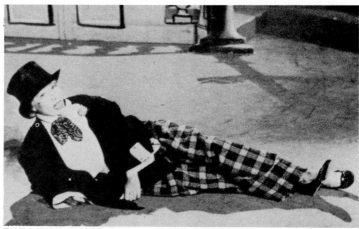

THE DINAH SHORE CHEVY SHOW: Dinah Shore (hostess)

THE DINAH SHORE CHEVY SHOW: Dinah Shore

MR. BROADWAY: May 11, 1957, NBC. James Dunn, Mickey Rooney, Gloria DeHaven, and Roberta Sherwood

CINDERELLA: March 31, 1957, CBS. Julie Andrews and Jon Cypher

OH, SUSANNA/THE GALE STORM SHOW: September 29, 1956-March 24, 1960, CBS, ABC. ZaSu Pitts and Gale Storm (Susanna Pomeroy)

CINDERELLA: Alice Ghostley, Kaye Ballard, Julie Andrews, and Ilka Chase

THE LAST WORD: January 6, 1957-October 18, 1959, CBS. Dr. Bergen Evans (moderator), Arthur Knight, June Havoc, and John Mason Brown

THE FLORIAN ZABACH SHOW: 1956, syndicated. Florian Zabach (host)

THE XAVIER CUGAT SHOW: February 27, 1957-May 24, 1957, NBC. Xavier Cugat and Abbe Lane

THE NAT KING COLE SHOW: November 5, 1956-December 17, 1957, NBC. Nat King Cole (host)

MR. ADAMS AND EVE: January 4, 1957–September 23, 1958, CBS. Ida Lupino (Eve Drake) and Howard Duff (Howard Adams)

THE ADVENTURES OF JIM BOWIE: September 7, 1956–August 29, 1958, ABC. Scott Forbes (Jim Bowie)

JUDGE ROY BEAN: 1956, syndicated. Edgar Buchanan (Judge Roy Bean)

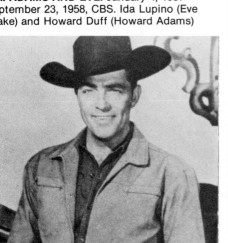

TALES OF WELLS FARGO: Dale Robertson

A DATE WITH THE ANGELS: May 10, 1957–January 29, 1958, ABC. Betty White and Bill Williams

DR. CHRISTIAN: 1956, syndicated. MacDonald Carey (Dr. Christian)

TALES OF WELLS FARGO: March 18, 1957–September 8, 1962, NBC. Dale Robertson

BROKEN ARROW: September 25, 1956–September 23, 1958, ABC. Michael Ansara and John Lupton

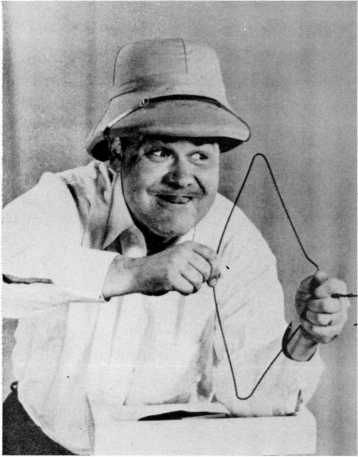

THE JONATHAN WINTERS SHOW: October 2, 1956–June 25, 1957, NBC. Jonathan Winters (host)

THE ADVENTURES OF HIRAM HOLIDAY: October 3, 1956–February 27, 1957, NBC. Angela Greene (guest) and Wally Cox (Hiram Holiday)

HEY, JEANNIE: Allen Jenkins and Jeannie Carson

THE ADVENTURES OF HIRAM HOLIDAY: Wally Cox and Carol Conn (guest)

THE JACK PAAR SHOW (TONIGHT SHOW): July 29, 1957–March 30, 1962, NBC. Jack Paar (host)

HEY, JEANNIE: September 8, 1956–May 4, 1957, CBS. Jeannie Carson (Jeannie) and Allen Jenkins

THE JACK PAAR SHOW (TONIGHT SHOW): Jack Paar and Hugh Downs (announcer)

THE JACK PAAR SHOW (TONIGHT SHOW): Jack Paar and Cliff Arquette (Charlie Weaver), guest

THE RAY ANTHONY SHOW: 1956, syndicated; October 12, 1956–May 3, 1957, ABC. Molly Bee (guest) and Ray Anthony

MEET McGRAW: July 2, 1957–June 24, 1958, NBC. Frank Lovejoy (McGraw) and unknown actress

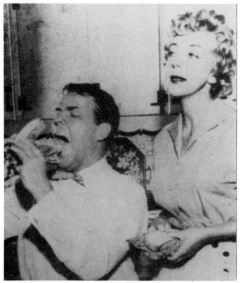

BLONDIE: January 4, 1957–September 27, 1957, NBC. Arthur Lake and Pamela Britton (Blondie)

THEATER TIME: July 25, 1957–September 26, 1957, ABC. Patricia Hardy and Ricardo Montalban in an episode

CIRCUS BOY: September 23, 1956–September 11, 1958, NBC, ABC. Mickey Braddock and Bimbo the elephant

THE MAN CALLED X: 1956, syndicated. Barry Sullivan and unknown actor

ON TRIAL/THE JOSEPH COTTEN SHOW: September 14, 1956–September 13, 1957, NBC. Baynes Barron (guest) and Joseph Cotten (host and occasional star)

THE ANDY WILLIAMS AND JUNE VALLI SHOW: July 2, 1957–September 5, 1957, NBC. June Valli (hostess) and Andy Williams (host)

1957-58

This season, television was completing its first decade of full prime-time network programming. During these 10 years, American homes with TV sets increased in truly meteoric fashion, going from less than 3 percent to almost 80 percent. And over these 10 seasons, viewers had become accustomed to several different entertainment formats: situation comedy, musical and comedy variety, drama anthology, episodic drama, and quiz and game shows.

Now television was ready to introduce to its vast audience a major new format (one that it previewed two seasons earlier), the adult Western. During TV's formative years, Westerns were exclusively the domain of kids. These cowboys-and-Indians series starred the traditional grade-B movie heroes: the Lone Ranger, Hopalong Cassidy, Gene Autry, Roy Rogers, and others. But now that television was growing up, so were the cowboys—the big ratings the first adult Westerns were receiving were nothing to kid about. So, as the season began, so did the shoot-out as the three networks premiered 10 Westerns for kids of all ages.

ABC already had two of the three pioneering adult Westerns—"Wyatt Earp," rated 13th this season, and "Cheyenne," seen on alternate weeks, rated 6th. Among the shows to join them on the network's schedule was "Maverick," with James Garner in his first starring series role. It was about an unconventional cowboy, and became quite a popular series. Also on ABC were "Tombstone Territory," starring Pat Conway as Sheriff Clay Hollister and set in Tombstone, Arizona; "Colt .45," starring Wayde Preston as government agent Christopher Colt, son of the inventor of the Colt revolver; and "Sugarfoot," played by Will Hutchins (he would later star in comedies "Hey Landlord" and "Blondie") as Ted "Sugarfoot" Brewster, an inept cowboy.

CBS, which continued as the network with the most top-rated programs, had earlier introduced the other initial adult Western, "Gunsmoke." This season it became the No. 1-rated show on television and remained there for four consecutive years. It was joined in the network lineup by two new entries. The first was "Have Gun, Will Travel," starring Richard Boone as Paladin, a dapper, well-educated professional trouble shooter whose services were available to all for a price. His distinctive calling card bore the image of a chess knight and simply read: "Have Gun, Will Travel . . . Wire Paladin, San Francisco." Boone had considerable control over the series, including script and cast approval. In addition, he directed some of the episodes. His judgment was very sound—in this, its first season, the show went to the top, rated 4th for the year. The series continued at the top, placing in the top five during its first four years on the air. In addition, even its theme song, "The Ballad of Paladin," became a top-selling single.

CBS's other new adult Western was "Trackdown," starring Robert Culp as Texas Ranger Hoby Gilman. Many of the stories in this two-season series were adapted from the files of the Texas Rangers, and the show had the official approval of the law-enforcement agency.

NBC, finally getting in on a good thing, offered a strong lineup of four adult Westerns: "Wagon Train," "Tales of Wells Fargo," "The Restless Gun," and "The Californians."

"Wagon Train" was one of television's all-time most popular Westerns. This hour-long series about the adventures of traveling West after the Civil War had its genesis from the 1950 John Ford-directed, RKO motion picture "The Wagonmaster." Ward Bond, who starred in the title role in the film, also played the role in this series. Other regulars were Robert Horton as scout Flint McCullough, Frank McGrath as cook Charlie Wooster, and Terry Wilson as assistant wagonmaster Bill Hawks. "Wagon Train" this season made the top-25-rated programs, then skyrocketed to the No. 2 spot for the next three years. And in the 1961–62 season, it dethroned "Gunsmoke" as the No. 1 show on television.

"Tales of Wells Fargo" was originally an episode on the "Schlitz Playhouse of Stars" in the previous season. Dale Robertson starred as agent Jim Hardie of the Wells Fargo Transport Company. NBC thought enough of the story line, and the star, to quickly turn it into a weekly series (it actually debuted late in the previous season). And they were rewarded: during the show's first two full years it ranked among the top 10 programs. An interesting note about this episodic series is that in its first five years, Robertson was the only regular cast member. Another Western drama on the "Schlitz Playhouse" last season was "The Restless Gun," starring John Payne. The network also decided to turn this story of Vint Bonner, a Civil War veteran who traveled throughout the country's Southwest territory, into a weekly series. This season it did well (8th-ranked), but it trailed off badly and was canceled after two seasons. "The Californians" was NBC's weakest link in its Western lineup. The series aired for two years, never quite catching on with the TV audience.

While three of the top 5 and five of the top 10 shows this season were Westerns, there were other new programs that would gain much popularity and have significant life spans.

"Perry Mason," the lawyer who never lost a case, was originally a character conceived by Erle Stanley Gardner for his mystery novels. From the pages of these popular books, the character became a radio serial in the forties, ran for 12 years, and left the airwaves in 1955. When the switch was made to television, several actors were considered for the meaty role. Among them were Fred MacMurray, William Hopper, Efrem Zimbalist, Jr., Richard Carlson of "I Led Three Lives" fame, and the eventual Perry Mason, Raymond Burr. Burr's fine performance during the show's nine years on CBS was complemented by Barbara Hale as Della Street, Mason's trusted secretary; William Hopper (son of famed columnist Hedda Hopper and originally up for the lead) as Paul Drake,

Mason's private investigator who always came up with the winning evidence at the last moment; William Talman as prosecutor Hamilton Burger, who was constantly frustrated because his adversary always made "Ham-burger" out of him in the courtroom; and Raymond Collins as Lt. Arthur Tragg of the Los Angeles Police Department. This fine cast helped make "Perry Mason" one of television's all-time favorite series.

Two hundred and eleven Pine Street, in Mayfield, was the residence of the Cleaver family, home for the situation comedy "Leave It to Beaver." The Cleavers were like many other TV families that existed in this decade. The mother, June (Barbara Billingsley), was always well dressed in her home that had the not-lived-in look. The father, Ward (Hugh Beaumont), was understanding and patient, never raised his voice, and was always having heart-to-heart talks with his children. And the sons, Theodore "Beaver" Cleaver (Jerry Mathers) and his older brother, Wally (Tony Dow), were mostly well behaved. But this series differed from other family sitcoms in two important ways. First, the basis of the stories was life as seen through the eyes of seven-year-old Beaver. And second, the realistic and credible portrayal of Beaver and Wally gave the show's young audience the opportunity to really identify with the characters. This reality enabled the program to build a strong and loyal following that watched the two boys grow up over the show's six-year run. In all, 234 episodes were aired before the show went into syndication.

Television's first successful rural situation comedy, "The Real McCoys," debuted on ABC and became the network's first sitcom to be placed in the top 10 (next season). The first of many rural comedies to appear on TV over the next several years, it starred three-time Academy Award winner Walter Brennan as Grandpa Amos McCoy. This was Brennan's first television series (he later went on to star in "The Tycoon," "The Guns of Will Sonnet," and "To Rome with Love"). In addition, young veterans Richard Crenna, as grandson Luke McCoy, and Kathy Nolan, as Luke's wife, Kate, co-starred. Crenna was a veteran of many radio shows and was known to viewers from his days as Walter Denton on "Our Miss Brooks." Nolan had appeared on Broadway and in an earlier sitcom, "Jamie." During the series' six-year run, 224 episodes were aired.

"Bachelor Father" was another program to originate from an episode on an anthology series. This time "General Electric Theater," in May 1957. This sitcom starred John Forsythe in the role of a wealthy Beverly Hills attorney, Bentley Gregg. During its five years, it was seen on all three networks: CBS first, followed by NBC and ABC.

In the police/detective genre, several interesting, though never top-rated, series began this season. "M Squad" starred Lee Marvin as a tough Chicago police detective assigned to investigate homicides and fight organized crime in the Windy City. It lasted three seasons. David Janssen starred in "Richard Diamond, Private Detective" (summer start), another of the many series that began on radio. On television, the program spent three years on CBS and NBC. "Meet McGraw" was about a tough private eye and starred Frank Lovejoy in the title role. In 1954, "McGraw," the character's only name, originally appeared as an episode on "Four Star Playhouse." Angie Dickinson made one of her earliest TV appearances in this series. And "The Thin Man," Dashiell Hammett's novel that was the basis for several films starring William Powell and Myrna Loy, began, with Peter Lawford and Phyllis Kirk as Nick and Nora Charles, the husband-and-wife detective team. The program was aired for two years on NBC (72 episodes) before going into syndication.

There was still more to this busy season. Frank Sinatra, lured by a huge contract, consented to do a variety/drama show for ABC. This second attempt to do a weekly series proved no better than the first, and the show was canceled after the season. Never again would Sinatra attempt weekly television. The documentary series "The Twentieth Century," with Walter Cronkite as the host/narrator, presented in-depth reports on a wide variety of historical and scientific subjects and enjoyed a long run on CBS. Singer Dean Martin starred in his first musical/variety special since splitting up with Jerry Lewis. A group of popular musical personalities were first-time hosts of their own variety shows: Rosemary Clooney (NBC), Pat Boone (three years on ABC), Gisele MacKenzie (NBC), and Guy Mitchell (ABC). And "American Bandstand," already on the air in Philadelphia for five years, began a daily daytime network run on ABC. The show's success resulted in a short-lived (13 weeks) prime-time version seen Mondays at 7:30 P.M. "Bandstand" is still going strong today after more than 30 years on television.

COLT .45: October 8, 1957–September 20, 1960, ABC. Wayde Preston

TOMBSTONE TERRITORY: October 16, 1957–October 9, 1959, ABC. Pat Conway

THE CALIFORNIANS: September 24, 1957–September 10, 1959, NBC. Richard Coogan

PERRY MASON: Raymond Burr (Perry Mason)

PERRY MASON: Raymond Burr and Barbara Hale

PERRY MASON: William Talman

PERRY MASON: September 21, 1957–September 4, 1966, CBS. William Hopper and Raymond Burr

LOVE THAT JILL: January 20, 1958–April 28, 1958, ABC. Ann Jeffreys (Jill Johnson) and Robert Sterling

THE BIG RECORD: September 18, 1957–June 11, 1958, CBS. Patti Page (hostess)

DECOY: 1957, syndicated. Unknown actor and Beverly Garland

M SQUAD: September 20, 1957–September 13, 1960, NBC. Lee Marvin

THE LUX SHOW STARRING ROSEMARY CLOONEY: September 26, 1957–June 19, 1958, NBC. Rosemary Clooney (hostess)

RESTLESS GUN: John Payne and Chuck Connors (guest)

SID CAESAR INVITES YOU: January 26, 1958–May 25, 1958, ABC. Imogene Coca and Sid Caesar

ZORRO: October 10, 1957–September 24, 1959, ABC. Guy Williams (Zorro) and Charles Korvin (guest)

RESTLESS GUN: September 23, 1957–September 14, 1959, NBC. John Payne

HAVE GUN, WILL TRAVEL: September 14, 1957–September 21,1963, CBS. Richard Boone

HAVE GUN, WILL TRAVEL: Richard Boone

DECISION: July 6, 1958–September 28, 1958, NBC. James Whitmore and June Lockhart in an episode

26 MEN: 1957, syndicated. Tris Coffin

NO WARNING: April 6, 1958–September 7, 1958, NBC. Alfred Toigo and Everett Sloane in an episode

CHARLIE CHAN: 1957–58, syndicated. J. Carrol Naish (Charlie Chan) and James Hong

THE THIN MAN: September 20, 1957–June 26, 1959, NBC. Phyllis Kirk and Peter Lawford

DUPONT SHOW OF THE MONTH: Denholm Elliott, Eric Portman, James Donald, Gracie Fields, Rosemary Harris, and Walter Fitzgerald in "A Tale of Two Cities"

DUPONT SHOW OF THE MONTH: James Donald, Don Murray, Roddy McDowall in "Billy Budd"

DUPONT SHOW OF THE MONTH: Margaret Leighton, John Gielgud in "The Browning Version"

DUPONT SHOW OF THE MONTH: Jackie Cooper, Rex Everhaut, John McCurry, Richard Harris, and Don Murray in "The Hasty Heart"

DUPONT SHOW OF THE MONTH: Marion Lorne, Art Carney in "Harvey"

DUPONT SHOW OF THE MONTH: September 29, 1957–March 21, 1961, CBS. Rosemary Harris, Christopher Plummer, and Rex Thompson in "The Prince and the Pauper"

THE FRANK SINATRA SHOW: October 18, 1957–June 27, 1958, ABC. Frank Sinatra (host)

SUSPICION: Warren Beatty, Barbara Turner, and David Wayne in an episode

SUSPICION: September 30, 1957–September 22, 1958, NBC. Bette Davis and Judson Pratt in an episode

WAGON TRAIN: Frank McGrath, John McIntire (replaced Ward Bond), Terry Wilson, and Robert Fuller

WAGON TRAIN: September 18, 1957–September 5, 1965, NBC, ABC. Robert Horton and Ward Bond

129

THE COURT OF LAST RESORT: October 4, 1957–February 17, 1960, NBC, ABC. John Anderson and Lorna Thayer (guests) with Lyle Bettger

SUGARFOOT: September 17, 1957–July 3, 1961, ABC. Will Hutchins (Tom "Sugarfoot" Brewster)

THE PAT BOONE SHOW: Pat Boone with the sons of Bing Crosby

THE PAT BOONE SHOW: October 3, 1957–June 23, 1960, ABC; October 17, 1966–June 30, 1967, NBC. Pat Boone (host)

O.S.S.: September 26, 1957–March 17, 1958, ABC. Ron Randell

THE BOB CROSBY SHOW: June 14, 1958–September 6, 1958, NBC. Bob Crosby (host)

THE O'HENRY PLAYHOUSE: 1957, syndicated. Thomas Mitchell (host)

THE GISELE MACKENZIE SHOW: September 28, 1957–March 29, 1958, NBC. Gisele MacKenzie (hostess)

DICK AND THE DUCHESS: Hazel Court, Eugene Deckers (guest), and Patrick O'Neal (Dick Starrett)

LEAVE IT TO BEAVER: Jerry Mathers Theodore "Beaver" Cleaver) and Tony Dow early years)

LEAVE IT TO BEAVER: Hugh Beaumont, Barbara Billingsley, and Jerry Mathers

DICK AND THE DUCHESS: September 28, 1957–May 16, 1958, CBS. Hazel Court (the duchess)

LEAVE IT TO BEAVER: October 4, 1957–September 12, 1963, CBS, ABC. (Clockwise) Tony Dow, Hugh Beaumont, Jerry Mathers, and Barbara Billingsley (later years)

HARBOR COMMAND: 1957, syndicated. Wendell Corey and unknown actor

TUGBOAT ANNIE: 1957, syndicated. Minerva Urecal (Annie Brennan)

MAVERICK: September 22, 1957–July 8, 1962, ABC. James Garner (Bret Maverick)

OFFICIAL DETECTIVE: 1957, syndicated. Everett Sloane

SALLY: September 15, 1957– March 30, 1958, NBC. Joan Caulfield (Sally Truesdale) and Johnny Desmond

WHIRLEYBIRDS: 1957, syndicated. Craig Hill and Kenneth Tobey

HARBOURMASTER: September 26, 1957–June 29, 1958, CBS, ABC. Barry Sullivan

MAVERICK: Jack Kelly, Adam West (guest) and James Garner (as Pappy Maverick)

MAVERICK: Jack Kelly (Bart Maverick)

MAVERICK: James Garner and Jack Kelly

THE EDDIE FISHER SHOW: September 24, 1957–March 17, 1959, NBC. Eddie Fisher (host) and Debbie Reynolds (guest)

E.S.P.: July 11, 1958–August 22, 1958, ABC. Vincent Price (host)

KEEP IT IN THE FAMILY: October 12, 1957–February 8, 1958, ABC. Bill Nimmo (host)

WIN WITH A WINNER: June 24, 1958–September 9, 1958, NBC. Marilyn Toomey (postcard girl) and Sandy Becker (host)

BACHELOR FATHER: September 15, 1957–September 25, 1962, CBS, NBC, ABC. John Forsythe and Noreen Corcoran

KEEP TALKING: July 15, 1958–May 3, 1960, CBS, ABC. Louis Nye, Ilka Chase, Danny Dayton, Roger Price, and Monte Hall (host)

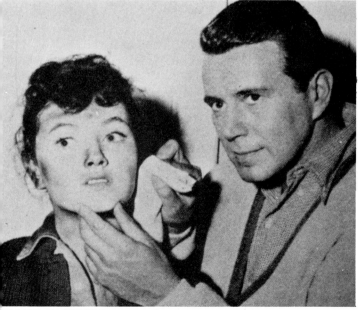

BACHELOR FATHER: Noreen Corcoran and John Forsythe

THE PRICE IS RIGHT: September 23, 1957–September 11, 1964, NBC, ABC. Bill Cullen (host)

AMERICAN BANDSTAND: October 7, 1957–December 30, 1957, ABC. Dick Clark (host)

AMERICAN BANDSTAND: Dick Clark and teenagers on American Bandstand

AMERICAN BANDSTAND: Dick Clark and teenagers on American Bandstand

AMERICAN BANDSTAND: Dick Clark and teenagers on American Bandstand

THE BIG GAME: June 13, 1958–September 12, 1958, NBC. Tom Kennedy (host)

DOTTO: July 1, 1958–August 12, 1958, NBC. Jack Narz (host)

IT COULD BE YOU: July 2, 1958–September 27, 1961, NBC. Bill Leyden (host)

TRACKDOWN: October 4, 1957–September 23, 1959, CBS. Robert Culp and Rita Moreno (guest)

TRAFFIC COURT: June 18, 1958–March 30, 1959, ABC.

ASSIGNMENT FOREIGN LEGION: October 1, 1957–December 24, 1957, CBS. Merle Oberon (hostess and occasional star) and Tom Conway (guest) in an episode

THE REAL McCOYS: October 3, 1957–September 22, 1963, ABC, CBS. Walter Brennan

THE REAL McCOYS: *(Front)* Tony Martinez; *(middle)* Lydia Reed, Walter Brennan, Michael Winkleman; *(back)* Richard Crenna, Kathy Nolan

HANSEL AND GRETEL: April 27, 1958, NBC. Barbara Cook, Red Buttons, Rudy Vallee, and Hans Conried

ANNIE GET YOUR GUN: November 27, 1957, NBC. John Raitt, William O'Neal, and Mary Martin

CRESCENDO: September 29, 1957, CBS. Carol Channing and Louis Armstrong

COMEDY AND MUSIC: February 19, 1958, CBS. Victor Borge (host)

THE PIED PIPER OF HAMLIN: November 26, 1957, NBC. Van Johnson and Kay Starr

THE RED MILL: April 19, 1958, CBS. Evelyn Rudie, Shirley Jones, and Donald O'Connor

THE AQUA SPECTACULAR OF 1957: September 29, 1957, NBC. Esther Williams

SEA HUNT: 1957–61, syndicated. Lloyd Bridges

LAS VEGAS MUSICAL SPECIAL: November 16, 1957, NBC. Sammy Davis, Jr.

BUCKSKIN: July 3, 1958–September 14, 1959, NBC. Pernell Roberts (guest), Michael Road, and Michael Lipton

SHIRLEY TEMPLE'S STORYBOOK: January 12, 1958–September 10, 1961, NBC, ABC. Shirley Temple (hostess and occasional star)

THE WALTER WINCHELL FILE: October 2, 1957–March 28, 1958, ABC. Jacques Aubuchon (guest), and Walter Winchell (host and narrator)

JEFFERSON DRUM: April 25, 1958–April 23, 1959, NBC. Jeff Richards (Jefferson Drum)

THE PATRICE MUNSEL SHOW: October 18, 1957–June 13, 1958, ABC. Patrice Munsel (hostess)

SHIRLEY TEMPLE'S STORYBOOK: Charlton Heston, Shirley Temple, and Claire Bloom in "Beauty and the Beast"

THE VERDICT IS YOURS: July 3, 1958–September 25, 1958, CBS. Jim McKay (court reporter)

THE PATRICE MUNSEL SHOW: Patrice Munsel

1958-59

This was the year television not only reported the news but made the news.

Over the years quiz shows had become a programming pillar of the industry because the format was easy to put together and therefore was quickly available to fill gaps in any network's lineup. These shows were inexpensive to produce and attracted high viewer support. This led to a plethora of game shows, each with a slightly different gimmick to keep a fickle audience tuned in. Just as important, though, was that sponsor support was also high; surveys indicated product identification to be much greater on these shows than on situation comedies or Westerns, for example.

But with the recent big-money quiz shows, the stakes were raised. And with that came a closer scrutiny of ratings. Which is when some disturbing figures were found. It seemed that these big-money shows were unstable. Their ratings varied from week to week in an unacceptable fashion. And it was reasoned that it wasn't the shows but the contestants that were causing the fluctuation. So it was determined that to assure a program's steady success, contestants who related well to the vast TV audience, or indeed became newsworthy, were a necessity. These "overnight" heroes were an instant way to provide the high continuing ratings these big-money shows needed.

That was the problem facing TV quiz-show producers. And they did something about it. They rigged the shows. They kept their popular contestants on the air by giving them the correct answers.

With the start of this season, what had been rumored for a while (an investigation of the daytime quiz show "Dotto," hosted by Jack Narz, was being conducted) exploded on page one across the country. And within a few weeks, all big-money shows were off the air.

What was on the air in greater-than-ever numbers were adult Westerns. Nine new series began this season: CBS led the way with four—"Wanted: Dead or Alive," "Rawhide," "Yancy Derringer,"

and "The Texan." NBC presented three—"Bat Masterson," "Buckskin" (summer start), and "Cimarron City." ABC introduced "The Rifleman" and "The Lawman." Five of these shows developed loyal followings almost immediately and would run at least three years.

The most popular of this crop was "The Rifleman," which went to the top of the charts, ranking fourth among all shows for the season. Chuck Connors starred as Lucas McCain, a widower trying to raise his young son, Mark, played by Johnny Crawford, on a ranch outside of North Fork, New Mexico, in the late 1880s. Lucas was known for his ability to use a special quick-action 44/40 Winchester rifle (he never used a six-shooter), with which he helped the town marshal to rid North Fork of undesirables. Paul Fix played Marshal Micah Torrance, and was the only other cast member who was featured throughout the series. "The Rifleman" was on for five years and 168 episodes were shown.

Steve McQueen had appeared in many drama anthologies, including "Studio One" and "Goodyear Playhouse," but never in a continuous series before "Wanted: Dead or Alive." And this was to be his only series before going on to become a film star of the first magnitude. McQueen was featured as bounty hunter Josh Randall, who used a potent 30/40 sawed-off rifle (carried on his hip in a holster) that he called his "Mare's Leg" as his trademark. The series caught on right away, ranking 16th this season and 9th next. During the program's three-year run, 117 half-hour episodes were aired.

"Rawhide" did well for CBS during its seven years; it was among the top 30 programs for most of that time. This series about the Old West's huge cattle drives opened each week with the voice of Frankie Laine singing the show's title theme while viewers watched a drive in progress. Eric Fleming played trail boss Gil Favor from this season until he left the series in 1965. Clint Eastwood, play-

ing Rowdy Yates, Favor's right-hand man, then became the trail boss. There were many in the cast over the years but only Eastwood, Paul Brinegar, as Wishbone the cook, and Steve Raines, as Quince, remained throughout the show's entirety. In total, 144 episodes were telecast on the network before the show went into syndication.

Gene Barry starred this season as "Bat Masterson," the Beau Brummel of TV's Western heroes. With his derby hat, gold-tipped cane (which housed a sword), and custom-built gun, Barry's portrayal of the legendary character (he was a real-life lawman who had been a deputy of Wyatt Earp) advocated using brains not brawn in his battle with criminals. Dyan Cannon and William Conrad each made their first prime-time dramatic appearances on this series. Barry was the only permanent cast member throughout the show's three years on NBC.

"The Lawman" was a four-year half-hour Western series about Marshal Dan Troop of Laramie, Wyoming, and his young deputy, Johnny McKay, both of whom were sworn to maintain law and order in their part of the Wild West. John Russell starred as the marshal and Peter Brown played the deputy. The series was on Sunday nights throughout its tenure and 156 episodes were produced.

"The Texan" was not part of the group of successful Westerns. It did start out as if it would enjoy a decent run on CBS (it ranked 15th this season), but fared badly the next season and was canceled. Rory Calhoun played Bill Longley, a fast gun who was always helping people in distress. After its two years on the network, it went into syndication.

A trio of popular police/detective series, each with its own distinct style, made the airwaves this season. The highest rated this first year was "Peter Gunn," starring Craig Stevens in the title role. Gunn was a suave ladies' man who was smart, aggressive, and worked well with the police. His office, most of the time, was a jazz nightclub called "Mother's," where his girlfriend, Edie

(Lola Albright), worked as the featured singer. Herschel Bernardi, as Lieutenant Jacoby, and Hope Emerson initially, then Minerva Urecal, as Mother, rounded out the cast. Henry Mancini's music provided the backdrop that captured the action. In fact, the show's title theme became a hit song and, with the other Mancini music featured, a successful album. "Gunn" was on for three years; first on NBC, then ABC.

"77 Sunset Strip" had action, humor, sex appeal, and a set of disparate characters who worked well together. The series concerned itself with the work of two private detectives based in a plush Hollywood office at the address of the show's title. Their office was next door to a posh restaurant with a hip-talking parking-lot attendant who wanted to be a private detective himself. Stuart Bailey and Jeff Spencer were the private eyes played by Efrem Zimbalist, Jr., and Roger Smith. Edd Byrnes was the parking-lot attendant, Gerald Lloyd Kookson III, better known as Kookie. The show started slowly, picked up momentum, and became a big hit in its second season, reaching 7th in the ratings. The success of "Strip" spawned several other series of this type in subsequent seasons for ABC, including "Bourbon Street Beat," "Hawaiian Eye," and "Surfside Six."

Unlike the previous shows, "Naked City" took a serious look at police work. Focusing on the day-to-day activities of one New York City precinct, the series was filmed entirely on location in New York. ABC first presented it as a half-hour series starring James Franciscus as Det. Jim Halloran, John McIntire as Lt. Dan Muldoon, his boss, and Harry Bellaver as Sgt. Frank Arcaro. McIntire left the series before the completion of this season and was replaced by Horace McMahon. Then the show took a year's hiatus and returned in a 60-minute format. McMahon and Bellaver also returned, but Paul Burke replaced Franciscus. It was on three consecutive years as an hour show and gave several future stars their first major TV role, including: Dustin Hoffman, Jon Voight, Sandy Dennis, and Peter Fonda. The series was based on a story by Mark Hellinger that had been made into a movie in 1948. The film's famous tag line—"There are eight million stories in the naked city. This has been one of them"—was used to conclude each episode.

With so many Westerns getting on the air, only two sitcoms of note debuted. The Stone family lived in Hilldale and was one of the most wholesome families ever to appear on television (it won many civic-affairs awards). The Stones were found in the series "The Donna Reed Show," starring Donna Reed as Donna Stone, Carl Betz as her husband, Dr. Alex Stone, Shelley Fabares as teenage daughter Mary, and Paul Peterson as son Jeff. Another award it should have won was for not getting canceled after this season: it ranked an unbelievable 86th among all prime-time programs, and yet it returned. The show was moved to another day and time in its second season and began a slow rise to ratings respectability. Ultimately, it reached 16th place in its sixth season. Several stars-to-be made their first major TV appearance in this series, including John Astin (later to star in "The Addams Family"), James Darren (one of the stars of "The Time Tunnel"), and George Hamilton. In total, the series ran eight years, in which 275 episodes were telecast.

Ann Sothern did not stay away too long from TV situation comedy after her first series "Private Secretary" concluded (1957). She was back now in "The Ann Sothern Show, this time playing a New York assistant hotel manager and working with a new cast (except for Ann Tyrrell) that included Ernest Truex, Jack Mullaney, Jacques Scott, and Reta Shaw. But things did not go well and the cast was changed in mid-season. Don Porter and Jesse White, from Sothern's original series, were brought in to join Ann Tyrrell. They, along with newcomers Louis Nye and Ken Berry, turned the show around. It ran for three seasons on CBS.

By no means is that all that happened this TV year. Fred Astaire made his long-awaited television debut (October 17, 1958) in an outstanding special titled, "An Evening with Fred Astaire," with dancing partner Barrie Chase. The show was such a sensation that it was repeated later in the season (February 11, 1959). The program won an Emmy as the Most Outstanding Single Program of the Year, and Astaire won an Emmy for the Best Single Performance by an Actor. "The Bell Telephone Hour" was a 19-year radio tradition that moved to television. This quality musical series featured many performers over the years, including Benny Goodman, Mahalia Jackson, Paul Whiteman, Carol Lawrence, Richard Tucker, Ray Bolger, and Bing Crosby. It began as a series of monthly specials then went biweekly and even weekly over the nearly 10 years it was on NBC. "Mike Hammer Private Eye," mystery writer Mickey Spillane's creation, came to television with Darren

McGavin in the title role. Comic-strip character "Steve Canyon," created by Milton Caniff, came alive this season. There were two adventure series: "Northwest Passage," starring Keith Larsen and Buddy Ebsen, was set during the French and Indian Wars, "The Rough Rider," with Kent Taylor, Jan Merlin, and Peter Whitney, was about three Civil War veterans (two Union, one Confederate) who combined their efforts at war's end to fight injustice. And country-and-Western singer Jimmie Rodgers, whose big hits "Honeycomb" and "Kisses Sweeter Than Wine" had made him one of the top recording artists, hosted a short-lived weekly musical/variety show. He was the only new personality this season to have his own prime-time show.

CASEY JONES: 1958, syndicated. Alan Hale, Jr. (Casey Jones)

BRAINS AND BRAWN: September 13, 1958–December 27, 1958, NBC. Fred Davis and Jack Lescoulie (co-hosts)

THE NAKED CITY: James Franciscus and John McIntire (early cast)

THE NAKED CITY: Harry Bellaver and John McIntire

MARKHAM: May 2, 1959–September 22, 1960, CBS. Cindy Robbins (guest) and Ray Milland (Roy Markham)

THE NAKED CITY: September 30, 1958–September 11, 1963, ABC. Paul Burke, Nancy Malone, and Horace McMahon (later cast)

MAN WITH A CAMERA: October 10, 1958–February 29, 1960, ABC. Charles Bronson

THE FURTHER ADVENTURES OF ELLERY QUEEN: September 26, 1958–September 4, 1959, NBC. George Nader (earlier Ellery Queen)

THE FURTHER ADVENTURES OF ELLERY QUEEN: Lee Philips (later Ellery Queen)

PURSUIT: October 22, 1958–January 14, 1959, CBS. Cameron Mitchell, Dennis Hopper, and Lyle Bettger in an episode

BRENNER: June 6, 1959–September 13, 1964, CBS. James Broderick and Edward Binns (Lt. Roy Brenner)

PURSUIT: Fernando Lamas and Robert Middleton in an episode

THE D.A.'S MAN: January 3, 1959–August 29, 1959, NBC. Howard Rasmussen and Frank Lavelle (guests) and John Compton

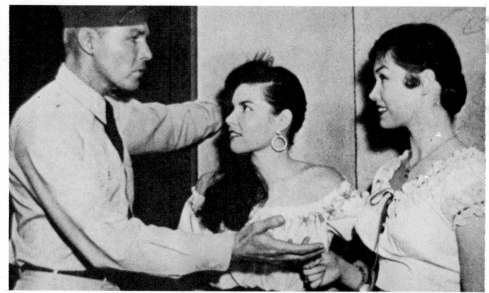

STEVE CANYON: September 13, 1958–September 8, 1959, NBC. Dean Fredericks (Steve Canyon) with guests Yvonne Preble and Mary Moore (later Mary Tyler Moore)

21 BEACON STREET: July 2, 1959–March 20, 1960, NBC, ABC. Dennis Morgan and Joanna Barnes

21 BEACON STREET: Dennis Morgan, James Maloney, Brian Kelly, and Joanna Barnes

77 SUNSET STRIP: October 10, 1958–September 9, 1964, ABC. Efrem Zimbalist, Jr.

77 SUNSET STRIP: Edd "Kookie" Byrnes

77 SUNSET STRIP: Roger Smith, Efrem Zimbalist, Jr., and Edd "Kookie" Byrnes

NORTHWEST PASSAGE: September 14, 1958–September 8, 1959, NBC. Keith Larsen and Buddy Ebsen

THE LAWLESS YEARS: April 16, 1959–September 22, 1961, NBC. Robert Karnes and James Gregory

ONE STEP BEYOND: January 20, 1959–October 3, 1961, ABC. John Newland (host)

ONE STEP BEYOND: Skip Homeier and Virginia Leith in "The Bride Possessed"

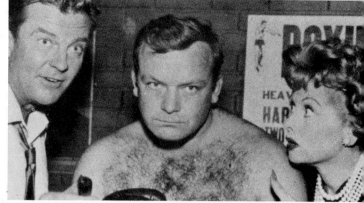

WESTINGHOUSE DESILU PLAYHOUSE: October 13, 1958–June 10, 1960, CBS. William Lundigan, Aldo Ray, and Lucille Ball in "Kayo Kitty"

PETER GUNN: September 22, 1958–September 25, 1961, NBC, ABC. Craig Stevens (Peter Gunn) and Lola Albright

WESTINGHOUSE DESILU PLAYHOUSE: Pier Angeli and Bruce Gordon in "Bernadette"

PETER GUNN: Hope Emerson and Craig Stevens

WESTINGHOUSE DESILU PLAYHOUSE: Neville Brand in "The Untouchables"

PETER GUNN: Craig Stevens, Lola Albright, and Herschel Bernardi

WESTINGHOUSE DESILU PLAYHOUSE: Desi Arnaz (host and occasional star) in "Thunder in the Night"

WESTINGHOUSE DESILU PLAYHOUSE: Keenan Wynn and Robert Stack in "The Untouchables"

THE TEXAN: September 29, 1958–September 12, 1960, CBS. Rory Calhoun

BAT MASTERSON: October 8, 1959–September 21, 1961, NBC. Gene Barry (Bat Masterson)

YANCY DERRINGER: October 2, 1958–September 24, 1959, CBS. Jock Mahoney (Yancy Derringer) and X Brands

BLACK SADDLE: January 10, 1959–September 30, 1960, NBC, ABC. Anna Lisa and Peter Breck

TALES OF THE TEXAS RANGERS: December 22, 1958–May 25, 1959, ABC. Willard Parker and Harry Lauter

THE RIFLEMAN: September 30, 1958–July 1, 1963, ABC. Johnny Crawford and Chuck Connors

OLDSMOBILE MUSIC THEATRE: March 26, 1959–May 7, 1959, NBC. Chester Morris, Hurd Hatfield, Carol Lawrence, and Roddy McDowell in "Too Bad About Sheila Troy"

HOW TO MARRY A MILLIONAIRE: 1958–59, syndicated. Barbara Eden, Merry Anders, and Lori Nelson

WHO PAYS?: July 2, 1959–September 24, 1959, NBC. Sir Cedric Hardwicke, Mike Wallace (host), Celeste Holm, and Gene Klavan

RAWHIDE: Clint Eastwood, Kathleen Crowley (guest), and Eric Fleming

THE INVISIBLE MAN: November 4, 1958–September 22, 1960, CBS. Deborah Watling and the Invisible Man

WANTED: DEAD OR ALIVE: Steve McQueen and Judith Ames (guest)

RAWHIDE: January 9, 1959–January 4, 1966, CBS. Clint Eastwood

WANTED: DEAD OR ALIVE: September 6, 1958–March 29, 1961, CBS. Steve McQueen

THE LAWMAN: October 5, 1958–October 2, 1962, ABC. Peter Brown and John Russell

CIMARRON CITY: October 11, 1958–September 26, 1959, NBC. George Montgomery

CIMARRON CITY: George Montgomery and Dan Duryea (guest)

THE WALTER WINCHELL SHOW: October 5, 1956–December 28, 1956, NBC. Joe DiMaggio, Dorothy Kilgallen, Sammy Davis, Jr., Lisa Kirk, Ernie Kovacs, Martha Raye, and Walter Winchell (host)

THE KRAFT MUSIC HALL: October 8, 1958–May 20, 1959, NBC. Milton Berle (host)

THE G.E. COLLEGE BOWL: *(Right)* Allen Ludden

THE G.E. COLLEGE BOWL: January 4, 1959–June 14, 1970, CBS, NBC. Allen Ludden (first host)

WONDERFUL TOWN: November 20, 1958, CBS. Rosalind Russell

AN EVENING WITH FRED ASTAIRE: October 17, 1958, NBC. Barrie Chase and Fred Astaire

MUSIC WITH MARY MARTIN: March 29, 1959, NBC, Easter Sunday evening. Mary Martin

MEET ME IN ST. LOUIS: April 26, 1959, NBC. Jeanne Crain, Ed Wynn, Myrna Loy, Walter Pidgeon, Jane Powell, and Tab Hunter

MAGIC WITH MARY MARTIN: March 29, 1959, NBC, Easter Sunday afternoon. Dirk Sanders and Mary Martin

CONCENTRATION: October 30, 1958–September 11, 1967, NBC. Hugh Downs (host)

PONTIAC STAR PARADE: February 28, 1959, NBC. Louis Jordan and Marge and Gower Champion

THE DONNA REED SHOW: September 24, 1958–September 3, 1966, ABC. *(Front)* Shelley Fabares, Carl Betz; *(back)* Donna Reed, Paul Peterson

LITTLE WOMEN: October 16, 1958, CBS. *(First row)* Zina Bethune, Margaret O'Brien *(Second row)* Jeannie Carson, Rise Stevens, Florence Henderson

THE BELL TELEPHONE HOUR: January 12, 1959–June 14, 1968, NBC. Duke Ellington and Ella Fitzgerald (guests)

THE ED WYNN SHOW: September 25, 1958–January 1, 1959, NBC. Sherri Alberoni and Ed Wynn

THE JIMMIE RODGERS SHOW: March 31–September 8, 1959, NBC; June 16–September 1, 1969, CBS. Jimmie Rodgers (host)

TOO YOUNG TO GO STEADY: Brigid Bazlen

PECK'S BAD GIRL: May 5, 1959–August 4, 1959, CBS. Marsha Hunt, Patty McCormick, and Wendell Corey (Steve Peck)

TOO YOUNG TO GO STEADY: May 14, 1959–June 25, 1959, NBC. Joan Bennett and Donald Cook

THE DAVE KING SHOW: May 27, 1959–September 23, 1959, NBC. Dave King (host)

PECK'S BAD GIRL: Wendell Corey, Marsha Hunt, and Patty McCormick

1959-60

As the decade came to a close, television was firmly established as the nation's pastime. More than 85 percent of all homes had TV sets and the average viewing time per household was more than five hours per day. There were now more than 560 commercial TV stations in operation, and virtually every city had at least one station. Each of the networks was continuing to increase the number of stations in its lineup: during the last three years, NBC, the largest, added 13; CBS added 25; and ABC, the smallest, increased its lineup by 26. ABC not only increased its station lineup the most, it increased its ratings the most, by offering a combination of Western, private detective, and action/adventure series that were well received by viewers.

Also coming to a close with the decade was the last residue of Hollywood-studio holdouts to TV. No longer did the movie capital view the new medium as detrimental to its industry. Instead, all of the studios were now releasing recent feature films for distribution to the networks and individual stations, and all were actively seeking to produce prime-time programming. And there was a third thing coming to a close with this decade: weekly sponsorship of the programs. Rising costs were causing advertisers to look more closely at their budgets, and full alternate-week sponsorship was already becoming the norm.

Programming this season was primarily made up of Westerns (naturally), private detective/police series, action/adventure shows, and situation comedies. And leading the way were three that would make most everyone's all-time most popular/important programs list: the Western "Bonanza," the police series "The Untouchables," and the anthology "The Twilight Zone."

It was difficult this season to know what a landmark series "Bonanza" would be. The show was not a traditional shoot-'em-up Western; it relied instead on the personal and business interaction between Ben Cartwright, owner of the vast Ponderosa Ranch, his three grown sons, and the characters they encountered each week. During its first two years, the show was positioned against stiff competition: "Perry Mason" on Saturday nights. It survived, then moved to Sunday nights, where, in its third season, it became the second-rated show on TV. From then on it was either at the top or close to it for the next 11 years. The Cartwright family of widower Ben, serious-minded eldest son Adam, cheerful and strong Hoss, and impulsive youngest son Little Joe was played by former Canadian newscaster Lorne Greene, Pernell Roberts, Dan Blocker, and Michael Landon, respectively. The cast worked very well together and Greene and Landon stayed with the series throughout its long run. Roberts left after six years and Blocker suddenly died as the show was going into its 14th season. His death and the program's subsequent move to Tuesday nights were the principal reasons for its demise. "Bonanza"'s original network run was the second longest ever for a Western. Only "Gunsmoke" surpassed it.

"The Untouchables" first appeared as a highly rated two-part story on the anthology series "Desilu Playhouse" (CBS) last season. Robert Stack starred as Treasury Agent Eliot Ness, who got the goods on gangster Al Capone (Neville Brand) and his right-hand man, Frank Nitti (Bruce Gordon), to have them sent to prison. Among TV executives, there was a feeling that stories taking place during the nation's Prohibition era would catch on with viewers. Late last season, NBC had already introduced two series that took place in the 1920s: "The Lawless Years," with James Gregory as Barney Ruditsky, a New York police detective, and "Pete Kelly's Blues," with William Reynolds as a musician who was always lending a hand to people in distress. So it was with high anticipation that ABC brought "The Untouchables" to television as an hour-long series. Stack once again starred in the featured role, although he was not the first choice of the producers; film actors Van Johnson and then Van Heflin had been asked and had declined. Newspaperman Walter Winchell, in his inimitable style, was the narrator.

Many factual events and characters of the time were woven into interesting, exciting episodes that benefited from an authenticity of clothing, autos, and props of the period. The network had a winning series with "The Untouchables," but almost from the start the show caught a lot of flak because of the excessive violence it presented each week. The show was also the target of Italian-American protest groups that felt that too many of the gangsters bore Italian surnames. After four seasons, it was gone.

Rod Serling, one of television's most gifted and prolific writers, and a contributor to most of the fine drama anthologies of the past decade, turned his talents to the world of science fiction this season. Serling, who had won Emmys for "Patterns," presented in 1955 on "The Kraft Television Theater," and for "Requiem for a Heavyweight," on "Playhouse 90" the following year, was now the creator, frequent writer, and host for "The Twilight Zone" on CBS. The series began with a 30-minute format in its first three seasons, expanded to an hour for a short time, and finally reverted back to the half-hour format. Many well-known performers appeared in the series, including Roddy McDowall, Inger Stevens, Robert Redford, Cliff Robertson, Burgess Meredith, David Wayne, Art Carney, and Ann Blythe. There were a total of 151 shows, of which close to two-thirds were written by Serling. These stories are still seen and enjoyed by a new generation of fans today through syndication.

Now a look at the popular genres this season. Other Westerns to debut were: "The Deputy," with Henry Fonda as Marshal Simon Fry; "Bronco," with Ty Hardin as Bronco Layne; "Hotel de Paree," with Earl Holliman as Sundance; "Law of the Plainsman," starring Michael Ansara as U.S. Marshal Sam Buckhart; "The Man from Blackhawk," with Robert

Rockwell as Sam Logan; "Wichita Town," starring Joel McCrea as Marshal Mike Dunbar; "Man Without a Gun," with Rex Reason as crusading editor Adam MacLean; "The Overland Trail," with William Bendix and Doug McClure; and "Tate," with David McLean playing a one-armed gunfighter. In addition, there was "The Rebel" on ABC and "Laramie" on NBC. The half-hour series "The Rebel" was a more solemn and cerebral show than most of this genre. Nick Adams, the only regular cast member, starred as Johnny Yuma, a former Confederate soldier after the Civil War who traveled from town to town in the West helping people in need while searching for his own inner peace. The show's theme song, "The Ballad of Johnny Yuma," was sung by Johnny Cash and, interestingly enough, the program was produced by Goodson and Todman Productions, this being one of their few non-game-show efforts.

"Laramie" had a big cast and was impressive to look at. This year it featured John Smith, Robert Fuller, Hoagy Carmichael, and Bobby Crawford, Jr. The series was set in the Wyoming territory of the 1870s and was centered around the life and experiences of the Sherman brothers (one of whom was only 14 years old), who were partners in a ranch and relay stagecoach depot for the Great Overland Mail Stageline. The series aired Tuesday nights throughout its four years on the network.

Besides "The Untouchables," there were six more private detective/police series: "Bourbon Street Beat," starring Richard Long, Rex Randolph, and Andrew Duggan; "Staccato," with John Cassavetes in the title role; "Dan Raven," featuring Skip Homeier as Lieutenant Raven; "Tightrope," with Mike Connors as undercover cop Nick Stone; "The Detectives"; and "Hawaiian Eye."

Film star Robert Taylor played Capt. Matt Holbrook, a tough, no-nonsense New York City police detective, in "The Detectives." Featured along with Taylor was Tige Andrews (later a police captain on "Mod Squad") as Lt. Johnny Russo, who was the only supporting player to remain throughout the show's tenure. Adam West, the future Batman, appeared in the series for one season, as did Taylor's real-life wife, Ursula Thiess. During its first two years, on ABC, the show was a half-hour. Upon moving to NBC for its third season, it expanded to a full hour.

Warner Brothers Studios had already set in motion its formula for detective shows with the successful launching of

"77 Sunset Strip" last season. This season's entry was "Hawaiian Eye." It employed many of the "Strip" elements, with Hawaii replacing Los Angeles; Kookie present in the person of young nightclub singer Cricket Blake (played by Connie Stevens in her first weekly series); Tom Lopaka and Tracy Steele, played by Robert Conrad (his first series) and Anthony Eisley, emulating the Spencer and Bailey team. The show's beautiful Hawaiian scenery was a TV first. Never before had a series been shot in this lovely locale. Chad Everett (later Dr. Joe Gannon on "Medical Center") made his TV debut in one episode of the hour-long series that ran on ABC for four years, in which 134 episodes were produced.

In the action/adventure group this season were: "Adventures in Paradise," with Gardner McKay as Adam Troy; "Riverboat," starring Darren McGavin as Capt. Grey Holden, with Burt Reynolds in his first series role as pilot Ben Frazer; "The Alaskans," with Roger Moore as Silky Harris, Dorothy Provine as Rocky Shaw, and Jeff York as Reno McKee; "Man and the Challenge," starring George Nadar as Dr. Glenn Barton; and "Mr. Lucky," starring John Vivian in the title role and co-starring Ross Martin as Andamo, Lucky's right-hand man. Mr. Lucky was actually Joe Adams, proprietor of the Fortuna, a luxury gambling yacht and supper club. The series was based on the 1943 movie of the same name starring Cary Grant in the title role. Ironically, though it was a well-rated show for CBS, the network received significant amounts of mail protesting the making of a national hero of a gambler, and so this was the series' only

year. Henry Mancini composed the show's wonderful music, which ultimately became two successful albums.

Situation comedies this season included: "The Betty Hutton Show," with Betty Hutton playing Goldie Appleby, a former showgirl; "The Dennis O'Keefe Show," with O'Keefe playing widower Hal Towne; "Fibber McGee and Molly," with Bob Sweeney and Cathy Lewis from the popular longtime radio show, which proved unsuccessful for television; "Love and Marriage," with William Demarest as the owner of a music-publishing company; "Happy," with Ronnie Burns in a series about a baby who could think out loud; the comedy/drama "Hennesey," starring Jackie Cooper; "Dennis the Menace"; and "The Many Loves of Dobie Gillis."

This season's highest rated new show was the popular comic-strip character come to life, "Dennis the Menace." Dennis was the mischievous young son of Henry and Alice Mitchell, who lived at 627 Elm Street, in Hillsdale. Jay North was marvelous in the role of Dennis, who was always trying to help out but usually made things worse. Herbert Anderson and Gloria Henry played the suffering parents who put up with him as best they could. Throughout the program's four years on CBS, it was seen at 7:30 on Sunday nights.

"The Many Loves of Dobie Gillis" was a show for the American teenager, and like most teenage boys, Dobie loved girls, cars, and money. During the series' four years, viewers watched Dobie and his beatnik friend, Maynard G. Krebs, finish their last two years of high school, go into the Army, resign from the Army, come back to civilian life, and enroll in

THE TROUBLESHOOTERS: September 11, 1959–June 17, 1960, NBC. Bob Mathias and Keenan Wynn

CORONADO 9: 1959, syndicated. Rod Cameron

college. Dwayne Hickman was Dobie and Bob Denver played Maynard. The large cast included Tuesday Weld as Thalia Menninger, the girl Dobie loved (but who didn't love him), Frank Faylen as Dobie's father, Herbert T. Gillis, Florida Friebus as his mother, and Sheila James as Zelda Gilroy, the girl who loved Dobie (but who he didn't love). Over the years, many others appeared in the cast including, for a short while, Warren Beatty in his only continuing role in a series.

In other highlights of this season, only one network drama anthology debuted, the half-hour ''The Dupont Show with June Allyson,'' which featured many top film stars but couldn't attract an audience the way similar dramatic presentations had once done. It lasted two seasons. ''Startime'' was a short-run dramatic and variety series with a wide range of productions. Ingrid Bergman and Alec Guinness each made their American TV dramatic debuts in this series and one of the show's presentations eventually became the popular series ''Sing Along with Mitch,'' with Mitch Miller. CBS and NBC increased their number of news and public-affairs programs in order to upgrade their image, which, they felt, was tarnished in the wake of the quiz-show scandals. CBS premiered ''CBS Reports,'' which began a decade-long weekly run, after which the program was seen at various times during the season and to this day is still on the air. The series has won many awards for broadcast journalism. NBC debuted ''Wide World '60,'' a public-affairs showcase for the network. Under this title the program had a short run, but it was the genesis for many future NBC documentaries.

MANHUNT: 1959, syndicated. Victor Jory and Patrick McVey

FIVE FINGERS: October 3, 1959–January 9, 1960, NBC. Luciana Paluzzi and David Hedison

THE DENNIS O'KEEFE SHOW: September 22, 1959–June 7, 1960, CBS. Dennis O'Keefe, Hope Emerson, and Rickey Kelman

FOUR JUST MEN: 1959, syndicated. Honor Blackman (guest) and Dan Dailey

STACCATO: September 10, 1959–September 25, 1960, NBC, ABC. John Cassavetes (Johnny Staccato)

STACCATO: Eduardo Ciannelli and John Cassavetes

SUNDAY SHOWCASE: (series of specials) September 20, 1959–May 1, 1960, NBC. Thomas Mitchell, Tony Randall, and Kim Hunter in "The Secret of Freedom"

THE MAN AND THE CHALLENGE: September 12, 1959–September 3, 1960, NBC. George Nader and Joyce Meadows (guest)

TIGHTROPE: September 8, 1959–September 13, 1960, CBS. Emerson Tracy (guest) and Mike Connors

PHILIP MARLOWE: September 29, 1959–March 29, 1960, ABC. Philip Carey (Philip Marlowe)

THE THIRD MAN: 1959–60, syndicated. Jonathan Harris and Michael Rennie

LOVE AND MARRIAGE: September 21, 1959–January 25, 1960, NBC. William Demarest and Stubby Kaye

THE MANY LOVES OF DOBIE GILLIS: September 29, 1959–September 18, 1963, CBS. Bob Denver and Dwayne Hickman (Dobie Gillis)

THE MANY LOVES OF DOBIE GILLIS: Bob Denver, Dwayne Hickman, Sheila James, and Steve Franken

OUR AMERICAN HERITAGE: (series of specials) 1959–61, NBC. Ann Harking, Sir Cedric Hardwicke, and Anne Francis in "Autocrat and Son"

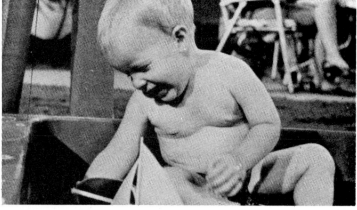

HAPPY: June 8, 1960–September 8, 1961, NBC. David/Steven Born, twins (Happy)

LOCK UP: 1959, syndicated. MacDonald Carey

MEN INTO SPACE: September 30, 1959–September 7, 1960, CBS. *(Right)* William Lundigan

OUR AMERICAN HERITAGE: Joseph Mell, Stephen Roberts, and Billy Vincent in "The Assassination Ploy at Teheran"

THE UNTOUCHABLES: Abel Fernandez, Nicholas Georgiade, Robert Stack, and Paul Picerni

THE UNTOUCHABLES: October 15, 1959–September 10, 1963, ABC. Paul Picerni and Robert Stack

JOHNNY RINGO: October 1, 1959–September 29, 1960, CBS. Don Durant (Johnny Ringo) and Karen Sharp

JOHNNY RINGO: Karen Sharp, Don Durant, and Mona Freeman (guest)

THE REBEL: October 4, 1959–September 17, 1961, ABC. Nick Adams

BOURBON STREET BEAT: October 5, 1959–September 26, 1960, ABC. Andrew Duggan, Richard Long, and Arlene Howell

LARAMIE: September 15, 1959–September 17, 1963, NBC. Robert Fuller, Bobby Crawford, Jr., and Hoagy Carmichael

THE DETECTIVES: October 16, 1959–September 21, 1962, ABC, NBC. Tige Andrews, Robert Taylor, Lee Farr, and Russell Thorson

SHOTGUN SLADE: 1959, syndicated. Scott Brady (Shotgun Slade)

TATE: June 8, 1960–September 28, 1960, NBC. David McLean (Tate)

THE MAN FROM BLACKHAWK: October 9, 1959–September 23, 1960, ABC. *(Center)* Robert Rockwell

HOTEL DE PAREE: October 2, 1959–September 23, 1960, CBS. Judi Meredith and Earl Holliman

THE OVERLAND TRAIL: February 7, 1960–September 11, 1960, NBC. William Bendix and Doug McClure

THE DEPUTY: September 12, 1959–September 16, 1961, NBC. Henry Fonda and Clay McCord

WICHITA TOWN: September 30, 1959–September 23, 1960, NBC. Jody McCrea and Joel McCrea

RIVERBOAT: September 13, 1959–January 16, 1961, NBC. Darren McGavin and Burt Reynolds

RIVERBOAT: Burt Reynolds *(center)* and Darren McGavin *(second from right)*

BRONCO: September 23, 1960–August 20, 1962, ABC. Ty Hardin (Bronco Layne)

BONANZA: Michael Landon, Dan Blocker, Pernell Roberts, and Lorne Greene

BONANZA: September 12, 1959–January 16, 1973, NBC. Dan Blocker, Lorne Greene, Pernell Roberts, and Michael Landon

DENNIS THE MENACE: Jay North and Joseph Karnes

DENNIS THE MENACE: October 4, 1959–September 22, 1963, CBS. Herbert Anderson, Jay North (Dennis Mitchell), and Gloria Henry

THE PLAY OF THE WEEK: 1959-61, syndicated. Zero Mostel, Morris Carnovsky, Nancy Walker, and Sam Levene in "The World of Sholom Aleichem"

THE PLAY OF THE WEEK: Mildred Natwick and Hugh Griffith in "The Waltz of the Toreadors"

HAWAIIAN EYE: October 7, 1959–September 10, 1963, ABC. Robert Conrad and Connie Stevens

HAWAIIAN EYE: Connie Stevens

MOON AND SIXPENCE: October 30, 1959, NBC. Jean Marsh and Laurence Olivier

ADVENTURES IN PARADISE: October 5, 959–April 1, 1962, ABC. Gardner McKay

ADVENTURES IN PARADISE: Gardner McKay in "Paradise" scene

WILIGHT ZONE: Franchot Tone and onathan Harris in "The Silence"

TWILIGHT ZONE: Richard Deacon in "The Brain Center at Whipples"

TWILIGHT ZONE: Earl Holliman in "Where Is Everybody?"

WILIGHT ZONE: October 2, 1959–September 18, 1964, CBS. od Serling (host)

TWILIGHT ZONE: Jonathan Winters and Jack Klugman in "A Game of Pool"

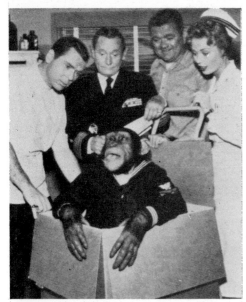

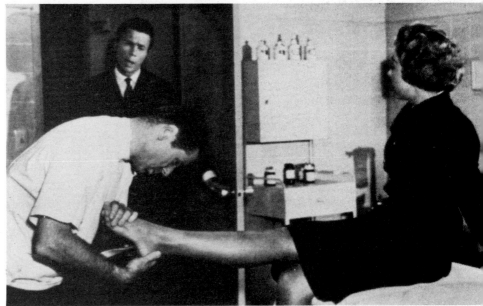

HENNESEY: Jackie Cooper, Roscoe Karnes, Henry Kulky, and Abby Dalton

HENNESEY: Jackie Cooper and patient

HENNESEY: September 28, 1959–September 17, 1962, CBS. Jackie Cooper (Lt. Chick Hennesey)

FIBBER McGEE AND MOLLY: September 15, 1959–January 19, 1960, NBC. Bob Sweeney and Cathy Lewis (Fibber and Molly McGee)

THE ALASKANS: October 4, 1959–September 25, 1960, ABC. Dorothy Provine and Roger Moore

THE BIG PARTY: October 8, 1959–December 31, 1959, CBS. Barbara Britton, Patrice Munsel, and Abe Burrows

PLAY YOUR HUNCH: April 15, 1960–September 26, 1962, NBC. Merv Griffin (host) and Liz Gardner (assistant)

1960-61

During 1960, it became evident that television had become a focal point in the political process. In the early part of the year the networks extensively covered the aspiring presidential candidates in each of the many primaries. In the latter part of the year a television landmark aired: the Great Presidential Debates. For the first time, the nation's voters were afforded the opportunity to witness—live, right in their homes—campaign debates staged specifically for them. The two presidential candidates, Republican Vice President Richard M. Nixon and Democratic Sen. John F. Kennedy, met in face-to-face confrontations.

As this season commenced, the first debate was telecast live from Chicago on all three networks and on many independent stations around the country. It was estimated that the audience for this event was 75 million, the largest ever to watch a TV program to that time. Three more live debates took place before the November election. Many analysts believe it was this series of contests that enabled Kennedy, who had a particular affinity for the camera, to emerge the victor in what was ultimately a very close election.

Also as this season commenced, ABC, after many years, finally emerged as a respectable third network. And as far as top-rated shows were concerned, the network actually placed more in the top 25 than TV's early powerhouse, NBC. Its success could be attributed to a willingness to try more innovative programming, which was beginning to really pay off.

But it was the network with the most top-rated shows, CBS, that placed the best-rated new series in its lineup, "The Andy Griffith Show." This situation comedy became a winner almost immediately and placed fourth for the year. Three other new programs made the top 25: "My Three Sons," "The Flintstones," and "Checkmate."

Mayberry, North Carolina, was the home for the immensely popular rural situation comedy, "The Andy Griffith Show." This was the first season for what was to become an eight-year Monday night ritual for millions of viewers. Sheriff Andy Taylor (Andy Griffith) was a widower with a six-year-old son, Opie (Ronny Howard), and an inept, hypertense cousin, Deputy Barney Fife (Don Knotts). The series revolved around the relationship between Andy and Barney and how they did their job of maintaining law and order in their virtually crime-free town. The other principal character in the cast was Aunt Bee Taylor (Frances Bavier), who lived with Andy and his son and was a combination housekeeper and mother influence for the young Opie. Over the years there were many characters in the cast, and one, gas-station attendant Gomer Pyle (Jim Nabors), eventually got a series of his own ("Gomer Pyle, U.S.M.C."). Griffith, Howard, and Bavier remained with the series throughout its full network life. Knotts left in 1965 to make movies. In total, there were 249 episodes produced. An interesting note: when it left the air, it was the No. 1 show on television.

From rural Mayberry we go to middle-class suburban Bryant Park, where we find another widower trying to raise his children in "My Three Sons," starring Fred MacMurray as Steve Douglas. This series went on to become TV's second-longest-running sitcom (12 years). The Douglas children were eldest son Mike (Tim Considine), Robbie (Don Grady), and youngest son Chip (Stanley Livingston). In addition, there was grandfather Michael Francis "Bub" O'Casey (William Frawley), and Tramp, the family dog. Frawley's character was sort of the mother of the clan and this was the only other continuing series the veteran actor was in (the first being "I Love Lucy"). Over the years there were many cast changes and even a second hometown for the show. The first major change took place in 1965, when Frawley left the show for health reasons and longtime film actor William Demarest joined the cast as Charley O'Casey, the boy's live-in uncle. The location change occurred when Steve, an aeronautical engineer,

was asked by his company to relocate with his family in North Hollywood. There were an incredible 369 episodes produced for the series. For five years it was on ABC, and then went to CBS for the next seven. And for most of that time it was among the top 25 shows each season.

ABC, whose reputation for innovative programming was growing, decided to include in its lineup this season the first prime-time animated series made especially for television. And once again they hit pay dirt. "The Flintstones" was a Stone Age parody on modern suburban life (complete with a "pet" dinosaur and "rock" music), and apparently the novelty of a cartoon series in prime time was a relief from much of the sameness found on television's schedule. The voices of the principal characters, Fred and Wilma Flintstone and their neighbors Barney and Betty Rubble, were provided by Alan Reed, Jean Vander Pyl, Mel Blanc, and Bea Benaderet. Amazingly, the program remained on the network for six years and became prime time's longest-running animated series.

The fourth show of this season's crop to make the top 25 was "Checkmate." Checkmate, Inc., was a private investigative agency based in San Francisco. Anthony George starred as Don Corey and Doug McClure as Jed Sills, while Sebastian Cabot was Dr. Carl Hyatt, a professor of criminology and a consultant to the firm. Notable performers who appeared on the show were Charles Laughton, in his final TV role, and Cyd Charisse, in her first TV dramatic role. The hour-long series' good showing this season on CBS wasn't repeated the next season, after which it left the air.

And now a potpourri of new programs presented this season:

Martin Milner and George Maharis starred as Tod Stiles and Buzz Murdock, two young men traveling the country searching for adventure in a sporty Corvette, in "Route 66." Stiles's background was of wealth while Murdock came from the streets of Hell's Kitchen in New York. They met because Murdock had been employed by the elder Stiles. When the elder man died, it was discovered that young Stiles's family wealth was all gone. At this point, the two young men decided to pool their resources and travel across the country with no real objective in mind. Maharis was in the series for the first two and a half seasons, but reasons of health prevented him from continuing. Glenn Corbett joined Milner for the program's final year-and-a-half run. Among the show's notable guest stars were Alan Alda, singer-dancer Joey Heatherton (her first TV dramatic role), Robert Redford, and Rod Steiger. Composer Nelson Riddle provided the title music, which became a hit in 1962.

Mitch Miller, composer, arranger, and record producer for many years, brought to television his musical-variety creation "Sing Along with Mitch." Home viewers were encouraged to participate in the sing-along—the lyrics of the familiar songs performed were superimposed at the bottom of their TV screens. The show had been introduced last season on "Startime," and this season it had a limited alternate-weekly run. Its success led to its becoming a weekly series the next season. The regulars were the Sing Along Gang, the Sing Along Kids, and soloists Leslie Uggams, Diana Trask, Gloria Lambert, and Louise O'Brien.

"Surfside Six" was another in the series of Warner Brothers private detective shows. Two of the studio's previous efforts, "77 Sunset Strip" and "Hawaiian Eye," were proving to be successful, and they applied the formula once again, this time on a houseboat that served as an office and home in Miami Beach. The trio of private eyes were Troy Donahue as Sandy Winfield, Van Williams (a survivor of last season's "Bourbon Street Beat," and the future "Green Hornet") as Ken Madison, and Lee Patterson as Dave Thorne. Diane McBain, as their friend Daphne Dutton, and Margarita Sierra, as nightclub singer Cha Cha O'Brien, were also featured. But the formula didn't work, and the show ran for only two seasons, in which 79 episodes were produced.

Pete Porter was the wisecracking neighbor who was always complaining about his daffy wife, Gladys, on the long-running "December Bride." Now Pete and his wife had their own sitcom, "Pete and Gladys," with Harry Morgan and Cara Williams in the lead roles. Also featured in the cast were Gale Gordon, formerly of "Our Miss Brooks," as Uncle Paul and two holdovers from the "Bride" cast, Verna Felton, repeating her role as Hilda Crocker, and Frances Rafferty, now

playing Gladys's friend Nancy. Unfortunately, Pete and Gladys on their own couldn't hold the audience. It lasted only two seasons.

"The Tall Man" was a series about two real-life Westerners, Sheriff Pat Garrett and William H. Bonney, better known as Billy the Kid. The setting was the territory of New Mexico in the 1870s. Barry Sullivan was Garrett and Clu Gulager played the Kid. The two characters had actually been close friends in real life despite often being on the opposite sides of the law. Garrett's reputation for honesty and straightforwardness and his motto—"My business is the law and I mean to mind it"—earned him the nickname that was the series' title.

On other news of the season, Milton Berle, whose previous short-lived show "Milton Berle Starring in The Kraft Music Hall" went off the air in May 1959, was now back as the host of "Jackpot Bowling." Berle had a 30-year contract with NBC that began in 1951, and while this was not really a show for him, the network felt his presence would help. It didn't. The show lasted 26 weeks. Another TV great, Jackie Gleason, had been absent from network television for two years when he returned as the host of a prime-time game show titled "You're in the Picture." The program was a total flop and did not survive after the first telecast. Gleason abandoned the format the following week and simply chatted with his studio audience and apologized to home viewers for the disaster. For the next two months, he conducted an informal talk show under the title "The Jackie Gleason Show." Each week he talked with one celebrity guest. Among them were Jayne Mansfield, Bobby Darin, and Mickey Rooney. Film star Barbara Stanwyck began hosting her own 30-minute anthology, "The Barbara Stanwyck Show," on NBC. Like Loretta Young, Stanwyck starred in many of the episodes, though the show only lasted this season. Near the close of the season, one of the last live dramatic anthologies made a short appearance. Live weekly drama was a rarity when NBC introduced "Great Ghost Tales," with Frank Gallop as host. Among the featured performers were Kevin McCarthy, Lee Grant, Arthur Hill, and Richard Thomas (in one of his earliest TV roles). ABC launched a weekend sports series, "Wide World of Sports." Jim McKay began hosting what was to become television's foremost sports anthology and does so to this day. This was also the season in which the newly appointed chairman of the Federal Communications Commission, Newton Minow, a

former Chicago law partner of Adlai Stevenson, gave a speech that shook the television industry. Addressing the National Association of Broadcasters in Washington, D.C., he described TV programming as a "vast wasteland." After this, whenever media critics wanted to condemn the medium, his was the succinct phrase they used.

THE AQUANAUTS: September 14, 1960–February 22, 1961, CBS. Ron Ely and Jeremy Slate

THE ASPHALT JUNGLE: April 2, 1961–September 24, 1961, ABC. Jack Warden

THE ROARING TWENTIES: October 15, 1960–September 21, 1962, ABC. Dorothy Provine

THE WITNESS: September 29, 1960–January 26, 1961, CBS. Anita Dangler pointing to Telly Savalas in an episode

THE BROTHERS BRANNAGAN: 1960, syndicated. Steve Dunn and Mark Roberts (Mike and Bob Brannagan)

THE JIM BACKUS SHOW (HOT OFF THE WIRE): 1960, syndicated. Bobs Watson and Jim Backus

THE CASE OF THE DANGEROUS ROBIN (DANGEROUS ROBIN): 1960, syndicated. Rick James and Jean Blake

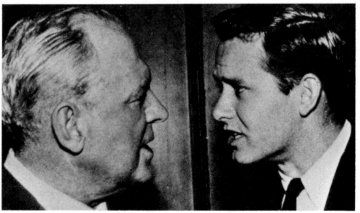

HARRIGAN AND SON: October 14, 1960–September 29, 1961, ABC. Pat O'Brien and Roger Perry (James Harrigan senior, and junior)

ROUTE 66: October 7, 1960–September 18, 1964, CBS. Martin Milner and George Maharis

ROUTE 66: George Maharis, Martin Milner, and their Corvette

THRILLER: September 13, 1960–July 9, 1962, NBC. Boris Karloff (host)

THRILLER: Boris Karloff in "The Incredible Dr. Markesan"

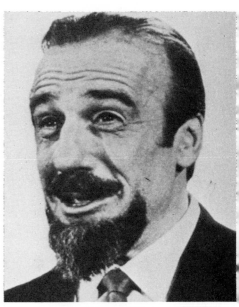

SING ALONG WITH MITCH: January 27, 1961–September 21, 1964, NBC. Mitch Miller

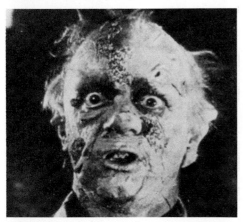

THRILLER: Harry Townes becomes grotesque in "The Cheaters"

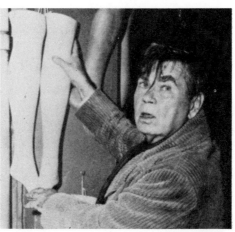

THRILLER: Oscar Homolka in "Waxworks"

MR. ED: Early 1961, syndicated; October 1, 1961–September 4, 1966, CBS. Alan Young and Mr. Ed

DANTE: October 3, 1960–April 10, 1961, NBC. Howard Duff (Willie Dante)

GUESTWARD HO!: September 29, 1960–September 21, 1961, ABC. J. Carrol Naish

HOLLYWOOD SINGS: (special), 1960. Tammy Grimes and Eddie Albert

MY THREE SONS: Fred MacMurray, Meredith MacRae, and Tim Considine

MY THREE SONS: September 29, 1960–August 24, 1972, ABC, CBS. Tim Considine, Stanley Livingston, Fred MacMurray, William Frawley, and Don Grady

167

THE FLINTSTONES: September 30, 1960–September 2, 1966, ABC. Barney and Betty Rubble, Wilma and Fred Flintstone

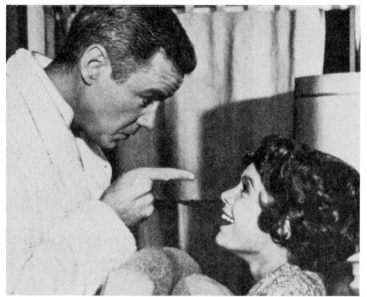

ANGEL: October 6, 1960–September 20, 1961, CBS. Marshall Thompson and Annie Farge (Angel)

HONG KONG: September 28, 1960–September 20, 1961, ABC. Rod Taylor

THE ANDY GRIFFITH SHOW: Andy Griffith and Anita Corsaut (Andy's wedding)

THE ANDY GRIFFITH SHOW: Don Knotts, Jim Nabors, and Andy Griffith

THE ANDY GRIFFITH SHOW: October 3, 1960–September 10, 1968, CBS. Don Knotts, Ron Howard, and Andy Griffith

GUNSLINGER: February 9, 1961–September 14, 1961, CBS. Tony Young

WHISPERING SMITH: May 15, 1961–September 18, 1961, NBC. Guy Mitchell and Audie Murphy (Tom "Whispering" Smith)

THE TALL MAN: September 10, 1960–September 1, 1962, NBC. Clu Gulager and Barry Sullivan

THE DOW HOUR OF GREAT MYSTERIES: (series of specials) 1960, NBC. Joseph Welch, host *(foreground)*, Helen Hayes, and Jason Robards, Jr., in "The Bat"

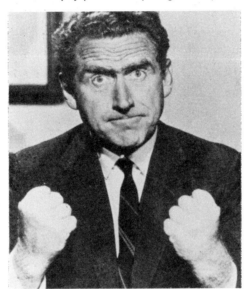

THE LAW AND MR. JONES: October 7, 1960–September 22, 1961, ABC. James Whitmore (Abraham Lincoln Jones)

MICHAEL SHAYNE: September 30, 1960–September 22, 1961, NBC. Richard Denning (Michael Shayne)

CHECKMATE: September 17, 1960–September 19, 1962, CBS. Doug McClure, Sebastian Cabot, and Anthony George

CHECKMATE: Anthony George, Joan Fontaine (guest), Doug McClure, and Sebastian Cabot

THE BUGS BUNNY SHOW: October 11, 1960–September 2, 1966, ABC. Bugs Bunny

PETE AND GLADYS: September 19, 1960–September 10, 1962, CBS. Harry Morgan (Pete Porter), Cara Williams (Gladys Porter), and Verna Felton

PETE AND GLADYS: Cara Williams, Harry Morgan, and Bill Hinnant

THE ISLANDERS: Wendy Barrie (guest), William Reynolds, and Hans Conried (guest)

THE ISLANDERS: October 2, 1960–March 26, 1961, ABC. *(Seated)* James Philbrook, William Reynolds; *(standing)* Daria Massey and Diane Brewster

SURFSIDE SIX: October 3, 1960–September 24, 1962, ABC. Troy Donahue

SURFSIDE SIX: Van Williams, Margarita Sierra, and Troy Donahue

1961-62

The attention of the world had been captured in the closing months of the 1960–61 television year when man first ventured into space. The U.S.S.R., on April 12, 1961, sent a *Vostok 1* spacecraft, with cosmonaut Yuri Gargarin on board, on a 89.1-minute orbit of the earth. Less than four weeks later (May 6), the United States launched its first manned spacecraft, with astronaut Alan B. Shepard, Jr., at the controls. And, unlike the Soviet launch, television cameras were there to enable the nation to share the experience live. Shepard's flight was suborbital, as was the subsequent flight that also took place before millions of TV viewers on July 21. These successful launchings were the prerequisites for the nation's premiere orbital flight of astronaut John Glenn at about the midpoint—February 20, 1962—of this TV season. As America's venture into space progressed, television was on hand to give the viewing public the opportunity to share the exciting journey.

As this season began, the television industry was still angry over FCC Commissioner Newton Minow's "vast wasteland" statement. But in truth, many felt television programming indeed was, at best, mediocre in recent years. One reason for this was the instant success achieved by the networks with their big-money game shows from the mid to late fifties. These shows were less costly, faster to produce, and attracted high ratings. The networks' emphasis on these easy-to-create shows caused a diminished interest in developing much-needed, but costly, quality programming. This was particularly true in the drama and comedy genres, which had been the highlights of the medium's earlier years.

But possibly the message was already getting through, because this season four outstanding series debuted: "The Defenders," "Dr. Kildare," "Ben Casey," and "The Dick Van Dyke Show."

CBS went back to a 1957 live presentation of a two-part legal drama on "Studio One" to come up with one of TV's outstanding weekly series, "The Defenders." The original story was scripted by Reginald Rose and starred Ralph Bellamy and William Shatner as a father-and-son attorney team. For the series, E. G. Marshall and Robert Reed were cast as the father-and-son team of Lawrence and Kenneth Preston. Marshall had been a frequent TV performer during the past decade; Reed was a relative newcomer to television. This series was the first continuing role for both actors. What made this a qualitative series, in addition to its high production values, was that it dealt realistically with sensitive issues of the day including abortion, blacklisting, and euthanasia. Also featured in the cast this season were Joan Hackett as Ken's girlfriend, Joan Miller, and Polly Rowles as the Prestons' secretary, Helen Donaldson. Gene Hackman, James Earl Jones, Robert Redford, Dustin Hoffman, Jon Voight, and, in their first major TV roles, James Farentino and Martin Sheen were among the many performers who appeared in the series. A total of 132 episodes were aired during the program's four-year run.

Less than a week separated the debut of TV's two finest medical series, "Dr. Kildare" on NBC and "Ben Casey" on ABC. "Dr. Kildare" had its genesis in a series of M-G-M movies made in the late thirties and early forties starring Lew Ayres and Lionel Barrymore. In the TV series, Raymond Massey played the Barrymore role of Dr. Leonard Gillespie, the senior staff physician at Blair General Hospital, and Richard Chamberlain played the young, idealistic intern, James Kildare. They were the only regular cast members during the show's five years. The series was presented in an hour format during its first four years and then as a half-hour show twice weekly in its last year.

"Ben Casey" was set in County General Hospital, where Chief of Surgery Dr. David Zorba (Sam Jaffe) and the young chief resident of neurosurgery, Dr. Ben Casey (Vince Edwards), very realistically went about the business of trying to save lives. The series had a regular cast consisting of Bettye Ackerman (Sam Jaffe's wife) as Dr. Maggie Graham, Harry Landers as Dr. Ted Hoffman, Nick Dennis as orderly Nick Kanavaras, and Jeanne Bates as Nurse Wills. Jaffe left the series in its last year and was replaced by Franchot Tone. "Casey," like "Kildare," had a five-season network run.

Comedy performer and writer Carl Reiner, one of Sid Caesar's second bananas on "Your Show of Shows," created a pilot for a situation comedy titled "Head of the Family" that was aired as part of the summer series "The Comedy Spot" in 1960. Reiner starred as comedy writer Robert Petrie in this, the first series, in which the central character worked for a television show. When "Head of the Family" was put on this season's CBS schedule it became "The Dick Van Dyke Show," starring Dick Van Dyke in the Petrie role, Mary Tyler Moore as his wife, Larry Mathews as his young son, and Morey Amsterdam and Rose Marie as his co-writers. Other cast members were Richard Deacon, Jerry Paris, Ann Morgan Guilbert, and Carl Reiner, now as Petrie's boss Alan Brady. Incredibly, the series survived an 80th-place finish this season and went on to become a top-10 show in subsequent years. It was on for five years and left the air as one of TV's best sitcoms ever.

There was also a group of popular, though less distinguished, situation comedies that arrived this year. "Mr. Ed," a series about a talking horse, starred Alan Young as Wilbur Post and ran for five years. The series was the brainchild of producer-director Arthur Lubin, who had directed the five "Frances the Talking Mule" films of the fifties. The show originated in syndication last season and this season it became one of the earliest examples of a syndicated program becoming a network series. Others in the cast were Connie Hines as Carol Post, Wilbur's wife; Larry Keating as next-door neighbor Roger Addison; and Edna Skinner as Roger's wife, Kay. The voice of Mr. Ed was provided by former cowboy star Allan "Rocky" Lane.

"Hazel," a sitcom about a maid who,

in her zeal, practically took over her employer's home, was based on the popular Ted Key cartoons that appeared in the *Saturday Evening Post*. Shirley Booth starred in the series, which had two formats. The first, on NBC, took place at 123 Marshall Drive in Hydsberg, New York, at the residence of George and Dorothy Baxter (Don DeFore and Whitney Blake) and their son, Harold (Bobby Buntrock). At the start of the show's fifth and last year, when it moved to CBS, Hazel also moved to 325 Sycamore Street, the home of George's brother's family. George had been transferred by his company and asked his brother Steve (Ray Fulmer) to let Harold stay with him so that his schooling would not be interrupted. Steve's family consisted of his wife, Barbara, played by Lynn Borden, and daughter, Susie, played by Julia Benjamin.

"The Joey Bishop Show" began a four-year stint that endured format and network changes (NBC, then CBS). This season Bishop played Joey Barnes, an unmarried Hollywood public-relations man. Also featured were Joe Flynn (the future Captain Binghamton in "McHale's Navy") as his brother-in-law Frank; Virginia Vincent as his older sister, Betty; Marlo Thomas (in her first continuing role) as his younger sister, Stella; Warren Berlinger as his kid brother, Larry; and Madge Blake as his widowed mother. The next season, Bishop played a married show-business personality. There was a whole new cast that included Abby Dalton as his wife, Ellie; Guy Marks as his manager, Freddy; and Corbett Monica as Larry, his writer. The show did reasonably well this year, placing among the top 25 programs.

A new era in network programming began when NBC debuted "Saturday Night at the Movies." This was the first program to telecast more recent post-1948 Hollywood films, and it led to many similar network movie programs in the years ahead. This came about because the studios, already working with the networks as the major supplier of filmed weekly series, made the inevitable decision to release more recent films. The premiere movie was a 1953 flick, *How to Marry a Millionaire*, starring Marilyn Monroe, Lauren Bacall, and Betty Grable. This movie series was a fixture on NBC for 17 years.

But there was still more to this season. Film star Dick Powell, already a TV veteran, was the host of, and occasional performer in, "The Dick Powell Show," a dramatic anthology. Many of the episodes were pilots for new TV programs, and two did become weekly

series the following season: "Amos Burke," starring Gene Barry, and "Saints and Sinners," with Nick Adams. "Alcoa Premiere" was another hour-long anthology, with Fred Astaire as the host and occasional performer. Some of the guest stars who appeared during its two years on ABC were Lee Marvin, Charlton Heston, Shelley Winters, Brian Keith, Robert Redford, Telly Savalas, and James Stewart. Standup comedian Bob Newhart hosted his own comedy/variety show. Newhart's routines were successful on records and his monologues, done in the form of telephone conversations, had been seen by viewers in his many TV guest appearances. As in all other seasons, there was a flock of one-season series: "Father of the Bride," "The Hathaways," "Ichabod and Me," "Margie," "Mrs. G Goes to College," "Oh, Those Bells," "Room for One More," "Window on Main Street," "87th Precinct," "The New Breed," "Target: The Corrupters," "Follow the Sun," and "Bus Stop." Tragedy struck when Ernie Kovacs, the medium's most innovative comic, was killed in an auto accident on January 13, 1962, one week before his forty-third birthday. And more tragedy occurred when boxer Benny "Kid" Parret died as a result of his Madison Square Garden Welterweight Championship match with Emil Griffith on ABC's "Fight of the Week," March 17, 1962.

FEATHERTOP: (Musical special), 1961. Jane Powell and Hugh O'Brian

THE BOB NEWHART SHOW: October 11, 1961–June 13, 1962, NBC. Bob Newhart (host)

MRS. G. GOES TO COLLEGE: October 4, 1961–April 5, 1962, CBS. Sir Cedric Hardwicke and Gertrude Berg (Sarah Green/Mrs. G)

STRAIGHTAWAY: October 6, 1961–July 4, 1962, ABC. Brian Kelly and John Ashley

BUS STOP: October 1, 1961–March 23, 1962, ABC. Marilyn Maxwell and Fabian (guest)

THE DICK VAN DYKE SHOW: *(Seated)* Ann Morgan Guilbert, Jerry Paris, and Dick Van Dyke; *(standing)* Rose Marie and Morey Amsterdam

INTERNATIONAL SHOWTIME: September 15, 1961–September 10, 1965, NBC.
Don Ameche (host)

THE DICK VAN DYKE SHOW: October 3, 1961–September 7, 1966, CBS. Dick Van Dyke and Mary Tyler Moore

THE DICK VAN DYKE SHOW: Dick Van Dyke and Larry Mathews

THE DICK VAN DYKE SHOW: *(Front)* Mary Tyler Moore and Dick Van Dyke; *(back)* Richard Deacon, Rose Marie, and Morey Amsterdam

THE DEFENDERS: September 16, 1961–September 9, 1965, CBS. E. G. Marshall, Sam Jaffe (guest), and Robert Reed

FATHER OF THE BRIDE: September 29, 1961–September 14, 1962, CBS. Myrna Fahey

THE DEFENDERS: J. D. Cannon (guest), E. G. Marshall, and Robert Reed *(seated)*

OH, THOSE BELLS: March 8, 1962–May 31, 1962, CBS. The Wiere Brothers — Herbert, Harry, and Sylvester

TARGET: THE CORRUPTERS: September 29, 1961–September 21, 1962, ABC. Stephen McNally

TARGET: THE CORRUPTERS: Robert Harland

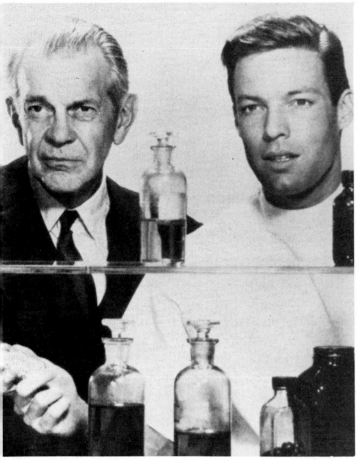

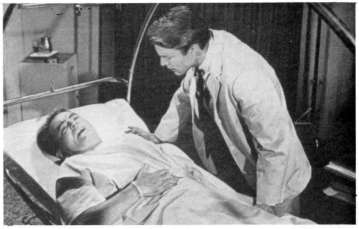

DR. KILDARE: Richard Chamberlain (Dr. James Kildare)

DR. KILDARE: September 28, 1961–August 30, 1966, NBC. Raymond Massey and Richard Chamberlain

DR. KILDARE: Richard Chamberlain and Raymond Massey

DR. KILDARE: Richard Chamberlain and Raymond Massey

SATURDAY NIGHT AT THE MOVIES: September 23, 1961–September 2, 1978, NBC. Marilyn Monroe, Lauren Bacall, and Betty Grable in "How to Marry a Millionaire" (premiere telecast)

87TH PRECINCT: September 25, 1961–September 10, 1962, NBC. Robert Lansing, Norman Fell, and Ron Harper

FRONTIER CIRCUS: October 5, 1961–September 20, 1962, CBS. Richard Jaeckel, Mickey Rooney (guest), and John Derek

THE JOEY BISHOP SHOW: September 20, 1961–September 7, 1965, NBC, CBS. Joey Bishop and Corbett Monica

THE NEW BREED: October 3, 1961–September 25, 1962, ABC. Leslie Nielsen, Greg Roman, John Clark, and John Beradino

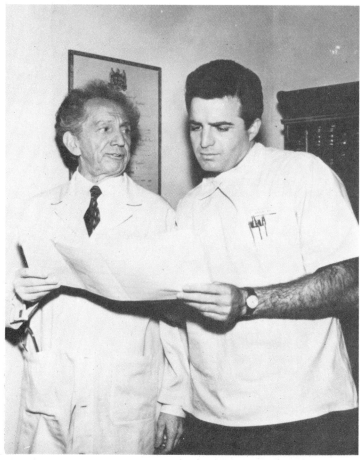

BEN CASEY: October 2, 1961–March 21, 1966, ABC. Sam Jaffe and Vince Edwards (Dr. Ben Casey)

FOLLOW THE SUN: September 17, 1961–September 9, 1962, ABC. Barry Coe and Gary Lockwood

BEN CASEY: Vince Edwards

BEN CASEY: Vince Edwards and unknown actress

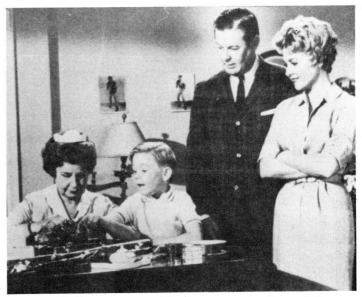

HAZEL: Hazel's first family—Shirley Booth, Bobby Buntrock, Don DeFore, Whitney Blake

HAZEL: September 28, 1961–September 5, 1966, NBC, CBS. Shirley Booth (Hazel Burke)

HAZEL: Hazel's second family—*(front)* Bobby Buntrock, Shirley Booth, and Julie Benjamin; *(back)* Lynn Borden and Ray Fulmer

HAZEL: Don DeFore, Bobby Buntrock, and Whitney Blake

PASSWORD: January 2, 1962–May 22, 1967, CBS. Carol Channing, Allen Ludden (host), Eli Wallach, and contestant

MARGIE: October 12, 1961–August 31, 1962, ABC. Wesley Tackitt, Cynthia Pepper, and Dave Willock

ROOM FOR ONE MORE: January 27, 1962–September 22, 1962, ABC. Timothy Rooney (Mickey's son) and Andrew Duggan

ICHABOD AND ME: September 26, 1961–September 18, 1962, CBS. Robert Sterling and Rod Serling (guest)

CAR 54, WHERE ARE YOU?: September 17, 1961–September 8, 1963, NBC. Fred Gwynne and Joe E. Ross

ICHABOD AND ME: Robert Sterling and Guy Raymond

THE HATHAWAYS: October 6, 1961–August 31, 1962, ABC. Jack Weston, Peggy Cass, and a Marquis Chimp

THE HATHAWAYS: Peggy Cass and the Marquis Chimps

178

1962-63

Shortly before the new season began, global television became more of a reality with the successful launching of the *Telstar 1* satellite, which was placed in orbit 22,300 miles above the earth. It permitted, for the first time, live television transmission between the United States and European countries. Future satellites would extend the range of live TV to other areas of the world.

As the new fall schedule commenced, President Kennedy was in the midst of desegregating the South's educational system. The focus of this event was the University of Mississippi, in Oxford, Mississippi, and the rioting and violence taking place appeared daily on TV screens in the homes of Americans. This was followed by a confrontation between the United States and the Soviet Union over the shipment of offensive military weapons to Cuba. Kennedy dramatically used television to tell the nation and the world about the danger of this missile crisis and what he intended to do about it.

In conjunction with these world and national events that were becoming so much a daily part of our lives, the networks provided more public-affairs programming than ever before. Six programs totaling four hours were now seen in prime time. ABC offered Howard K. Smith on "News and Comment," along with "Bell and Howell Closeup." CBS provided "CBS Reports" and "Eyewitness." And NBC aired "David Brinkley's Journal" and "Chet Huntley Reporting."

On the lighter side, personalities were also in the limelight. Jack Paar gave up hosting "The Tonight Show" after almost five years in favor of a weekly prime-time variety show. On October 1, 1962, both Johnny Carson and Merv Griffin began hosting their own talk shows on NBC. Carson took over "The Tonight Show" and Griffin began hosting a 55-minute daily afternoon program. Jackie Gleason returned to television on Saturday nights in a variety program titled "Jackie Gleason and His American Scene Magazine." The show featured topical humor and musical productions, in addition to

his new sidekick, comedian Frank Fontaine. Many of Gleason's standard characters were back, and one, Joe the Bartender, appeared regularly. Joe was joined each week by a slightly smashed character, Crazy Guggenheim, played by Fontaine. With this show Gleason recaptured high ratings and became a Saturday-night fixture on CBS for the next eight years.

There were the usual large number of one-season (or less) programs this year. Among the situation comedies were NBC's "Don't Call Me Charlie," with John Hubbard, Josh Peine, Alan Napier (the future Alfred the Butler of "Batman"), and Arte Johnson (of future "Laugh-In" fame); "It's a Man's World," with Glenn Corbett, Randy Boone, and Ted Bessell (later Donald on "That Girl"); "McKeever and the Colonel," with Scott Lane as Cadet Gary McKeever, Allyn Joslyn, and Jackie Coogan (later Uncle Fester on "The Addams Family"); and "Ensign O'Toole," starring Dean Jones with J. C. Flippen, Jack Mullaney, Jack Albertson, Harvey Lembeck, and Beau Bridges. ABC's schedule included the large-casted "Fair Exchange," the first hour-long sitcom, with Eddie Foy, Jr., Audrey Christie, Lynn Loring, Flip Mark, Victor Maddern, Diana Chesney, Judy Carne (the future Sock-It-To-Me girl on "Laugh In"), and Dennis Waterman; "Our Man Higgins," starring veteran British music-hall comic Stanley Holloway (Eliza Doolittle's father in "My Fair Lady"), with Audrey Totter (who originated the role of Millie in "Meet Millie" on radio in 1951); "Going My Way," starring Gene Kelly, Leo G. Carroll (years ago Cosmo in "Topper" and the future Mr. Waverly in "The Man from U.N.C.L.E."), and Dick York (later the husband of Samantha Stevens on "Bewitched"); and "The New Loretta Young Show," starring Loretta Young in her only continuing role. CBS had two entries: "Mr. Smith Goes to Washington" (based on the 1939 film starring James Stewart), starring Fess Parker, who had last been seen as Davy Crockett, and "I'm Dickens—He's Fenster," with Marty In-

gels and John Astin (later Gomez, head of "The Addams Family").

Westerns that didn't fare any better included: "Stoney Burke," starring Jack Lord in the title role, with Bruce Dern, Warren Oates, and Robert Dowdell (later Lieutenant Commander Morton on "Voyage to the Bottom of the Sea"); "The Wide Country," starring Earl Holliman and Andrew Prine; "The Dakotas," with Larry Ward, Chad Everett, Jack Elam, and Michael Greene; and "Empire," with Richard Egan, Anne Seymour, Terry Moore, and Ryan O'Neal.

Among drama shows that did not survive this season were: "G. E. True," with Jack Webb as host; "The Lloyd Bridges Show," with Bridges as narrator and star; "Saints and Sinners," with Nick Adams, John Larkin, Richard Erdman (formerly of "The Ray Bolger Show" and "The Tab Hunter Show"), and Barbara Rush; "Sam Benedict," starring Edmond O'Brien in the title role of this courtroom drama; and "The Gallant Men," a World War II series with William Reynolds (future agent Colby on "The F.B.I.") and a large cast.

Enough of the losers. Now a look at the winners.

"The Beverly Hillbillies" opened to some of the worst reviews in the history of television. Critics tore the show apart for its poor story line and childish dialogue. There should have been no way for this show to survive if you listened to the critics. But what they failed to admit was that this series about a rich hillbilly family was very funny. Viewers had no problem seeing that, and within a very short time, they made it the No. 1 show. This was one of the few times in TV history a series had captured the country's fancy so quickly. Buddy Ebsen, formerly Davy Crockett's sidekick George Russell, played widower Jed Clampett, head of the clan. Irene Ryan was Granny Daisey Moses, his mother-in-law; Donna Douglas was daughter Elly May; and Max Baer, Jr. (son of the onetime heavyweight champion) played Jethro Bodine, Jed's nephew. Other regulars were Raymond Bailey as Milton

Drysdale, president of the Commerce Bank, where Jed kept his family fortune, and Nancy Kulp as Jane Hathaway, Mr. Drysdale's secretary. Some tidbits about the show: the theme song, "The Ballad of Jed Clampett," composed and played by Lester Flatt and Earl Scruggs, made it to the top of the song charts in 1963; The Clampetts lived at 518 Crestview Drive, Beverly Hills; the family dog's name was Duke. The series ran for nine seasons, was the No. 1 show during its first two, and thereafter was usually among the top 12.

The island of Taratupa in the South Pacific was the setting for the wacky situation comedy "McHale's Navy" during its first three years on ABC. Ernest Borgnine played Lt. Cmdr. Quinton McHale, commander of Squadron 19 and PT Boat 73. Joe Flynn was Capt. Wallace B. Binghamton (known as "Old Lead Bottom"), McHale's commanding officer. Tim Conway was Ens. Charles "Chuck" Parker, a bumbler who was always trying to do the right thing but somehow always got into trouble. McHale's motley crew included Carl Ballantine as Lester Gruber, Gary Vinson as Christy Christopher, Billy Sands (Private Paparelli on "Sergeant Bilko") as Harrison "Tinker" Bell, Gavin MacLeod (the future Murray Slaughter on "The Mary Tyler Moore Show" and Capt. Merrill Stubing on "The Love Boat") as Happy Haines, Edson Stroll as Virgil Farrell, and Yoshio Yoda as Fuji. Bob Hastings played Lt. Elroy "Carpy" Carpenter, Binghamton's aide. McHale and company were transferred to Voltafiore, in southern Italy, for the show's last season. In total, 138 episodes were aired and can still be seen in syndication today.

Lucille Ball returned to situation comedy, without Desi this time, and began a six-year CBS run in her own series, "The Lucy Show." It was a very big hit throughout its entire stint and was among the top eight programs every season. Lucy played Lucy Carmichael, a widowed bank secretary with two children who was always looking for a husband. The show had a large cast and there were many changes over the years. The original supporting cast consisted of her old pal Vivian Vance, Charles Lane (veteran of many sitcoms), Candy Moore, Jimmy Garrett, Ralph Hart, and Dick Martin (of future "Laugh-in" fame). Within the first year, Gale Gordon replaced Lane in the cast.

NBC premiered television's first 90-minute Western, "The Virginian," based on Owen Wister's novel that had been made into three motion pictures.

The pilot for the series appeared on an NBC summer-replacement show, "Decision," four years earlier. James Drury was cast as the spartan title-role character (who didn't have any other name), foreman of the sprawling Shiloh Ranch in Medicine Bow, Wyoming. Besides Drury, only one actor had a role that was sustained throughout the series' long run, Doug McClure, who was Trampas, the ranch's assistant foreman. Some of the others in the large cast over the years included: Lee J. Cobb, Roberta Shore, Pippa Scott, Randy Boone, Clu Gulager, Charles Bickford, John McIntire, David Hartman, Stewart Granger, and Lee Majors. The show ran for eight years under the original title; for the ninth and final season, the title was changed to "The Men from Shiloh." A total of 249 episodes were broadcast before the series left the air.

"Combat" was the first, and eventually longest-running, of the several World War II drama series that were seen during this decade. The story centered on the experiences of a U.S. infantry platoon after its D-day landing at Normandy Beach in Europe. Vic Morrow was featured as Sgt. Chip Saunders and Rick Jason as Lt. Gil Hanley, leader of the platoon. Actual World War II battle footage was used to set the background and add a sense of realism to the series. The show was on for five seasons on ABC, with 152 episodes produced.

The success of "Dr. Kildare" and "Ben Casey" last year led the way for two new medical series this season: "The Nurses" on CBS and "The Eleventh Hour" on NBC. "The Nurses" was set in Alden General Hospital in New York City and starred Shirl Conway (one of the regulars for awhile on the old "Caesar's Hour") as Supervisor Nurse Thorpe, with young Zina Bethune (17 years old) as Nurse Gail Lucas. Expectations were high that the show would do well in the ratings because it was dramatically sound and finely acted, but it proved a disappointment. The "experts" rationalized that this was probably due to the lack of a sexy male doctor or two. So Joseph Campanella and Michael Tolan were brought in for the third season and the series was retitled "The Doctors and the Nurses." The new format fared worse, and the series was canceled. A half-hour daytime serial based on the prime-time show began in 1965 and ran for a year and a half on ABC.

"The Eleventh Hour" starred Wendell Corey as Dr. Theodore Bassett and Jack Ging as Dr. Paul Graham, two psychiatrists sharing an office. This was one of the earliest medical series to focus on

mental health and its story content generally appealed to a more sophisticated audience. For the show's second and final season, veteran TV actor Ralph Bellamy replaced Corey.

STONEY BURKE: October 1, 1962–September 2, 1963, ABC. Jack Lord (Stoney Burke) and James Mason (guest)

EMPIRE (REDIGO): September 25, 1962–September 6, 1964, NBC, ABC. Richard Egan (Redigo)

IT'S A MAN'S WORLD: September 17, 1962–January 28, 1963, NBC. Glen Corbett, Jan Norris, and Randy Boone

THE BEVERLY HILLBILLIES: *(Front)* Buddy Ebsen, Max Baer, Jr.; *(back)* Donna Douglas, Irene Ryan

THE BEVERLY HILLBILLIES: *(Front)* Donna Douglas, Buddy Ebsen; *(back)* Irene Ryan, Max Baer, Jr.

THE BEVERLY HILLBILLIES: September 26, 1962–September 7, 1971, CBS. Max Baer, Jr., Buddy Ebsen, Donna Douglas, and Irene Ryan

THE BEVERLY HILLBILLIES: Harriet MacGibbon and Raymond Bailey

THE BEVERLY HILLBILLIES: Irene Ryan, Buddy Ebsen, and Donna Douglas

COMBAT: October 2, 1962–August 29, 1967, ABC. Rick Jason and Vic Morrow

THE LUCY SHOW: October 1, 1962–September 16, 1968, CBS. Ralph Hart, Vivian Vance, Lucille Ball (Lucy Carmichael), Jimmy Garrett, and Candy Moore

COMBAT: October 2, 1962–August 29, 1967, ABC. Vic Morrow

THE LUCY SHOW: Lucille Ball and Gale Gordon

THE ELEVENTH HOUR: October 3, 1962–September 9, 1964, NBC. Wendell Corey

RIPCORD: 1962, syndicated. Larry Pennell

OUR MAN HIGGINS: October 3, 1962–September 11, 1963, ABC. Stanley Holloway (Higgins)

THE VIRGINIAN (THE MEN FROM SHILOH):
Roberta Shore

THE VIRGINIAN (THE MEN FROM SHILOH):
Clu Gulager

THE VIRGINIAN (THE MEN FROM SHILOH):
Lee J. Cobb

THE VIRGINIAN (THE MEN FROM SHILOH):
Randy Boone

THE VIRGINIAN (THE MEN FROM SHILOH):
Doug McClure

THE VIRGINIAN (THE MEN FROM SHILOH): September 19, 1962–September 8, 1971, NBC.
James Drury (the Virginian)

SAM BENEDICT: September 17, 1962–
September 7, 1963, NBC. Edmond O'Brien
(Sam Benedict)

McHALE'S NAVY: October 11, 1962–August 30, 1966, ABC. *(Front)* Carl Ballantine, Billy Sands, Ernest Borgnine, Tim Conway, and Gavin MacLeod; *(back)* John Wright, Gary Vinson, and Edson Stroll

McHALE'S NAVY: *(Seated)* Carl Ballantine, Ernest Borgnine (Lt. Cmdr. Quinton McHale); *(standing)* Joe Flynn, Gary Vinson, Tim Conway

I'M DICKENS—HE'S FENSTER: September 28, 1962–September 13, 1963, ABC. Marty Ingels (Arch Fenster). John Astin was Harry Dickens

JULIE AND CAROL AT CARNEGIE HALL: September 11, 1962, CBS. Carol Burnett and Julie Andrews

HOOTENANNY: April 6, 1963–September 12, 1964, ABC. Jack Linkletter was the host

WIDE COUNTRY: September 20, 1962–September 12, 1963, NBC. Earl Holliman

THE TONIGHT SHOW STARRING JOHNNY CARSON: October 2, 1962-present, NBC. Johnny Carson (host)

THE TONIGHT SHOW STARRING JOHNNY CARSON: Ed McMahon

THE TONIGHT SHOW STARRING JOHNNY CARSON: Skitch Henderson, Johnny Carson, and Ed McMahon

THE NURSES: September 27, 1962-September 7, 1965, CBS. Shirl Conway and Zina Bethune

THE DAKOTAS: January 7, 1963-September 9, 1963, ABC. Mike Greene, Larry Ward, Jack Elam, and Chad Everett

THE NURSES: Zina Bethune, Shirl Conway, Michael Tolan, and Joseph Campanella

BIOGRAPHY: 1962, syndicated. Mike Wallace (host)

THE ROY ROGERS AND DALE EVANS SHOW: September 29, 1962–December 29, 1962, ABC. Roy Rogers (host), Trigger, and Dale Evans (hostess)

THE JETSONS: September 23, 1962–September 8, 1963, ABC. Jane, Elroy, George, and Judy Jetson

FAIR EXCHANGE: September 21, 1962–December 28, 1962, CBS. *(Front)* Victor Maddern, Diana Chesney; *(back)* Judy Carne, Dennis Waterman

FAIR EXCHANGE: *(Front)* Dennis Waterman, Lynn Loring; *(back)* Victor Maddern, Diana Chesney

ENSIGN O'TOOLE: September 23, 1962–September 10, 1964, NBC. Dean Jones (Ensign O'Toole)

1963-64

A sense of optimism, vigor, and high-spiritedness existed in the country as this television year was about to begin. The upbeat national mood was due in part to the reduction of tensions between the United States and the Soviet Union in the wake of the Cuban missile crisis, the fact that we were finally on the road to winning the "space race," and, primarily, to President Kennedy's youthful vitality and personal charisma with which he led the nation—making these the days of Camelot.

This attitude was tragically short-lived: within weeks after the new season commenced, the unthinkable occurred. At approximately 1:30 P.M. Eastern Standard Time on Friday, November 22, 1963, while the CBS daytime soap opera "As the World Turns" was being telecast, Walter Cronkite appeared on TV screens to announce that the President had been shot in Dallas. Within minutes, all three networks ceased regular programming and began four days of commercial-free reporting. Americans were stunned as they sat in front of their sets and watched the tragedy unfold. Another horrifying event took place in their living rooms two days after the assassination. The accused assassin, Lee Harvey Oswald, was shot and killed before a nationwide audience. But viewers also were witness to the stability of the democratic process as the change of a presidential administration took place in just 99 minutes. Television, in these dark days, more than ever demonstrated that it had the capability to inform and unify the nation as never before, and indeed, that it was an integral part of daily life.

This season brought with it a group of programming innovations, some successful, others not. CBS made the inevitable move and expanded its evening news program with Walter Cronkite from 15 to 30 minutes on September 2. One week later, NBC followed and expanded "The Huntley-Brinkley Report" also to a half hour. ABC, hoping to get the jump on its competition, introduced all of its new shows for the season in one "Sneak Preview Week," September 15–21. This had never been done before. In programming, ABC introduced "Arrest and Trial," a series that was really two back-to-back 45-minute shows with a common plot. It lasted only for the season. ABC also extended prime time to 11:30 P.M. for a two-hour weekly variety show, "The Jerry Lewis Show." It, too, failed.

There were many other entries that did not survive past the season: Among the drama shows was "The Richard Boone Show" (NBC), an anthology series in which Boone hosted and performed. "The Lieutenant" (NBC), with Gary Lockwood and Robert Vaughn, was created and produced by Gene Roddenberry (later to gain fame as the creator of "Star Trek"). "Breaking Point" (ABC), a series trying to follow in the footsteps of other popular medical shows, starred Paul Richards and Eduard Franz. Thirty episodes were produced, and in one, Robert Redford made one of his last TV appearances. "The Greatest Show on Earth" (ABC) was based on the 1952 Cecil B. DeMille film of the same name. It starred Jack Palance and Stu Erwin. Two guest stars were Brenda Vaccaro (in her first major television role) and veteran film star Ruby Keeler (in a rare TV appearance). "Channing" (ABC) starred Jason Evers and Henry Jones.

Westerns that fared poorly included "The Travels of Jamie McPheeters" (ABC), the adventures of a twelve-year-old boy and his father on a westward-bound wagon train, featuring Kurt Russell, in the title role, and Dan O'Herlihy. "Temple Houston" (NBC) featured Jeffrey Hunter as the lawyer son of Texas hero Sam Houston. "Destry" (ABC), previously in film and on the Broadway stage, should seemingly be a winner as a series—but it didn't even last the season. John Gavin played the title role in this Western that bit the dust.

Among the sitcom losers were: "Glynis" (CBS), with Glynis Johns and Keith Andes; "Harry's Girls" (NBC), with Larry Blyden, Dawn Nickerson, Susan Silo, and Diahn Williams; "Grindl" (NBC), starring Imogene Coca; and "The New Phil Silvers Show" (CBS), starring Silvers.

Among the season's entries that lasted two seasons were: "Mr. Novak" (NBC), a drama about a high-school teacher, with James Franciscus and Dean Jagger (this season), and Burgess Meredith (next season); "Kraft Suspense Theater" (NBC), an anthology that aired "Rapture at Two-Forty," the pilot for the 1965 series "Run For Your Life"; "The Outer Limits" (ABC), a science-fiction anthology with a unique, eerie opening—"There is nothing wrong with your television set. Do not adjust the picture. We are controlling transmission," an imposing voice intoned—and closing—"We now return control of your television set to you until next week when the Control Voice will take you to The Outer Limits"; and half-hour sitcom "The Bill Dana Show," with Dana as José Jiménez and Don Adams in his first continuing TV role.

Now for a look at this season's shows that fared better; whether they were longer running, more acclaimed, or higher rated.

"East Side/West Side" (CBS) was a critically acclaimed dramatic series starring George C. Scott as social worker Neil Brock. The program dealt in a tough, realistic way with many controversial issues plaguing urban America, including child abuse, drug addiction, problems of the aged, race relations, and crime. Cicely Tyson and Elizabeth Wilson made up the supporting cast. Tyson was the first black cast member on TV in a non-comedy series. While critics lavished praise on "East Side/West Side," television audiences were not ready for serious social issues to be brought into their living rooms, and the show was dropped after this season.

"That Was the Week That Was," commonly referred to as "TW3," was a fiercely satirical, well-executed half-hour show that reviewed the previous week's national and world events. This kind of biting humor debuting (on January 10) just a few weeks after the Kennedy assassination, considering the somber mood of the nation, was a gutsy programming decision by NBC. Among the company of regulars were Elliot Reid, David Frost, Henry Morgan, Phyllis Newman, Buck Henry, Pat Englund, Doro Merande, and Burr Tillstrom's puppets. Nancy Ames was the TW3 Girl who sang the opening and closing numbers, and Skitch Henderson and his orchestra provided the music. This was an innovative show that throughout its one-and-a-half seasons was always up against stiff competition.

On September 17, 1963, Dr. Richard Kimble returned home to find a one-armed man running from his house. Rushing inside, he was shocked to find his wife, Helen, dead. Kimble, unable to prove his innocence, was charged and convicted of murder. En route to prison, the train he was on derailed and he escaped, thus beginning his four-year search for his wife's murderer. ABC's "The Fugitive" enjoyed great popularity and starred David Janssen as Kimble and Barry Morse as Lt. Philip Gerard, who was obsessed with pursuing Kimble. Bill Raisch was the one-armed killer, Fred Johnson, and Diane Brewster was Helen Kimble. The series actually came to a conclusion on August 29, 1967, in the 120th episode. When Kimble found Johnson, and Gerard found both of them, the lieutenant realized he was wrong about Kimble and exonerated him of the crime. This last episode ranks as one of the top-rated single episodes in the history of television.

Hooterville was the setting for "Petticoat Junction" (CBS), a rural comedy that was a spinoff from last year's "Beverly Hillbillies." Bea Benaderet played Kate Bradley, a widow with three beautiful daughters who owned the Shady Rest Hotel. Pat Woodell, Jeannine Riley, and Linda Kaye played daughters Bobbie Jo, Billie Jo, and Betty Jo. The girls helped with the chores of running the hotel, along with Uncle Joe Carson (Edgar Buchanan). In 1968, Benaderet died, and June Lockhart (formerly Mrs. Martin in "Lassie" and the future Mrs. Robinson in "Lost in Space") joined the cast. The series was the top-rated new program this year and ran for seven seasons.

CBS's other new top-10 show was "My Favorite Martian," with Bill Bixby (later to star in "The Courtship of Eddie's Father," "The Magician," and "The Incredible Hulk") and Ray Walston (his only series). This sitcom was a fantasy about a Martian whose one-passenger spaceship crashed onto Earth. His humorous experiences (he disguised his true identity) made use of some of the

best special effects seen on TV to this point. The series had a three-year run before the 107 episodes went into syndication.

"The Hollywood Palace" was an hour-long extravagant, and costly, variety show in the Ed Sullivan tradition. Each week a different guest host was featured, and over the years many big names made multiple appearances as host. These included Fred Astaire, Milton Berle, Jimmy Durante, Sid Caesar and Imogene Coca, Sammy Davis, Jr., and Don Adams. Bing Crosby hosted the premiere telecast and went on to make more appearances—more than 30—than any other performer in the six years the show was on ABC.

Among other significant happenings this season, former vocalist Mike Douglas, who for the past two years had been hosting a daily 90-minute Cleveland talk show, saw his program syndicated nationally. It remained on the air until 1982. Two very popular entertainers, Danny Kaye and Judy Garland, hosted their own shows, both on CBS. Kaye's musical variety show was well received and remained on the network for four years. Garland's, on the other hand, was a big disappointment and did not survive the season. Only 26 shows were aired. The program's demise was generally attributed to the producers' not finding the right format for their star, and to the competition from TV's No. 2 show, "Bonanza." There were, however, some memorable individual programs, including one with Ethel Merman and Barbra Streisand, one with Judy's two daughters, Liza Minnelli and Lorna Luft, and one with Danny Kaye. Ed Sullivan signed a British rock 'n' roll group that was virtually unknown in the United

States, the Beatles, for two live appearances on his show. While they did have an international reputation, there was an indifference to them in this country. Between the time he booked them and their February 9 and 16, 1964, performances, the promotion and publicity generated was such that it resulted in Sullivan achieving two of the all-time highest-rated individual shows in the history of the medium. Sullivan again demonstrated his talent for knowing what the American public wanted to see.

CHANNING: September 18, 1963–April 8, 1964, ABC. Jason Evers

THE LIEUTENANT: September 14, 1963–September 5, 1964, NBC. Gary Lockwood

GLYNIS: September 25, 1963–December 18, 1963, CBS. Keith Andes and Glynis Johns (Glynis Granville)

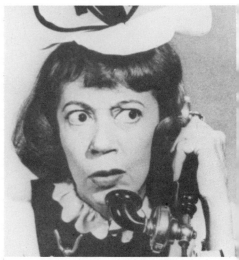

GRINDL: September 15, 1963–September 13, 1964, NBC. Imogene Coca (Grindl)

THE GREATEST SHOW ON EARTH: September 17, 1963–September 8, 1964, ABC. Jack Palance

BREAKING POINT: September 16, 1963–September 7, 1964, ABC. Paul Richards and Eduard Franz

ARREST AND TRIAL: September 15, 1963–September 6, 1964, ABC. John Larch, Chuck Connors, and Ben Gazzara

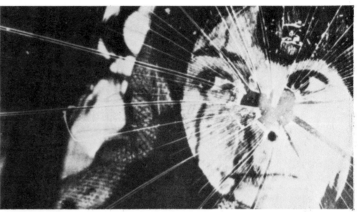
KRAFT SUSPENSE THEATER: October 10, 1963–September 9, 1965, NBC.

THE FUGITIVE: September 17, 1963–August 29, 1967, ABC. David Janssen

THE FUGITIVE: David Janssen

THE OUTER LIMITS: September 16, 1963–
January 16, 1965, ABC. Jacqueline Scott and
Cliff Robertson in "The Galaxy Being"

THE OUTER LIMITS: Creatures in "The Zanti
Misfits"

THE OUTER LIMITS: Robert Culp in "Corpus
Earthling"

THE OUTER LIMITS: Creature in
"The Galaxy Being"

THE OUTER LIMITS: Jay Novello, Jerry Douglas, Ralph Meeker, and
Henry Silva in "Tourist Attraction"

THE OUTER LIMITS: Barbara
Rush in an episode

EAST SIDE/WEST SIDE: September 23, 1963–September 14, 1964,
CBS. George C. Scott

EAST SIDE/WEST SIDE: George C. Scott and Elizabeth Wilson

190

PETTICOAT JUNCTION: September 24, 1963–September 12, 1970, CBS. Jeannine Riley, Pat Woodell, Linda Kaye, and Bea Benaderet *(seated)*

PETTICOAT JUNCTION: Jeannine Riley, Edgar Buchanan, and Pat Woodell

PETTICOAT JUNCTION: Bea Benaderet and Linda Kaye

THE HOLLYWOOD PALACE: January 4, 1964–February 7, 1970, ABC. Maurice Chevalier (guest host)

THE JUDY GARLAND SHOW: September 29, 1963–March 29, 1964, CBS. Judy Garland (hostess)

BURKE'S LAW (AMOS BURKE, SECRET AGENT): September 20, 1963–August 31, 1965, ABC. Gene Barry (Amos Burke)

BURKE'S LAW (AMOS BURKE, SECRET AGENT): Gene Barry, Ellen O'Neal, and Gary Conway

THAT WAS THE WEEK THAT WAS: January 10, 1964–May 4, 1965, NBC. Elliot Reid and Nancy Ames (TW3 regulars)

MR. NOVAK: September 24, 1963–August 31, 1965, NBC. James Franciscus (Mr. Novak) and Dean Jagger

THE BILL DANA SHOW: September 22, 1963–January 17, 1965, NBC. Virginia Kennedy (guest) and Bill Dana

MR. NOVAK: James Franciscus

MR. NOVAK: Dean Jagger

BOB HOPE PRESENTS THE CHRYSLER THEATER: October 6, 1963–September 6, 1967, NBC. Bob Hope (host)

ELIZABETH TAYLOR IN LONDON: October 6, 1963, CBS. Elizabeth Taylor

THE TRAVELS OF JAMIE McPHEETERS: September 15, 1963–March 15, 1964, ABC. James Westerfield, Robert Carricart, and Kurt Russell (Jamie)

THE DANNY KAYE SHOW: September 25, 1963–June 7, 1967, CBS. Lucille Ball (guest) and Danny Kaye (host)

THE ART LINKLETTER SHOW: February 18, 1963–September 16, 1963, NBC. Art Linkletter

193

THE FARMER'S DAUGHTER: September 20, 1963–September 2, 1966, ABC. Inger Stevens and William Windom

THE PATTY DUKE SHOW: September 18, 1963–August 31, 1966, ABC. Patty Duke in a dual role (Cathy Lane and Patty Lane)

THE FARMER'S DAUGHTER: Inger Stevens

THE PATTY DUKE SHOW: *(Front)* Patty Duke Paul O'Keefe; *(back)* Jean Byron, William Schallert

MY FAVORITE MARTIAN: September 29, 1963–September 4, 1966, CBS. Ray Walston

MY FAVORITE MARTIAN: Bill Bixby and Ray Walston

HARRY'S GIRLS: September 13, 1963–January 3, 1964, NBC. Larry Blyden (Harry Burns)

1964-65

On July 16, 1964, the 28th Republican National Convention in San Francisco chose Senator Barry M. Goldwater of Arizona as its candidate for president. In past years, CBS generally came out on top in the ratings battle among the networks in coverage of this event. This time, NBC's Huntley-Brinkley team broke the hold CBS, led by Walter Cronkite, had enjoyed since 1952 on presidential-convention coverage. As CBS prepared for the Democratic National Convention to be held in late August, it decided to replace Cronkite. Senior correspondent Robert Trout, with CBS radio since 1932, and Roger Mudd, a relative newcomer, were assigned the task of covering the Democrats in Atlantic City. As expected, President Johnson and his running mate, Sen. Hubert Humphrey, were easily nominated to run in November. And also as expected, Trout and Mudd fared no better against Huntley and Brinkley. There followed a public outcry to have Cronkite back, and CBS reinstated America's most trusted newscaster for the election returns in November.

Television once again played an important role in the campaign itself. But this time it was in the domain of the TV commercial. The Democratic Party was vicious in its attack on hawkish Goldwater, and it produced, among others, a campaign commercial that alleged that he was a man who would kill children by the irresponsible and indiscriminate use of nuclear weapons. Commercials such as this strongly conveyed the message that by not voting for Johnson, the country would be led into nuclear disaster. The Democratic Party won by a landslide.

Among goings-on this season, NBC followed ABC's lead of the previous year by introducing all of its new fall programming in a one-week preview. NBC, in collaboration with Universal Studios, also premiered the first two-hour made-for-TV movie, "See How They Run," starring John Forsythe, Jane Wyatt, Franchot Tone, and Senta Berger. NBC also introduced "90 Bristol Court," a 90-minute series consisting of three separate half-hour comedies tied together by having the principal characters in each segment living in the same apartment complex in southern California. The individual titles of the programs were "Karen," "Harris Against the World," and "Tom, Dick and Mary." Each sitcom was weak. Only "Karen" lasted the season; the others folded at midseason. After 18 years on network television, boxing ended its run as a weekly event. And the most inventive programming concept of this season was the introduction of "Peyton Place," a 30-minute series aired twice per week (Tuesday and Thursday) on ABC. This was the medium's first prime-time soap opera since the short-lived "Faraway Hill" in 1946, and it was the only successful evening serial for many years (more about this series later).

Another thing going on this season was music. Rock 'n' roll came to prime-time TV early this season in the form of a 30-minute, usually live, show on ABC, "Shindig." Jimmy O'Neill, a popular West Coast disc jockey, was the host. Regularly featured were Bobby Sherman, the Righteous Brothers (Bill Medley and Bob Hatfield), the Wellingtons, Glen Campbell, and Donna Loren. By midyear, the show expanded to an hour, and NBC introduced its own hour show, "Hullabaloo." Each week a different guest host was featured as top recording stars performed their current hits backed by elaborate productions that usually included the Hullabaloo Dancers. These six gals and four guys were the only regulars on the show. Two other rock shows debuted, "Shebang" and "Shivaree." Both were short-run syndicated programs. In sharp contrast, "The King Family Show" commenced on ABC with its several dozen members all singing on stage together. This huge wholesome clan descended from its oldest member, 79-year-old William King Driggs, a veteran vaudevillian. The Kings entertained TV audiences for only this season in a regularly scheduled program, then for the next few seasons appeared in specials. Finally, in the second half of the season, one of the new generation of musical greats had her first network-television special: Barbra Streisand in "My Name Is Barbra."

As in all other years, there was a long list of shows that did not survive past the season. These included sitcoms: "The Baileys of Balboa" (CBS), "My Living Doll" (CBS), "The Tycoon" (ABC), "The Bing Crosby Show" (ABC), "No Time for Sergeants" (ABC), "Broadside" (ABC), "Wendy and Me" (NBC), and "Valentine's Day" (ABC). Among the drama/adventure series that didn't last were: "For the People" (CBS), with William Shatner, Howard Da Silva, and Jessica Walter (had this show become a success, Shatner would not have been available to play the future Captain Kirk of "Star Trek"); "The Reporter" (CBS), with Harry Guardino and Gary Merrill; "Mr. Broadway" (CBS), with Craig Stevens; "The Rogues" (NBC), with David Niven, Gig Young, Charles Boyer, and Robert Coote; and "Kentucky Jones" (NBC), starring Dennis Weaver. "Slattery's People" (CBS), starring Richard Crenna, survived the season, got a new supporting cast, and within a few weeks of its second season was canceled for poor ratings.

Now for the shows that were a cut above the rest. "Peyton Place" was based on the Grace Metalious novel, which had been made into a movie in 1957, and was set in the New England town of the same name. The program's success this season (both weekly episodes were in the top 20) prompted the network to run it three times a week for most of its second season. But as a result of diminished ratings, it reverted back to two per week. The continuing story line centered on the infidelity of the people living in this small town. There was a very large cast over the years, including performers already well known to television viewers and others who would become well known. Among the former were Dorothy Malone, Ed Nelson, Warner Anderson, Lee Grant, John Kerr, Gena Rowlands, Dan Duryea, and Barbara Rush. Newcomers were Mia Farrow, Ryan O'Neal, Christopher Connelly, Barbara Parkins, and Mariette Hartley. After five seasons the series left the air but returned within three years as a daytime soap that enjoyed a two-and-a-half-year run on NBC.

"Daniel Boone," starring Fess Parker in the title role of the American folk hero, began a six-year stint on NBC. Parker had previously shot to fame as another hero, Davy Crockett, on "Disneyland." He wanted to do his own Crockett series but couldn't because the Disney Studios, which owned the rights, wasn't interested. As a result, Parker and his associates created the Boone series in much the same manner as Crockett: coonskin caps, buckskin clothing, etc. This season's supporting cast included Albert Salmi as Yadkin, his sidekick; Ed Ames as Mingo, his college-educated Indian friend; Patricia Blair as his wife, Rebecca; Veronica Cartwright as his daughter, Jemima; and Darby Hinton in the role of his son, Israel. The series usually was among the top 30, and 165 episodes were produced.

The United Network Command for Law and Enforcement was the CIA-type organization that employed agents Napoleon Solo and Illya Kuryakin in the spy-adventure series "The Man from U.N.C.L.E." The show was conceived by producer Sam Rolfe and author Ian Fleming, the creator of James Bond. Originally, it was to be titled "Mr. Solo," with the character being more of a James Bond type, but Fleming took ill and could not be involved in the rigors of a weekly series. Robert Vaughn starred as Solo, David McCallum (years later to star in the short-run series "The Invisible Man") played Kuryakin, and Leo G. Carroll was the elderly Alexander Waverly, head of the organization. The show was on NBC three and a half years and ranked, in its second season, 13th among prime-time programs.

Creator/producer Irwin Allen, later to gain fame for his disaster movies *The Poseidon Adventure* and *The Towering Inferno,* brought his 1961 science-fiction film *Voyage to the Bottom of the Sea* to television as a weekly series. Richard Basehart played Adm. Harriman Nelson, David Hedison (formerly of the short-run series "Five Fingers") played Capt. Lee Crane, and Robert Dowdell was Lt. Cmdr. Chip Morton. Last but not least of the stars was the submarine *Seaview*, on which the crew traveled the seven seas. This well-done, entertaining series was on for four seasons on ABC before it went into syndication. The 110 episodes are still watched today by many of its fans.

The situation comedy "Bewitched" was the top-rated new show of the season and, over all, the No. 2 program this year. The series concerned itself with an apparently typical suburban family, the Stevens: Samantha and Darrin. She was beautiful, with a beautiful home to match; he was an advertising executive for a New York agency. The only catch was that Samantha was a witch who did not want to be a witch—the kind who preferred to use her broom for cleaning her home at 1164 Morning Glory Circle in Westport, Connecticut, not for flying. The Stevens eventually had a daughter, Tabitha, born on the January 13, 1966, episode, and she, too, possessed supernatural powers. Elizabeth Montgomery was Samantha, Dick York and later Dick Sargent played Darrin; Agnes Moorehead played Endora, Samantha's meddling mother; and David White was Larry Tate, head of the ad agency. The series was among the top 12 in the ratings during its first five years and ran for a total of eight seasons on ABC. Thereafter, the 306 episodes went into syndication.

"Gomer Pyle, U.S.M.C." was a spinoff from "The Andy Griffith Show," and it certainly was a big winner for CBS. This situation comedy about a former gas-station attendant from Mayberry, North Carolina, who decided to join the Marines ranked 3rd this year, 2nd the next year, then dropped to 10th, moved back to 3rd, and in its final season ended up as the No. 2 show, behind "Rowan & Martin's Laugh-In." Jim Nabors starred as Gomer and Frank Sutton as Sgt. Vince Carter, the platoon leader.

KENTUCKY JONES: September 19, 1964–September 11, 1965, NBC. Dennis Weaver (Kentucky Jones)

THE TYCOON: September 15, 1964–September 7, 1965, ABC. Walter Brennan and Van Williams

SECRET AGENT: April 3, 1965–September 10, 1966, CBS. Patrick McGoohan

BROADSIDE: September 20, 1964–September 5, 1965, ABC. Kathy Nolan, Joan Staley, Lois Roberts, and Sheila James

THE MAN FROM U.N.C.L.E.: David McCallum and Robert Vaughn

THE MAN FROM U.N.C.L.E.: September 22, 1964–January 15, 1968, NBC. Robert Vaughn

THE MAN FROM U.N.C.L.E.: Leo G. Carroll

FLIPPER: Brian Kelly

FLIPPER: September 19, 1964–September 2, 1967, NBC. Flipper

FLIPPER: Tommy Nordon and Luke Halpin

THE CARA WILLIAMS SHOW: September 23, 1964–September 10, 1965, CBS. Frank Aletter and Cara Williams

THE CARA WILLIAMS SHOW: Frank Aletter (photo) and Cara Williams

HARRIS AGAINST THE WORLD: October 5, 1964–January 4, 1965, NBC. Jack Klugman (Harris)

HARRIS AGAINST THE WORLD: Patricia Barry

GOMER PYLE, U.S.M.C.: Frank Sutton and Jim Nabors

GOMER PYLE, U.S.M.C.: September 25, 1964–September 19, 1969, CBS. Jim Nabors (Gomer Pyle) and Frank Sutton

THE ROGUES: September 13, 1964–September 5, 1965, NBC. Charles Boyer and Gig Young (David Niven was the other rogue)

MR. BROADWAY: September 26, 1964–December 26, 1964, CBS. Craig Stevens (Mike Bell/Mr. Broadway)

MR. BROADWAY: Craig Stevens and unknown actress

THE ROGUES: Gladys Cooper

THE ROGUES: Robert Coote

THE BING CROSBY SHOW: September 14, 1964–June 14, 1965, ABC. Diane Sherry and Bing Crosby

TWELVE O'CLOCK HIGH: September 18, 1964–January 13, 1967, ABC. Robert Lansing

TWELVE O'CLOCK HIGH: Paul Burke

GILLIGAN'S ISLAND: September 26, 1964–September 4, 1967, CBS. (Seated) Russell Johnson, Bob Denver, Alan Hale, Jr., Dawn Wells; (standing) Jim Backus, Natalie Schafer, Tina Louise

BRANDED: January 24, 1965–September 4, 1966, NBC. Chuck Connors

BRANDED: Chuck Connors

MICKEY: September 16, 1964–January 13, 1965, ABC. Mickey Rooney (Mickey Grady) and Sammee Tong

MICKEY: Mickey Rooney

THE BAILEYS OF BALBOA: September 24, 1964–April 1, 1965, CBS. Les Brown, Jr., and Judy Carne

THE BAILEYS OF BALBOA: Paul Ford (Sam Bailey)

THE MUNSTERS: The Munster's family car, Fred Gwynne, and Yvonne DeCarlo

THE MUNSTERS: Al Lewis

TOM, DICK AND MARY: Joyce Bulifant (Mary)

TOM, DICK AND MARY: Steve Franken (Dick)

THE MUNSTERS: September 24, 1964–September 1, 1966, CBS. Butch Patrick, Yvonne DeCarlo, Fred Gwynne, Pat Priest, and Al Lewis

TOM, DICK AND MARY: October 5, 1964–January 4, 1965, NBC. Don Galloway (Tom)

SLATTERY'S PEOPLE: September 21, 1964–November 26, 1965, CBS. Richard Crenna (James Slattery), and Elsa Lanchester (guest)

MY LIVING DOLL: September 20, 1964–September 8, 1965, CBS. Julie Newmar and Bob Cummings

THE ADDAMS FAMILY: September 18, 1964–September 2, 1966, ABC. John Astin and Carolyn Jones

MY LIVING DOLL: Julie Newmar and Michael Jackson (guest)

THE ADDAMS FAMILY: *(Front)* Lisa Loring, Carolyn Jones, Ken Weatherwax; *(back)* Jackie Coogan, John Astin, Blossom Rock

PEYTON PLACE: September 15, 1964–June 2, 1969, ABC. Mia Farrow

PEYTON PLACE: Barbara Parkins and Ryan O'Neal

PEYTON PLACE: Christopher Connelly

PEYTON PLACE: Warner Anderson

PEYTON PLACE: Ed Nelson and Gena Rowlands

THE REPORTER: September 25, 1964–December 18, 1964, CBS. Harry Guardino and Janice Rule (guest)

BEWITCHED: September 17, 1964–July 1, 1972, ABC. Elizabeth Montgomery (daughter of Robert Montgomery), Dick York (1964–69), and Agnes Moorehead

BEWITCHED: Dick Sargent (1969–72), Elizabeth Montgomery, Erin Murphy, and Agnes Moorehead

BEWITCHED: David White and Dick York

BEWITCHED: Erin Murphy, Dick York, Elizabeth Montgomery, and Agnes Moorehead

KAREN: October 5, 1964–August 30, 1965, NBC. Debbie Watson (Karen)

MR. MAGOO: September 19, 1964–August 7, 1965, NBC.

KAREN: Guy Raymond

MY NAME IS BARBRA: April 28, 1965, CBS. Barbra Streisand

VOYAGE TO THE BOTTOM OF THE SEA: Richard Basehart

SOPHIA LOREN IN ROME: November 12, 1964, ABC. Sophia Loren

THE KING FAMILY: January 23, 1965–January 8, 1966; March 12, 1969–September 10, 1969, ABC. Some of the 37 King Family members: *(front)* Donna, Alyce, Maxine, Marilyn; *(back)* Luise, Yvonne

VOYAGE TO THE BOTTOM OF THE SEA: September 14, 1964–September 15, 1968, ABC. Richard Basehart and David Hedison

DANIEL BOONE: September 24, 1964–August 27, 1970, NBC. Fess Parker (Daniel Boone) and Patricia Blair

PROFILES IN COURAGE: November 8, 1964–May 9, 1965, NBC. John F. Kennedy (series based on his Pulitzer Prize book of the same title)

PROFILES IN COURAGE: Sidney Blackmer as Sen. Oscar W. Underwood in an episode

PROFILES IN COURAGE: Brian Keith as Sen. Thomas Hart Benton in an episode

DANIEL BOONE: Ed Ames

NO TIME FOR SERGEANTS: September 14, 1964–September 6, 1965, ABC. Sammy Jackson

DANIEL BOONE: Albert Salmi

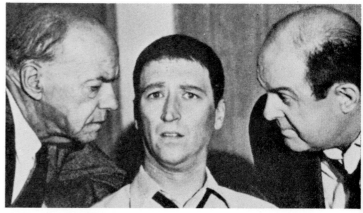

MANY HAPPY RETURNS: September 21, 1964–April 12, 1965, CBS. Russell Collins, Mickey Manners, and John McGiver

1965-66

As the new season commenced, the war in Vietnam began to really escalate. The president ordered 50,000 more troops to that far-off country and doubled the monthly draft quota. This increase brought the total of American military men engaged in war to 125,000. Paralleling this increase was the networks' increased coverage of the war, which many Americans still knew little about. From the start, U.S. intervention in Vietnam was expected to last only a matter of months and so much of the media coverage, as this season began, was still imbued with an adventurous spirit. Correspondents were right there in the jungle side by side with the troops, filming their stories for the nightly news in an effort to bring it into American homes before it was over.

Another conflict was also occurring at this time: race riots had broken out in American cities. In Watts, a suburb of Los Angeles, 35 people died, more than $200 million in property damage was incurred, and television cameras were there to graphically record the event as no other communications medium could. With all this strife and violence, TV viewers longed to be entertained.

Toward that end, the networks bombarded their audience with the most massive introduction of new fall shows ever (almost 40). Plus, for the first time, all three networks premiered their lineups simultaneously. During that week viewers were confronted with the enjoyable, but difficult, task of selecting what to watch from this huge crop of new programs in addition to the opening episodes of returning shows.

Ten years after the first color-TV sets had been sold, consumers were finally beginning to buy them in quantity. At this time, approximately 6 percent of all homes had color TV. Looking for a ratings edge, NBC heavily promoted the fact that nearly all its programming was already in color. By now CBS had reached the 50 percent level of color programming, while ABC was far behind and suffered in the ratings for the early weeks of this season. One thing was already

clear: people with color sets watched those shows telecast in color more than the national average.

Now a look at this very busy season. A group of performers already known to viewers had their own shows for the first time: Robert Goulet starred as a double agent in the short-lived spy series "Blue Light" on ABC; Anne Francis played her first continuing role as one of TV's earliest female private detectives, "Honey West," also on ABC; comedians Dan Rowan and Dick Martin (later of "Laugh-In" fame) co-hosted a short-run, hour-long variety show "The Rowan and Martin Show" on NBC; and Steve Lawrence hosted his own musical/variety show on CBS for 13 weeks. For a short time, Sammy Davis, Jr., also hosted his own musical variety show. Until this time no other black performer had been the host of a similar program during this decade.

Other short-run series were "Convoy," a World War II drama series on NBC with John Gavin, and "Court-Martial," another war drama, with Bradford Dillman and Peter Graves. Rod Serling, TV's most prolific writer, tried his hand at a Western and created and produced "The Loner," starring Lloyd Bridges. The show ran for one season on CBS.

Charles Schultz's famous comic-strip characters, Charlie Brown and the Peanuts gang, came to TV this year. "A Charlie Brown Christmas" was the first of many animated Peanuts specials on CBS. Snoopy, Lucy, and the rest of the bunch are still seen today in various specials.

The world of comic books brought forth a superhero who garnered super ratings this season—"Batman." The most unique series of the year, if not the decade, it was originally scheduled to air in the fall of 1966 but was moved up by ABC as a midseason replacement this season. The caped crusader and boy wonder, Robin, were presented in two 30-minute segments on Wednesday and Thursday evenings at 7:30. The series was an instant hit: both segments made

the top-10 list for the year. As in old-time movie serials, the Wednesday-night segment would always end in a cliffhanger, usually with Batman or Robin, or both, about to face something calamitous. The following night's episode would begin with the dynamic duo somehow escaping the clutches of death.

Adam West (formerly Sergeant Nelson in "The Detectives") starred as Bruce Wayne, Gotham City millionaire, alias Batman, and Burt Ward played Dick Grayson, Wayne's adopted teenage ward, alias Robin. Others in the regular cast were Alan Napier as Alfred Pennyworth, the butler and only character who knew the true identity of the duo; Neil Hamilton as Police Commissioner Gordon; Stafford Repp as Police Chief O'Hara; and Madge Blake as Harriet Cooper, Wayne's aunt. The show's immediate popularity made it a must-do for many well-known performers who did not mind being cast in the role of a villain. Guest evildoers were: Burgess Meredith (the Penguin), Victor Buono (King Tut), Cesar Romero (the Joker), Vincent Price (Egghead), Maurice Evans (the Puzzler), Liberace (Shandell), Joan Collins (the Siren), and Milton Berle (Louie the Lilac). Some of the comic-book characters played by more than one performer were Catwoman (Julie Newmar, Lee Meriwether, and Eartha Kitt), Mr. Freeze (George Sanders, Eli Wallach, and Otto Preminger), and the Riddler (Frank Gorshin and John Astin).

"Batman" was essentially a one-season phenomenon. Ratings began to decline in the second season and the program was cut back to one episode a week. At that time a new character was added, Barbara Gordon, daughter of the commissioner, alias Batgirl, played by Yvonne Craig. She teamed up with the duo to fight crime, and they never knew each other's real identities. The series, in contrast to its hyped debut, quietly left the air after less than two and a half seasons, in which 120 episodes had been produced, and went into syndication.

While "Batman" was an example of a

short-lived series that was "successful" (if any short series can be considered a success), the real measure of TV achievement is longevity; a run of at least three years. This season had more than its share of those TV winners.

Those that aired three seasons were: "Lost in Space" (CBS), a science-fiction adventure about a space-faring family trying to get home to Earth, starring Guy Williams and June Lockhart, and "Run for Your Life" (NBC), starring Ben Gazzara as a man who only had a short time to live and was determined to make the most of it. Also, there was "Daktari" (CBS), the Swahili word for doctor, an hour-long adventure series set in Africa and based on the 1965 film *Clarence the Cross-eyed Lion*. As in the film, Marshall Thompson (formerly John Smith in "Angel") was featured as Dr. Marsh Tracy, a veterinarian, and Cheryl Miller was Paula, his daughter. The story took place in the Wameru Game Preserve and Research Center, which was also the home of Clarence and a chimpanzee named Judy.

Comedian Bill Cosby became the first black actor to star in a non-comedy series when he and Robert Culp teamed up to do "I Spy" on NBC. This hour-long espionage series departed from the traditional perception of how spies and undercover agents operate and was filmed on location in many parts of the world. Culp was agent Kelly Robinson, whose cover was being a tennis pro, and Cosby was agent Alexander Scott, his trainer.

There were two series that began four-year runs this season. The first, ABC's "The Big Valley," was conceived with the idea of its being another "Bonanza." Barbara Stanwyck starred as Victoria Barkley, the matriarch of the Barkley clan; the family ran a 30,000-acre ranch in California's San Joaquin Valley. The cast remained with the show throughout the entire series. Richard Long was the oldest son, Jarrod, a lawyer; Peter Breck played Nick, the hotheaded second son; Lee Majors (in his first series) was the third son, Heath; Charles Briles was the youngest son, Eugene; Linda Evans (later of "Dynasty" fame) played the impulsive and beautiful daughter, Audra; and Napoleon Whiting was Silas, the family servant. A total of 112 episodes were produced.

Robert Conrad starred as James West, special undercover agent for President Ulysses S. Grant, in the Western series "The Wild Wild West" on CBS. West, the James Bond/Napoleon Solo of his time, was aided by his friend and fellow agent Artemus Gordon (Ross

Martin), a master of disguises. The two traveled the country in a special railroad car equipped with all sorts of gadgets to ward off any adversaries they encountered. Occasionally, James Gregory was seen in the role of Grant.

The two series that were to last five years were "Get Smart" and "I Dream of Jeannie." Created by funnymen Mel Brooks and Buck Henry, "Get Smart" was a spoof on spy shows and films. Don Adams starred as Maxwell Smart (also known as Agent 86), a bumbler who worked for CONTROL, an international spy organization based at 123 Main Street in Washington, D.C. Barbara Feldon co-starred as Smart's partner, Agent 99 (previously, she appeared in Revlon cosmetic commercials and was a winner on the "$64,000 Question"). Edward Platt was featured as the head of CONTROL and was known as the Chief. Others in the cast from time to time were Dick Gautier as Hymie, the robot; Bernie Kopell as Conrad Siegfried, the head of KAOS (the evil organization CONTROL was dedicated to destroying); Stacy Keach was Carlson, a CONTROL scientist; and Fang, CONTROL's dog, Agent K-13. This show created some expressions that became popular with its many viewers: "Would you believe . . .?" "Sorry about that, Chief," and "I find that hard to believe." The series first was on NBC (four years) and then on CBS before it went into syndication, where, to this day, Max is still bumbling along.

Larry Hagman, in his first continuing role (the future J. R. Ewing of "Dallas"), was Capt. Tony Nelson, an astronaut who crash-landed on a desert island in the South Pacific and found a bottle that contained a beautiful two-thousand-year-

old genie in "I Dream of Jeannie." Barbara Eden, also in her first continuing role, played Jeannie in this fantasy sitcom on NBC. Others in the original cast included Bill Daily (later Howard Borden on "The Bob Newhart Show") as Capt. Roger Healey, Tony's friend; Hayden Rorke as Dr. Alfred Bellows, a NASA psychiatrist; and Barton MacLane as Gen. Martin Peterson. During the show's first three seasons, Jeannie and Tony had a platonic relationship, but things heated up and early in the fourth year they were married. One of the mysteries of the series was that Jeannie, who was always seen with a bare midriff, did not have a navel. In all, 138 episodes were produced before it went into syndication.

Two sitcoms that ran six years debuted this season. Stalag 13 was the POW camp from which "Hogan's Heroes" operated. Col. Robert Hogan and his talented group of Allied soldiers, while officially prisoners of the Nazis, actually ran the camp. Although they could have escaped at any time, they were more valuable as prisoners because of the useful information they passed along to the Allies. Included in the cast were Bob Crane as Hogan; Werner Klemperer as Col. Wilhelm Klink, the camp commandant; John Banner as Sgt. Hans Schultz, Klink's aide who always walked around saying "I know nothing"; Robert Clary as Cpl. Louis LeBeau, a Frenchman; Richard Dawson (later of "Family Feud" fame) as Cpl. Peter Newkirk, an Englishman; Ivan Dixon as Cpl. Kinchloe, an American; and Leon Askin as Gen. Alfred Burkhalter. After its years on CBS, it went into syndication and is still seen today.

The other six-year show, "Green

THE SAMMY DAVIS, JR., SHOW: January 7, 1966–April 22, 1966, NBC. Sammy Davis, Jr., and Trini Lopez (guest)

TRIALS OF O'BRIEN: September 18, 1965–May 27, 1966, CBS. Peter Falk (Daniel J. O'Brien) and Joanna Barnes

Acres," on CBS, was really "The Beverly Hillbillies" in reverse. Eddie Albert and Eva Gabor starred as wealthy Oliver and Lisa Douglas, who moved from a big-city life-style to a rural life. The show was closely associated with the popular "Petticoat Junction" because Albert and Gabor originated their roles as the Douglases on that series. Others in the cast were Pat Buttram as Mr. Haney, Frank Cady as Sam Drucker, Hank Patterson as Fred Ziffel, and Tom Lester as Ed Dawson.

Finally, there were two shows that stayed around nine seasons. J. Edgar Hoover, the Director of the Federal Bureau of Investigation, was the enthusiastic supporter behind "The FBI," ABC's longest-running crime drama, which was based on the bureau's actual files. Efrem Zimbalist, Jr., was the cool, businesslike Inspector Louis Erskine, who, along with Philip Abbott as Arthur Ward, the assistant director, were the only cast members with the series throughout its entire run. An interesting aspect of the program was that many telecasts closed with a segment in which Zimbalist, out of character, asked the home audience for information leading to the arrest of people on the FBI's Most Wanted list. And because the Ford Motor Company sponsored the series for all its years, bureau agents were always seen in Fords.

Singer/comedian Dean Martin began hosting his own musical variety show on NBC and his relaxed style went over very well with viewers. During the program's nine-year tenure there were many regulars, including Tom Bosley, Rodney Dangerfield, Dom DeLuise, Nipsey Russell, and pianist Ken Lane.

I SPY: Bill Cosby and Robert Culp

I SPY: September 15, 1965–September 2, 1968, NBC. Robert Culp and Bill Cosby

F TROOP: Ken Berry

F TROOP: September 14, 1965–August 31, 1967, ABC. Larry Storch and Forrest Tucker

THE WILD, WILD WEST: September 17, 1965–September 19, 1969, CBS. Ross Martin and Robert Conrad

HONEY WEST: September 17, 1965–September 2, 1966, ABC. Anne Francis (Honey West)

THE WACKIEST SHIP IN THE ARMY: September 19, 1965–September 4, 1966, NBC. Jack Warden and Gary Collins

DAKTARI: January 11, 1966–January 15, 1969, CBS. Ross Hagen, Erin Moran, and Marshall Thompson

MONA McCLUSKEY: September 16, 1965–April 14, 1966, NBC. Juliet Prowse (Mona McCluskey) and Denny Miller

PLEASE DON'T EAT THE DAISIES: September 14, 1965–September 2, 1967, NBC. *(First row)* Brian Nash, Patricia Crowley, Kim Tyler; *(second row)* Jeff Fithian, Joe Fithian; *(top row)* Lad, the family dog, and Mark Miller

PLEASE DON'T EAT THE DAISIES: Mark Miller and Patricia Crowley

HANK: September 17, 1965–September 2, 1966, NBC. Dick Kallman (Hank Dearborn)

210

THE DEAN MARTIN SHOW: September 16, 1965–May 24, 1974, NBC. Dean Martin and Louis Armstrong (guest)

THE BIG VALLEY: September 15, 1965–May 19, 1969, ABC. Peter Breck, Barbara Stanwyck, and Richard Long

GET SMART: September 18, 1965–September 11, 1970, NBC, CBS. Don Adams and Barbara Feldon

GET SMART: Don Adams, Barbara Feldon, and Edward Platt (86 and 99 get married)

GET SMART: Don Adams (Maxwell Smart) and unknown actor

THE JOHN FORSYTHE SHOW: September 13, 1965–August 29, 1966, NBC. Ann B. Davis, John Forsythe, and Elsa Lanchester

MR. ROBERTS: September 17, 1965–September 2, 1966, NBC. Roger Smith (Lt. [j.g.] Douglas Roberts) and Richard Sinatra

BATMAN: Burgess Meredith (the Penguin), Cesar Romero (the Joker), Burt Ward (Robin), Adam West (Batman), Frank Gorshin (*behind Batman*, The Riddler), and Lee Meriwether (Catwoman)

BATMAN: Batgirl (Yvonne Craig)

THE STEVE LAWRENCE SHOW: September 13, 1965–December 11, 1965, CBS. Steve Lawrence and Eydie Gormé

BATMAN: January 12, 1966–March 14, 1968, ABC. Robin (Burt Ward) and Batman (Adam West)

HOGAN'S HEROES: September 17, 1965–July 4, 1971, CBS. Werner Klemperer and Bob Crane (Col. Robert Hogan)

HOGAN'S HEROES: John Banner, Werner Klemperer, and Bob Crane (Hogan)

THE AVENGERS: Linda Thorson

CAMP RUNAMUCK: September 17, 1965–September 2, 1966, NBC. Nina Wayne, Arch Johnson, Alice Nunn, and Dave Ketchum

BLUE LIGHT: January 12, 1966–August 31, 1966, ABC. Robert Goulet

THE AVENGERS: March 28, 1966–September 16, 1969, ABC. Patrick Macnee and Diana Rigg

THE F.B.I.: September 19, 1965–September 8, 1974, ABC. Philip Abbott, Efrem Zimbalist, Jr., and William Reynolds

THE F.B.I.: William Reynolds and Efrem Zimbalist, Jr.

MY MOTHER THE CAR: September 14, 1965– September 6, 1966, NBC. Jerry Van Dyke

GIDGET: Sally Field

THE F.B.I.: Steven Brooks, Lynn Loring, and Efrem Zimbalist, Jr.

MY MOTHER THE CAR: Jerry Van Dyke

GIDGET: September 15, 1965–September 1, 1966, ABC. Don Porter and Sally Field (Gidget)

214

CONVOY: September 17, 1965–December 10, 1965, NBC. John Gavin, Linden Chiles, and John Larch

I DREAM OF JEANNIE: Larry Hagman

I DREAM OF JEANNIE: Larry Hagman and Barbara Eden

RUN FOR YOUR LIFE: September 13, 1965–September 11, 1968, NBC. Ben Gazzara and MacDonald Carey (guest)

I DREAM OF JEANNIE: September 18, 1965–September 1, 1970, NBC. Barbara Eden (Jeannie)

COURT MARTIAL: April 8, 1966–September 2, 1966, ABC. Bradford Dillman and Peter Graves

LAREDO: September 16, 1965–September 1, 1967, NBC. Neville Brand, Peter Brown, and William Smith

GREEN ACRES: September 15, 1965–September 7, 1971, CBS. Eva Gabor and Eddie Albert

LOST IN SPACE: September 15, 1965–September 11, 1968, CBS. *(Foreground)* Marta Kristen; Mark Goddard, June Lockhart, and Guy Williams

GREEN ACRES: Eddie Albert and Eva Gabor

LOST IN SPACE: Billy Mumy

THE LEGEND OF JESSE JAMES: September 13, 1965–September 5, 1966, ABC. Allen Case and Christopher Jones (Jesse James)

1966-67

Nine years into the space race, and shortly before the networks' annual ratings race, the United States and the Soviet Union successfully landed unmanned spacecraft on the moon within the same week. For the first time, the nation and the world could see photographs sent from the bleak lunar surface. America's Surveyor 1 landed in the area where future American astronauts would walk. Back on Earth, also for the first time, TV cameras were able to telecast live pictures of a manned spacecraft descent (Gemini 9) for a nationwide audience. This was just the next step for the country's space heroes, and for TV viewers, in the quest for the ultimate mission of landing men on the moon.

Astronauts were not the only heroes on television this year. The new season brought forth a spate of heroes. Some were short-lived, others endure (in syndication) to this day.

Among the one-season heroes was ABC's "The Green Hornet." This old-time radio hero (1936) was created by George Trendle, who also developed the Lone Ranger. For television, this crime fighter was updated, using a sleek automobile loaded with features such as built-in guns, a TV camera, a smoke screen, and infrared lights to ward off pursuers. Van Williams (formerly of "Bourbon Street Beat," "Surfside Six," and "The Tycoon") played Britt Reid (the Green Hornet), publisher of the *Daily Sentinel*. Bruce Lee (later to star in many martial-arts films) played Kato, his servant. Others in the cast included Wende Wagner as Lenore "Casey" Case, Reid's personal secretary, and Walter Brooke as D.A. Frank Scanlon, the only person besides Kato and Casey who knew that Reid was the Hornet.

"Captain Nice" (NBC), created by Buck Henry, starred William Daniels (much later Dr. Craig on "St. Elsewhere") as Carter Nash. Nash was a police chemist who developed a secret formula that, when taken, transformed him into superstrong Captain Nice. This comedy spoof featured Alice Ghostly

(veteran TV sitcom performer) as his wife and Ann Prentiss as Policewoman Candy Kane, his girlfriend.

"Mr. Terrific" (CBS), another spoof, was Stanley Beamish, who, with his partner, Hal Walters, owned a gas station in Washington, D.C. Beamish was a nebbish, but he was also an agent for the Bureau of Secret Projects. When on assignment, he took a special pill (he was the only one the pill would work on) that gave him super powers for one hour and turned him into a crime fighter *extraordinaire*. Stephen Strimpell was Beamish, Dick Gautier (Hymie the robot on "Get Smart") played Walters, and John McGiver (a veteran TV performer) was Barton J. Reed, director of the bureau. Coincidentally, both "Captain Nice" and this series debuted and concluded on the same dates.

"Tarzan" (NBC), after appearing both in silent and sound films and becoming popular on radio, came to television this season. Edgar Rice Burroughs's hero of the jungle began an hour-long adventure series with Ron Ely (formerly on "The Aquanauts") in the title role. This was an expensive show to produce because all the episodes were filmed on location in Brazil and Mexico. The series did reasonably well this season, returned for a second, and then went into syndication.

Simon Templar, also known as "The Saint," was a popular fictional crime fighter created by Leslie Charteris. During the thirties and forties several movies were made about this hero, and a radio series starred Vincent Price and later Barry Sullivan. The TV series was produced in England and first seen in the early sixties in syndication in the United States. This season the series came to network television as NBC put new episodes of the familiar character on its schedule. Roger Moore, already known to TV audiences (and the future James Bond), played the title role. The series is still seen today in syndication.

The Impossible Missions Force was a group of heroes who performed heroics on the hour-long CBS series, "Mission: Impossible." The show, about the ex-

ploits of a clandestine government agency, became famous for its unique weekly opening in which the I.M.F. leader, during this season Dan Briggs (Steven Hill) and thereafter Jim Phelps (Peter Graves), arrived at some obscure location to listen to a secret tape-recorded message giving background information on the I.M.F.'s next assignment. The message always concluded with the warning: "As always, should you or any member of your I.M. Force be caught or killed, the secretary will disavow any knowledge of your actions. This tape will self-destruct in five seconds." Up in smoke went the recorder, and by show's end, down came this week's villain.

Except for the change of leader, the original cast remained intact for the first three seasons: Martin Landau as Rollin Hand, a master of disguise; Barbara Bain as Cinnamon Carter, a versatile combination of beauty and brains (in real life, Landau and Bain were married); Greg Morris as Barney Collier, an electronics wizard; and Peter Lupus as Willie Armitage, the brawn of the group. As the fourth year began, Landau and Bain left the series and Leonard Nimoy was added. Lesley Ann Warren and later Linda Day George were also featured players. Morris and Lupus were the only cast members to remain for the full series run.

The show's musical theme, composed by Lalo Schiffrin, was released as a single and was a hit for almost four months. After its seven-year network stay, the series went into syndication in the United States and was dubbed in 15 languages and shown in 70 countries.

The heroic crew of the starship *Enterprise* was commanded "to boldly go where no man has gone before," and each week, for three seasons, that's where "Star Trek" journeyed. Many consider it television's all-time-best adult science-fiction adventure series, and it has proved to be one of the medium's all-time most popular programs. Of course, this happened not when it was on NBC, where its potential was never clearly seen by network executives, but after its 78 episodes went into syndication. That's when it became a phenomenal success and resulted in Paramount Studios—a decade after the network had canceled the series—reassembling the cast to produce a feature-length film. The popularity of the movie motivated a second feature, released in 1982, and at this writing a third film is in the works, with a tentative release date of late 1984. While all this was happening, the original series continued in reruns and, at last count, is seen on 140 stations in the United States and in 47 countries. The large cast has a loyal "Trekkie" following and includes William Shatner as Capt. James T. Kirk; Leonard Nimoy as Mr. Spock, the Vulcan science officer; DeForest Kelly as Dr. Leonard "Bones" McCoy, the chief medical officer; James Doohan as Lt. Cmdr. Montgomery Scott, chief engineer; Nichelle Nichols as Lieutenant Uhura, the communications officer; George Takei as Mr. Sulu, a navigator; Majel Barrett as Christine Chapel, chief nurse; and Walter Koenig as Ensign Chekov, also a navigator. Occasionally seen was Grace Lee Whitney as Yeoman Rand.

But for all the hoopla this year with heroes, it took two comedy shows to win the biggest audiences.

The situation comedy "Family Affair," starring Brian Keith as a successful construction-company executive who becomes a bachelor father, placed 15th for the year. After an accident befell his brother and sister-in-law, Bill Davis found himself with a family of three children to raise. Fortunately for him, he was ably assisted by his manservant, Giles French, played by Sebastian Cabot. The children were teenager Cissy, played by Kathy Garver, and twins Jody and Buffy, played by Johnnie Whitaker and Anissa Jones. The series did even better in subsequent seasons, ranking fifth for three consecutive years on its way to five years on CBS.

The Smothers Brothers had previously starred in their own one-season situation-comedy series, but this year they returned in a program format more suited to their talents, a comedy variety show titled "The Smothers Brothers Comedy Hour." Their irreverent style of comedy, which included social and political satire, endeared them to a large, predominantly youthful audience that provided them with big ratings. However, the censors at CBS did not take kindly to their liberated philosophy on many sensitive issues of the day, and after two seasons this top-rated show (16th this season) went off the air.

The following were the only other

shows of this season to return the following season.

"That Girl," starring Marlo Thomas (Danny Thomas's daughter) as Ann Marie, was the first of the independent, self-reliant-women sitcoms. The series concerned itself with her attempt to make a career as an actress in New York City after she moved from her parents' home in the suburbs. Ted Bessell co-starred as her boyfriend, Donald Hollinger, a reporter for *Newsview* magazine. The series was on ABC for five years, with 136 episodes produced.

"The Rat Patrol" was one of the better World War II drama series of this decade. Fighting its way across Africa, this small unit consisted of three Americans and an Englishman. Christopher George was Sgt. Sam Troy, the leader of the pack; Gary Raymond was Sgt. Jack Moffitt, a British demolitions expert; Lawrence Casey played Pvt. Mark Hitchcock; and Justin Tarr was Pvt. Tully Pettigrew. The series ran for two seasons on ABC before going into syndication.

"Felony Squad" was a half-hour police drama, also on ABC. The cast included Howard Duff as veteran Det. Sam Stone; Dennis Cole as Det. Jim Briggs, Stone's young partner; and Ben Alexander as Desk Sgt. Dan Briggs, Jim's father. The action took place in Los Angeles, and 73 episodes aired during its two and a half years on the network—after which it went into syndication.

Finally, in other news this season, ABC, usually third in the ratings, introduced its new fall schedule just after Labor Day (to get a jump on the competition), the earliest ever. This helped it in the early-season ratings, but it could not sustain the edge for the remainder of the television year. Before this season, prime-time movies had made a successful impact on viewers. Now the networks increased the number of movie nights to five per week. Monday and Wednesday

nights were the exception but, by midseason, the latter would also become a movie night. CBS and NBC simultaneously telecast the first football Superbowl. The NFL Green Bay Packers and the AFL Kansas City Chiefs battled each other, with Green Bay winning 35–10. In the other battle, CBS topped NBC 24.6–17.0 in the Superbowl ratings. Starting the next season, the two networks alternated the yearly coverage of this big event.

HAWK: September 8, 1966–December 29, 1966, ABC. Burt Reynolds (John Hawk)

TARZAN: September 8, 1966–September 13, 1968, NBC. Ron Ely (Tarzan) with guests Julie Harris and Woody Strode

OCCASIONAL WIFE: September 13, 1966–August 29, 1967, NBC. Michael Callan and Patricia Harty

PISTOLS 'N' PETTICOATS: September 17, 1966–August 19, 1967, CBS. Gary Vinson and Douglas Fowley

MISSION: IMPOSSIBLE: *(Front)* Peter Lupus, Greg Morris, Martin Landau; *(back* Barbara Bain, Peter Graves (second cast)

THE MAN WHO NEVER WAS: September 7, 1966–January 4, 1967, ABC. Robert Lansing

MISSION: IMPOSSIBLE: September 17, 1966–September 8, 1973, CBS. Peter Lupus, Steven Hill, Martin Landau, Barbara Bain, and Greg Morris (original cast)

MISSION: IMPOSSIBLE: *(Seated)* Leonard Nimoy, Peter Graves; *(standing)* Greg Morris, Peter Lupus, Lesley Ann Warren, and Sam Elliott (later cast)

FAMILY AFFAIR: September 12, 1966–September 9, 1971, CBS. Brian Keith, Kathy Garver, Sebastian Cabot, Anissa Jones, and Johnnie Whitaker

FAMILY AFFAIR: Johnnie Whitaker, Sebastian Cabot, Brian Keith, Anissa Jones, and Kathy Garver

THE INVADERS: January 10, 1967–September 17, 1968, ABC. Roy Thinnes

THE INVADERS: Alien invader in process of being destroyed

THE INVADERS: Suzanne Pleshette and Roy Thinnes in "The Mutation"

THE GREEN HORNET: September 9, 1966–July 14, 1967, ABC. The Black Beauty, the Hornet's car

THE GREEN HORNET: The Green Hornet (Van Williams) and Kato (Bruce Lee)

THE GREEN HORNET: Van Williams

THE RAT PATROL: September 12, 1966–September 16, 1968, ABC. Christopher George, Gary Raymond, Lawrence Casey, and Justin Tarr

THE RAT PATROL: Christopher George

STAR TREK: William Shatner

STAR TREK: Leonard Nimoy

STAR TREK: DeForest Kelly

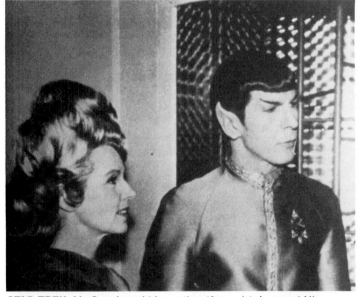

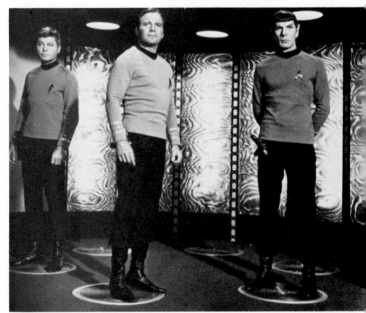

STAR TREK: Mr. Spock and his mother (Amanda), Leonard Nimoy and Jane Wyatt

STAR TREK: DeForest Kelly, William Shatner, and Leonard Nimoy

STAR TREK: September 8, 1966–September 2, 1969, NBC. *(Front)* DeForest Kelly, William Shatner, Leonard Nimoy; *(back)* James Doohan, Walter Koenig, Majel Barrett, Nichelle Nichols, and George Takei

STAR TREK: Nichelle Nichols

THE MONKEES: September 12, 1966–August 19, 1968, NBC. David Jones, Mike Nesmith, Peter Tork, and Micky Dolenz

STAR TREK: George Takei

THE TIME TUNNEL: September 9, 1966–September 1, 1967, ABC. Robert Colbert

THE TIME TUNNEL: Robert Colbert, Lee Meriwether, and James Darren

STAR TREK: Walter Koenig

THE TIME TUNNEL: Robert Colbert and James Darren in "The Day the Sky Fell Down"

THE GIRL FROM U.N.C.L.E.: Stefanie Powers

THE GIRL FROM U.N.C.L.E.: September 13, 1966–August 29, 1967, NBC. Stefanie Powers and Noel Harrison (son of Rex Harrison)

THAT GIRL: September 8, 1966–September 10, 1971, ABC. Marlo Thomas and Ted Bessell

DRAGNET '67: January 12, 1967–September 10, 1970, NBC. Jack Webb and Harry Morgan

THE SMOTHERS BROTHERS COMEDY HOUR: February 5, 1967–June 8, 1969, CBS. Tom and Dick Smothers (co-hosts)

THE SAINT: May 21, 1967–September 12, 1969, NBC. Roger Moore

IT'S ABOUT TIME: September 11, 1966–August 27, 1967, CBS. Joe E. Ross, Imogene Coca, Frank Aletter, and Jack Mullaney

FELONY SQUAD: September 12, 1966–January 31, 1969, ABC. Dennis Cole and Howard Duff

MR. TERRIFIC: Stephen Strimpell (Mr. Terrific)

MR. TERRIFIC: January 9, 1967–August 28, 1967, CBS. Dick Gautier and Stephen Strimpell

THE NEWLYWED GAME: January 7, 1967–August 30, 1971, ABC. Bob Eubanks (host)

ABC STAGE 67: September 14, 1966–May 11, 1967, ABC. (Guests) Albert Finney and Sir Laurence Olivier

CAPTAIN NICE: January 9, 1967–August 28, 1967, NBC. William Daniels (Captain Nice)

ABC STAGE 67: (Guests) David Frost and Peter Sellers

HEY LANDLORD: September 11, 1966–May 14, 1967, NBC. Will Hutchins and Sandy Baron

LOVE ON A ROOFTOP: September 13, 1966–August 31, 1967, ABC. Judy Carne and Peter Deuel

1967-68

Two decades after television began full prime-time evening programming, and a decade after adult Westerns became a new genre, this season began with the medium in a relative state of uniformity. Many of the usual personalities and programs that scored big for years were still scoring big: Ed Sullivan, Red Skelton, Jackie Gleason, Lucille Ball, Andy Griffith, Lawrence Welk, "Gunsmoke," "Walt Disney," "Bonanza," "My Three Sons," and "The Beverly Hillbillies." Even the popular fifties police drama "Dragnet," with Jack Webb, had been brought back in an updated version as a midseason replacement last year and was now starting the new TV year.

But within all this traditional television fare there debuted one of the most outstanding, highest-rated, and original programs in TV history. "Rowan and Martin's Laugh-In." First broadcast as a one-time special on September 9, viewer response was so strong that NBC was eager to include it in the schedule at the first opportunity. By midseason it was making America laugh. The show was an innovative, fast-paced, trend-setting program that took full advantage of the entire range of TV's technical capabilities. Ridiculous skits, snappy one-liners, and cameo appearances by top performers and celebrities (including President-to-be Richard Nixon saying one of the show's famous lines, "Sock it to me!"), made up each week's show.

There were 40 regular cast members over the years who prior to the show had been virtual unknowns. As a result of the program's success, many became stars in their own right: Goldie Hawn, Lily Tomlin, Eileen Brennan, Richard Dawson, Arte Johnson, Henry Gibson, Jo Anne Worley, Dave Madden, Teresa Graves, and Judy Carne. Besides Dan Rowan and Dick Martin, only two others were with the show throughout its run: Gary Owens and Ruth Buzzi. Some other memorable punch lines: "You bet your bippy," "Ring my chimes!" "Look it up in your Funk and Wagnalls," and "Here comes de judge!" "Laugh-In," was the

No.1-rated program during its first two full seasons. It ran its course after five years.

Four other shows, created more in the traditional mold, began long runs this season.

Multitalented performer Carol Burnett became familiar to TV audiences during the late fifties and early sixties on "The Garry Moore Show" (day and evening versions), "Stanley," a sitcom that starred Buddy Hackett, and "The Entertainers." This season she hosted and starred in her own variety show, supported by a talented group of performers who remained together for many years: Harvey Korman, Lyle Waggoner, Vickie Lawrence (her look-alike whom she discovered), and Tim Conway, who was a frequent guest before becoming a regular. Burnett's homey style and candor, which would be on display each week as she answered questions from the studio audience, endeared her to fans. The show became one of the longest-running prime-time variety series in history, lasting 11 seasons on CBS. Today, the show can be seen in syndication.

Mike Connors (formerly Nick Stone in "Tightrope") was the star of the hour-long private-detective series "Mannix." This season Joe Mannix worked as an investigator for Intertect, a sophisticated, computerized detective firm. Joseph Campanella was featured as his boss, Lou Wickersham. Starting in the second season, the private eye went out on his own, set up an office where he lived in Los Angeles, and hired Peggy Fair, played by Gail Fisher, as his secretary/assistant. The other regular cast member in this new format was Robert Reed as Lt. Adam Tobias. The series was created by Bruce Geller, who developed "Mission: Impossible," and 194 episodes aired during its eight-year tenure on CBS.

Raymond Burr just could not relax after his nine years as "Perry Mason." A year after it concluded he was back as Robert Ironside, the former chief of detectives of San Francisco's police

department, in the hour-long NBC police drama "Ironside." Although wounded in an assassination attempt and left paralyzed from the waist down (he was confined to a wheelchair), he became a special consultant to the department and was given living accommodations in the headquarters building, as well as a staff. Don Galloway was Sgt. Ed Brown, Barbara Anderson was Policewoman Eve Whitfield (replaced later by Elizabeth Baur as Policewoman Fran Belding), and Don Mitchell was Mark Sanger, an ex-con who was Ironside's personal assistant. The series ran for eight years and went into syndication as "The Raymond Burr Show."

"The High Chaparral" was another Western conceived in the "Bonanza" mold. Leif Erickson was John Cannon, owner of the High Chaparral ranch during the 1870s in the Arizona territory. As patriarch of his family, he was determined to establish a cattle empire. His wife, Victoria (Linda Cristal), was the daughter of Don Sebastian Montoya, owner of another big ranch in the territory. Together, the two families united their efforts to tame the vast land that was Arizona. Other Cannon family members were sons Buck and Billy Blue, played by Cameron Mitchell and Mark Slade. Frank Silvera was Montoya and his son, Manolito, was played by Henry Darrow. The series was on for four years on NBC.

There was a dearth of situation comedies: only six debuted (the smallest number in years), and of those, only two survived past the season.

"The Flying Nun" (ABC) was a fantasy comedy about a novitiate nun who, as the title states, could fly. Sally Field (formerly "Gidget") starred as Elsie Ethrington, a young, demonstrative woman who joined the Convent of San Tanco in Puerto Rico and became Sister Bertrille. Others in the cast were Marge Redmond (formerly Florence in the Red Buttons sitcom, "The Double Life of Henry Phyfe") as Sister Jacqueline, Madeleine Sherwood as Mother Superior, and Alejandro Rey (formerly Mike Valera in "Slattery's

People'') as Carlos Ramirez, a playboy and owner of the local discotheque. The series was seen for three seasons.

Eve Arden was back in a sitcom after an absence of almost 10 years. The series was about the Hubbards and the Buells, who were neighbors, in the aftermath of the marriage of the former's son to the latter's daughter. This was the setting for ''The Mothers-in-Law'' on NBC. The cast included Arden as Eve Hubbard; Herbert Rudley as her lawyer husband, Herb; Kaye Ballard as Kaye Buell; Roger C. Carmel (and later Richard Deacon) as Kaye's TV-writer husband, Roger; Jerry Fogel as the Hubbards' son, Jerry; and Deborah Walley as the Buells' daughter, Susie. This two-season series was set on Ridgewood Drive in Hollywood.

Concluding this season, the top-rated new program, ranking 19th, was one whose star was a 650-pound black bear, ''Gentle Ben,'' on CBS. The show's human star was Dennis Weaver as game warden Tom Wedloe, and although the series did well this year, it was canceled after the next season. Jerry Lewis, after being away from TV for several years, returned to host his own comedy variety series on NBC. ''The Jerry Lewis Show'' lasted two years, considerably longer than his previous three-month ABC show. Prime-time movies continued to be a big plus for the three networks. With fewer new series doing well in recent years, the networks allocated more time in their schedules for these Hollywood efforts. By mid-season, viewers for the first time had the opportunity to watch a network movie every night of the week. Late in the TV year, there was a feeble attempt to launch a fourth network. Bill Dana hosted ''The Las Vegas Show,'' which was to be the foundation for The United Network. Within a few weeks, the show—and the plans for the new network—vanished.

MANNIX: September 16, 1967–August 27, 1975, CBS. Mike Connors (Joe Mannix) and Gail Fisher

COWBOY IN AFRICA: September 11, 1967–September 16, 1968, ABC. Chuck Connors and Kamala Devi (guest)

THE HIGH CHAPARRAL: September 10, 1967–September 10, 1971, NBC. Frank Silvera (Leif Erickson was the star)

JUDD FOR THE DEFENSE: September 8, 1967–September 19, 1969, ABC. Katherine Justice (guest) and Carl Betz (Clinton Judd)

JUDD FOR THE DEFENSE: Carl Betz and Stephen Young

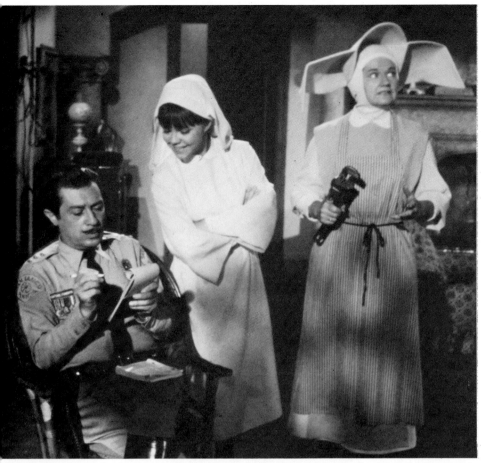

THE FLYING NUN: September 7, 1967–September 18, 1970, ABC. Vito Scotti, Sally Field, and Marge Redmond

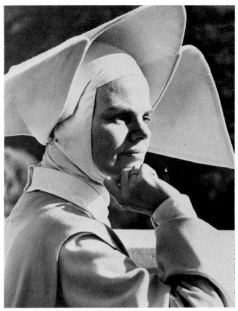

THE FLYING NUN: Madeleine Sherwood

GENTLE BEN: September 10, 1967–August 31, 1969, CBS. Dennis Weaver and Clint Howard *(right foreground)*

THE CAROL BURNETT SHOW: September 11, 1967–August 9, 1978, CBS. Vickie Lawrence, Tim Conway, Carol Burnett, and Harvey Korman

THE CAROL BURNETT SHOW: Carol Burnett

THE CHAMPIONS: June 10, 1968–September 9, 1968, NBC. William Gaunt and Stuart Damon

MAYA: September 16, 1967–February 10, 1968, NBC. Sajid Kahn and Jay North

THE MOTHERS-IN-LAW: September 10, 1967–September 7, 1969, NBC. Eve Arden and Kaye Ballard

THE CHAMPIONS: Alexandra Bastedo, Stuart Damon, and William Gaunt

THE MOTHERS-IN-LAW: Herb Rudley and Eve Arden

IT TAKES A THIEF: January 9, 1968–September 14, 1970, ABC. Robert Wagner and Malachi Throne

ROWAN AND MARTIN'S LAUGH-IN: January 22, 1968–May 14, 1973, NBC. Dan Rowan and Dick Martin (co-hosts)

ROWAN AND MARTIN'S LAUGH-IN: Goldie Hawn

ACCIDENTAL FAMILY: September 15, 1967–January 5, 1968, NBC. Lois Nettleton and Jerry Van Dyke with kids Teddy Quinn and Susan Benjamin

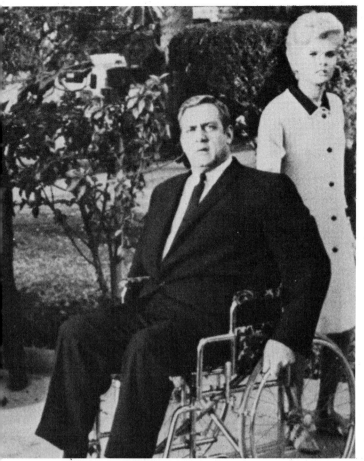

FRANK SINATRA: November 13, 1967, NBC. Frank Sinatra and Ella Fitzgerald (guest)

IRONSIDE: September 19, 1967–January 16, 1975, NBC. Raymond Burr (Robert Ironside) and Barbara Anderson

HE AND SHE: September 6, 1967–September 18, 1968, CBS. Richard Benjamin and unknown actress

IRONSIDE: Barbara Anderson, Raymond Burr; *(top)* Don Galloway and Don Mitchell

LET'S MAKE A DEAL: Monte Hall

LET'S MAKE A DEAL: May 21, 1967–August 30, 1971, NBC, ABC. Monty Hall (host)

CUSTER (THE LEGEND OF CUSTER): September 6, 1967–December 27, 1967, ABC. *(Front)* Slim Pickens, Michael Dante; *(back)* Peter Palmer, Robert F. Simon, Wayne Maunder (Lt. Col. George A. Custer), Grant Woods

THE PRISONER: June 1, 1968–September 11, 1969, CBS. Patrick McGoohan

HONDO: September 8, 1967–December 29, 1967, ABC. Royal Dano and James MacArthur (guests), and Ralph Taeger

THE PRISONER: Patrick McGoohan

THE SECOND HUNDRED YEARS: September 6, 1967–September 19, 1968, ABC. Monte Markham

HONDO: Ralph Taeger (Hondo Lane)

CIMARRON STRIP: September 7, 1967–September 7, 1971, CBS. Stuart Whitman

HOLLYWOOD SQUARES: January 12, 1968–September 13, 1968, NBC, 1972, syndicated. Peter Marshall (host)

HOLLYWOOD SQUARES: Hollywood Squares panel

1968-69

Nineteen sixty-eight will always be remembered as the year in which television provided much more than mere entertainment. It was, more than ever before, a true communications medium that gave the nation the opportunity to share in the many historical events that occurred before, and during, the new fall season.

In April, Dr. Martin Luther King, Jr., the nation's foremost champion of non-violence and racial brotherhood, was assassinated during a civil-rights campaign in Memphis, Tennessee. Whites as well as blacks went into mourning and spiritual depression. Television conveyed the somber mood of the many thousands marching in silence at King's funeral and permitted the millions watching to walk those same Atlanta streets. This moving gesture of respect was one of the greatest ever bestowed upon a person who had not been a high government official. And in the aftermath, as rioting broke out in cities across the country, television continued to focus on black America's frustration.

In June, another tragedy befell the nation. U.S. Sen. Robert Kennedy was shot and killed at a political rally in Los Angeles as he celebrated his California presidential-primary victory. This was the first time a candidate for the presidency had ever been assassinated, and television was there once again to inform the shocked nation.

The presidential primaries were going on before and after these calamitous events, and television was providing greater coverage than ever of these quadrennial happenings. As the conventions approached, a veteran political warrior was making a strong comeback. Richard M. Nixon, who six years earlier had told the press, after his gubernatorial defeat in California, that they would not have him to kick around anymore, got the Republican nomination on the first ballot. The convention, in Miami Beach, was given full coverage by NBC (Huntley and Brinkley) and CBS (Walter Cronkite), while ABC (Frank Reynolds) provided 90-minute selected coverage

nightly from 9:30 to 11:00.

Later, the Democratic convention in Chicago—in sharp contrast to the orderly Republican gathering—was disruptive inside the convention hall and violent outside on the streets. Home viewers saw thousands of antiwar demonstrators battle police and witnessed vivid scenes of police brutality never before seen by a TV audience. And when the cameras focused on the proceedings inside, they saw Hubert H. Humphrey get the nomination.

Election night was historic because it proved to be the longest coverage ever, lasting until nearly noon the next day before Nixon was declared the winner by a thin margin. The former vice-president had made one of the greatest comebacks in American politics.

In December, on Christmas Eve, the nation and the world shared an unprecedented television experience. Apollo 8, the first manned spacecraft ever to orbit the moon, sent back live, close-up black-and-white pictures of the lunar surface, a breathtaking sight! Astronauts Frank Borman, Jim Lovell, and Bill Anders read passages from the Book of Genesis as the spellbound TV audience watched the barren world pass below. The astronauts ended their telecast with "God bless all of you on the good Earth."

National election years usually mean increased public interest in news and events. This understanding motivated CBS to launch a prime-time, in-depth news-magazine show, "60 Minutes." The program had hard news, feature stories, and, in true magazine style, a letters-to-the-editor segment. Initially it was seen on alternate Tuesday nights, then shifted to early Sunday evenings (where many times it was preempted by football), and then broadcast only during the winter and spring. Finally, in 1975, it became a year-round weekly series, and its ratings began to climb until it became the highest-rated public-affairs program in TV history. Furthermore, in recent years, "60 Minutes" has become one of the top rated of all regularly seen programs.

The show originally had two correspondents/hosts, Mike Wallace and Harry Reasoner. Reasoner left for ABC in 1970 and Morley Safer replaced him. In 1975, Dan Rather joined the show and at the start of the 1978–79 season, Reasoner returned. Andy Rooney was added, with a feature titled "A Few Minutes with Andy Rooney." The only personnel change since then was the replacement of Rather by Ed Bradley. Rather took over for the retiring Walter Cronkite as anchorman for the "CBS Evening News" on March 9, 1981.

There were four successful sitcoms this season. Lucille Ball continued on the air but changed "The Lucy Show" to "Here's Lucy," with a new cast and format. She changed her name from Lucille Carmichael to Lucille Carter and moved from suburban Danfield, Connecticut, to Los Angeles. She was still a widow with two children, but now their names were Kim and Craig and they were, in fact, her real-life children, Lucy and Desi. But one thing that didn't change were the ratings; as usual, they were among the tops. During the six years "Here's Lucy" was on CBS, the series finished in the following order: 9th, 6th, 3rd, 11th, 15th, and 29th—after which Lucy said good-bye.

Doris Day's debut on television proved successful but volatile. During the five seasons of "The Doris Day Show," there were four different formats. This season she was a widow with two children who had moved from a hectic city life-style to a slower-paced country farm. In the second season she took a job as an executive secretary at *Today's World* magazine and became a commuter. In the third season she and her children gave up the farm life and moved back to the city. The fourth year had the most startling change of all: she was now working as a reporter for the magazine, but suddenly there were no children; instead, she was a single, carefree, independent career woman. This format lasted for the show's two final seasons. Day's character, Doris Martin, was the only permanent one throughout the five years on CBS.

"Mayberry R.F.D." was the top-rated new show of the season and, over all, fourth for the year. This very successful start was because it was the direct successor to the top-rated "The Andy Griffith Show" of the previous few seasons. When Griffith decided to give up being the sheriff of Mayberry, North Carolina, most of the cast were kept together and a new lead, the character of Councilman Sam Jones, played by Ken Berry, was selected, along with the new title. Included in the held-over cast were Frances Bavier as Aunt Bee; George Lindsey as Goober Pyle (Gomer's cousin); Jack Dodson as Howard Sprague, the county clerk; Paul Hartman as Emmett Clark, the repair-shop owner; Arlene Golonka as Millie Swanson, Sam's girlfriend; and Buddy Foster as Sam's son, Mike. "Mayberry R.F.D." was a top-rated show throughout its three years on CBS. It was canceled in 1971 when the network decided to discontinue all of its rural-type programming (the advertising demographics were poor), and its 78 episodes went into syndication.

Singer/actress Diahann Carroll starred in "Julia," the first situation comedy in which a black woman played a leading role since Ethel Waters, and later Louise Beavers, starred in "Beulah" in the early fifties. "Julia" was the story of Julia Baker, a widowed nurse who worked in the medical wing of an aerospace company while raising her young son, Corey, in Los Angeles. It had an integrated cast that featured Lloyd Nolan (who was "Martin Kane") as her boss, Dr. Morton Chegley; Lurene Tuttle (formerly Vinnie Day in "Life with Father" and Doris Dunston in "Father of the Bride") as Chief Nurse Hannah Yarby; Marc Copage as son Corey; and Paul Winfield as Julia's boyfriend, Paul Cameron. He was replaced by Fred Williamson as Steve Bruce, her romantic interest in the show's last season. The series ran three years on NBC.

Each of the networks introduced a successful police series this season. "Hawaii Five-O" was filmed on location in the nation's 50th state. It brought together the right combination of cast, scenery, and action to hold its CBS viewers 12 years. The stories were about the Hawaiian State Police's special Five-O branch, whose members reported only to the governor. There was little turnover among the cast during the show's long tenure: Jack Lord starred as Steve McGarrett, the no-nonsense head of the group; James MacArthur was Detective Danny Williams, the chief assistant; Kam Fong was Detective Chin Ho Kelly (Fong tired of the role after 10 seasons and

was written out by having his character killed); Richard Denning was Gov. Phillip Grey; Peggy Ryan was Jenny Sherman, McGarrett's second secretary (his first, May—played by Maggie Parker—lasted only this year); and Al Eban was Doc Bergman, Five-O's pathologist. A major reason for the cast staying together was Hawaii's pleasant working conditions: they were too good to give up. The series' hour-long episodes did not go into syndication immediately after it left the network. However, as of this writing, syndication had commenced.

"Adam-12" was a 30-minute police drama, produced by Jack Webb, that focused on the everyday events in the life of two uniform officers assigned to patrol car Adam-12. Martin Milner starred as veteran officer Pete Malloy (badge 2340) and Kent McCord co-starred as his rookie partner, Jim Reed (badge 744). Others in the cast were William Boyett as Sergeant MacDonald, their commanding officer, and Gary Crosby as Officer Ed Wells. One hundred and seventy-four episodes aired during its seven-year NBC run, and it continues today in syndication.

Something new in police shows was introduced this season. "The Mod Squad" was about a trio of young hippie cops who came together as an undercover unit of the Los Angeles Police Department. Its three members were from different segments of society: Pete Cochran (Michael Cole) came from a wealthy family, Linc Hayes (Clarence Williams III) was raised in the ghetto, and Julie Barnes (Peggy Lipton) was the vagrant daughter of a prostitute. Each of the group had earlier encounters with the law but their raw energy, resourcefulness, street smarts, and desire to make something of themselves was molded successfully by Capt. Adam Greer (Tige

Andrews), the squad's leader. The series was on for five seasons, after which its 124 episodes went into syndication.

Last, and definitely least, were the imitators of "Laugh-In." First, ABC introduced "Turn-On," which became one of the biggest flops in TV history. It lasted for only one show. Then ABC tried again with "What's It All About, World?" hosted by Dean Jones. That too was canceled after just several telecasts.

THE JOHNNY CASH SHOW: June 7, 1969–May 5, 1971, ABC. Johnny Cash (host) and June Carter Cash

THE OUTCASTS: September 23, 1968–September 15, 1969, ABC. Don Murray and Kay Reynolds (guest)

THE OUTSIDER: September 18, 1968–September 3, 1969, NBC. Darren McGavin

HERE COME THE BRIDES: September 25, 1968–September 18, 1970, ABC. Robert Brown

THE GHOST AND MRS. MUIR: September 21, 1968–September 18, 1970, NBC, ABC. *(Left)* Charles Nelson Reilly, Kellie Flanagan *(bottom); (right bottom)* Harlen Carraher, Hope Lange, Edward Mulhare

THE GHOST AND MRS. MUIR: Hope Lange (Mrs. Carolyn Muir)

THE GHOST AND MRS. MUIR: Kellie Flanagan and Harlen Carraher

HEE HAW: June 18, 1969–July 13, 1971, CBS; 1971, syndicated. Buck Owens and Roy Clark (co-hosts)

HEE HAW: Buck Owens and the "Hee Haw" regulars

THE MOD SQUAD: September 24, 1968–August 23, 1973, ABC. Clarence Williams III, Tige Andrews, Peggy Lipton, and Michael Cole (early years)

THE MOD SQUAD: Michael Cole, Peggy Lipton, and Clarence Williams III (later years)

THE QUEEN AND I: January 16, 1969–May 1, 1969, CBS. Larry Storch and Billy DeWolfe

THE BEAUTIFUL PHYLLIS DILLER SHOW: September 12, 1968–December 22, 1968, NBC. Phyllis Diller (hostess)

HAWAII FIVE-O: September 26, 1968–April 5, 1980, CBS. Jack Lord

THIS IS TOM JONES: February 7, 1969–January 15, 1971, ABC. Tom Jones (host) and Cass Elliott (guest)

THE GOOD GUYS: September 25, 1968–January 12, 1970, CBS. Joyce Van Patten, Bob Denver, and Herb Edelman

HAWAII FIVE-O: Khigh Dhiegh (Wo Fat)

ADAM-12: Kent McCord and Martin Milner

ADAM-12: September 21, 1968–August 26, 1975, NBC. Kent McCord and Martin Milner

LAND OF THE GIANTS: September 22, 1968–September 6, 1970, ABC. Deanna Lund, Stefan Arngrim, and Kurt Kasznar

THE DORIS DAY SHOW: September 24, 1968–September 10, 1973, CBS. Doris Day (Doris Martin)

LAND OF THE GIANTS: *(foreground)* Don Marshall, Gary Conway; *(background)* Stefan Arngrim, Kurt Kasznar, Deanna Lund

MAYBERRY R.F.D.: Buddy Foster and Arlene Golonka

MAYBERRY R.F.D.: Ken Berry, Buddy Foster, and Arlene Golonka

MAYBERRY R.F.D.: September 23, 1968–September 6, 1971, CBS. Ken Berry and Paul Hartman

JULIA: Diahann Carroll

JULIA: September 17, 1968–May 25, 1971, NBC. Don Ameche (guest), Diahann Carroll (Julia Baker), Lloyd Nolan

60 MINUTES: September 24, 1968–present, CBS. Harry Reasoner

THE MERV GRIFFIN SHOW: August 16, 1969–February 11, 1972, CBS; 1972-present, syndicated. Arthur Treacher (announcer) and Merv Griffin (host)

60 MINUTES: Morley Safer and Mike Wallace

THE MERV GRIFFIN SHOW: Vice-President Spiro Agnew and Merv Griffin

60 MINUTES: Morley Safer, Dan Rather, Mike Wallace, and Harry Reasoner

BLONDIE: Jim Backus and Will Hutchins

THE DAVID FROST SHOW: David Frost and Shirley MacLaine (guest)

60 MINUTES: Ed Bradley

BLONDIE: September 26, 1968–January 9, 1969, CBS. Peter Robbins, Will Hutchins, Patricia Harty (Blondie), and Pamelyn Ferdin

THE DAVID FROST SHOW: July 7, 1969–July 14, 1972, syndicated. David Frost (host)

THE DONALD O'CONNOR SHOW: 1968, syndicated. Donald O'Connor (host) and Shari Lewis (guest)

HERE'S LUCY: September 23, 1968–September 2, 1974, CBS. Desi Arnaz, Jr., Gale Gordon, and Lucille Ball (Lucy Carter)

THE NAME OF THE GAME: September 2, 1968–September 10, 1971, NBC. Robert Stack, Gene Barry, and Tony Franciosa

THE NAME OF THE GAME: Tony Franciosa and Jill St. John (guest)

LANCER: September 24, 1968–June 22, 1970, CBS. Andrew Duggan (Murdoch Lancer)

LANCER: James Stacy, Wayne Maunder, Andrew Duggan, and Elizabeth Baur

1969-70

As the turbulent sixties came to a close, television had demonstrated to all that it was as much an information and communications medium as an entertainment vehicle. Society was more aware than ever before of what was going on locally, nationally, and internationally because of the deeds of television. People still read newspapers, but by this time more and more of us were turning to television as our primary source of news. The medium achieved this lofty success in a relatively short time. By the start of this season, more than 95 percent of all American homes were equipped with black-and-white sets, and almost 40 percent of all households now had color sets—all this in little more than two decades. Television had changed the daily lives of people, given national exposure to local events, transformed the political apparatus of the nation, among other things, and made available more information, more quickly, then could previously have been imagined.

The essence of the medium's omnipresence was summed up several weeks before the commencement of the new fall season. All three networks stayed on the air for 30 consecutive hours with live coverage of an epochal event: man's setting foot on the moon. A dream for thousands of years, and still almost unimaginable just a generation ago, this achievement attracted the largest audience in world history. Seven hundred and twenty-five million people watched all or part of the 2-hour-and-21-minute moon walk by Neil A. Armstrong, commander of the Apollo 11 mission, and Col. Edwin "Buzz" Aldrin, Jr. Covering the event for the networks were Jules Bergman (ABC), Walter Cronkite (CBS), and Frank McGee (NBC), each having covered America's space adventure since the early sixties.

The excitement, drama—and coverage—of the first lunar landing was repeated a short time after the new television year began as men walked on the moon a second time. This time there was to be a live color telecast from space, but the camera failed and the transmission was again in black and white. The third mission to the moon became the first colorcast.

Less excitement existed with the introduction of the new fall programming. In the past few years there had been an increasing outcry from political and private groups protesting what they considered to be an excessive display of violence on many TV shows. Bowing to this pressure, the networks, for the first time, did not debut one new police, detective, spy, or Western series. And going further, all the existing series of these types were toned down. But this policy led the networks into a quandary as to what to do for new shows. The answer was to bring back less-offensive programming that had proved successful: doctor shows, lawyer shows, general drama, dramatic anthologies, and good situation comedies.

The most popular of these were shows about doctors. The University Medical Center in Los Angeles was the setting for "Medical Center." This was the story of two doctors: Dr. Paul Lochner, the hospital chief of staff, played by James Daly, and Dr. Joe Gannon, the associate professor of surgery, played by Chad Everett. The interaction between the older Lochner and the younger Gannon was similar to Dr. Ben Casey and Dr. David Zorba in the earlier successful "Ben Casey." There were a number of doctors and nurses who came and went in the series, including Jayne Meadows as Nurse Chambers and Audrey Totter as Nurse Wilcox. The show ran for seven years on CBS. One hundred and forty-four episodes were aired before it went into syndication.

"Marcus Welby, M.D." was also set in California, this time in Santa Monica, and starred Robert Young (of "Father Knows Best") as a homey general practitioner who had his office in his home, made house calls, and was associated with the local hospital. His assistant and colleague was young Dr. Steven Kiley, played by James Brolin. The Welby-Kiley paternalistic relationship was similar to the Gillespie-Kildare professional involvement of the other early-sixties popular medical program, "Dr. Kildare." The only other regular cast character was Consuelo Lopez, the doctors' receptionist and nurse, played by Elena Verdugo. "Marcus Welby, M.D." was among the top 10 shows this season and became the No. 1-rated program the following year. It was the first ABC series to be in that spot for a full season. After seven years and 172 episodes it left the network and went into syndication under the title "Robert Young, Family Doctor."

"The Bold Ones" was a dramatic series that consisted of three rotating programs, one of which was "The New Doctors." Taking place at the David Craig Institute of New Medicine, this medical series starred E. G. Marshall (Dr. Craig), David Hartman (later of "Good Morning, America" fame), John Saxon, and, during its fourth and final season on NBC, Robert Walden (the future Joe Rossi on "Lou Grant").

In the next three areas, lawyers, general drama, and dramatic anthology, only two shows need be mentioned. Another segment of "The Bold Ones" was "The Lawyers." The members of the firm of Nichols, Darrell and Darrell were a well-rounded, successful trio played by Burl Ives, Joseph Campanella, and James Farentino. The show ran for three years on NBC. And on ABC, the new format for dramatic anthology began on "The ABC Movie of the Week." One-and-a-half- to two-hour "World Premiere" films, made expressly for television, were shown each week. The series made the top 25 this season.

ABC also came up with three winning sitcoms this year. "The Brady Bunch" enjoyed five years as a prime-time comedy, appeared as a Saturday-morning cartoon that was followed by a short daily network rerun of the series, and finally evolved into a variety show in the late seventies. The story was about a lovely lady, Carol Martin, a widow who was bringing up three lovely girls, and a man named Michael Brady, a widower with three boys of his own. Of course, this being sitcom-land, Brady met the lady and they all became "The Brady Bunch." This was all explained in the show's theme song. Robert Reed and Florence Henderson were Mr. and Mrs. Brady. Maureen McCormick, Eve Plumb, and Susan Olsen played daughters Marcia, Jan, and Cindy. Barry Williams, Christopher Knight, and Michael Lookinland were sons Greg, Peter, and Bobby. And Ann B. Davis was housekeeper Alice Nelson. Throughout its network run, the series was seen on Friday nights. It is still seen in syndication.

Pete Dixon, played by Lloyd Haynes, was a black teacher at Walt Whitman High, an integrated school in Los Angeles, who taught American history in "Room 222." This half-hour dramatic series was well regarded in the educational community for its sound dealing with such relevant problems as drugs and racial prejudice, among other controversial matters. Others in the cast were Karen Valentine as Alice Johnson, a student teacher; Michael Constantine as school principal Seymour Kaufman; and Denise Nicholas as Liz McIntyre, the school's guidance counselor and Pete's girlfriend. The series was on for four and a half years before going into syndication.

In "The Courtship of Eddie's Father," *Tomorrow* magazine editor Tom Corbett, played by Bill Bixby (the future Dr. David Banner, who turns into "The Incredible Hulk"), was another of TV's many widowers. He had a young son, Eddie, played by six-year-old Brandon Cruz, who was always trying to get him romantically involved with various beautiful women. The Corbetts had a Japanese housekeeper, Mrs. Livingston (Miyoshi Umeki), who was dependable but

generally confused. In addition, there was James Komack as Norman Tinker, Tom's friend and a photographer at the magazine, and Kristina Holland as Tom's secretary, Tina Rickles. Eddie and his father had a three-year network relationship with viewers, after which their 78 episodes went into syndication.

At the conclusion of the TV year, longtime NBC anchorman Chet Huntley said "good night" to David Brinkley for the last time, and the "Huntley-Brinkley Report" was no more. Huntley retired to pursue businesss interests, including the development of the Big Sky Resort in Montana, which did not open until after his death in 1974.

THE DEBBIE REYNOLDS SHOW: September 16, 1969–September 1, 1970, NBC. Debbie Reynolds

TO ROME WITH LOVE: September 28, 1969–September 1, 1971, CBS. Joyce Menges and John Forsythe

TO ROME WITH LOVE: Joyce Menges and Vito Scotti (guest)

PARIS 7000: January 22, 1970–June 4, 1970, ABC. George Hamilton and E. G. Marshall (guest)

THE ENGELBERT HUMPERDINCK SHOW: January 21, 1970–September 19, 1970, ABC. Engelbert Humperdinck (host)

THE BARBARA McNAIR SHOW: 1969–70, syndicated. Gordon MacRae (guest), Barbara McNair (hostess), and Rich Little (guest)

BRACKEN'S WORLD: September 19, 1969–January 1, 1971, NBC. Karen Jansen, Linda Harrison, and Laraine Stephens

THE JIM NABORS HOUR: September 25, 1969–May 20, 1971, CBS. Andy Griffith (guest) and Jim Nabors (host)

THE GOVERNOR AND J.J.: September 23, 1969–December 30, 1970, CBS. Julie Sommars and Dan Dailey

THE BRADY BUNCH: September 26, 1969–August 30, 1974, ABC. *(Bottom)* Ann B. Davis, Florence Henderson, Michael Lookinland, and Maureen McCormick; *(top)* Eve Plumb, Barry Williams, Susan Olsen, Robert Reed, and Christopher Knight

MARCUS WELBY, M.D.: September 23, 1969–May 11, 1976, ABC. Robert Young (Marcus Welby), Elena Verdugo, and James Brolin

MARCUS WELBY, M.D.: Robert Young and James Brolin

MARCUS WELBY, M.D.: James Brolin and Robert Young

MARCUS WELBY, M.D.: Robert Young, Pamela Hensley, and James Brolin (Dr. Kiley's wedding)

BEAT THE CLOCK: 1969, syndicated. Sheila MacRae (guest) and Jack Narz (host)

MEDICAL CENTER: September 24, 1969–September 6, 1976, CBS. Chad Everett

MEDICAL CENTER: James Daly and Lee Grant (guest)

MEDICAL CENTER: Victoria Federova (guest) and Chad Everett

THE BOLD ONES: September 14, 1969–January 9, 1973, NBC. John Saxon, David Hartman, and E. G. Marshall on "The New Doctors" segment

THE BOLD ONES: David Hartman

THE BOLD ONES: Edmund G. (Pat) Brown (guest), Joseph Campanella, and Burl Ives on "The Lawyers" segment

THEN CAME BRONSON: September 17, 1969–September 9, 1970, NBC. Michael Parks (Jim Bronson)

ROOM 222: Karen Valentine

ROOM 222: Lloyd Haynes

ROOM 222: September 17, 1969–January 11, 1974, ABC. Karen Valentine, Lloyd Haynes, and Denise Nicholas

THE DES O'CONNOR SHOW (KRAFT MUSIC HALL): May 20, 1971–September 1, 1971, NBC. Des O'Connor (host) and Phil Harris (guest)

THE SURVIVORS: September 29, 1969–September 17, 1970, ABC. George Hamilton and Lana Turner

THE DICK CAVETT SHOW: December 29, 1969–January 1, 1975, ABC. Dick Cavett (host)

THE COURTSHIP OF EDDIE'S FATHER: September 17, 1969–June 14, 1972, ABC. Bill Bixby, Brandon Cruz (Eddie), and Miyoshi Umeki

LOVE, AMERICAN STYLE: September 29, 1969–January 11, 1974, ABC. Michael Callan (center) with Penny Fuller and Dave Ketchum in a short story

LOVE, AMERICAN STYLE: Robert Cummings and Jane Wyatt in a short story

THE BILL COSBY SHOW: September 14, 1969–August 31, 1971, NBC. Bill Cosby

THE BILL COSBY SHOW: Bill Cosby

LOVE, AMERICAN STYLE: Flip Wilson and Mantan Moreland in a short story

1970-71

The American politician was consistently on home screens in this midterm-election year. The vigorous political battles taking place throughout the nation were fought on television to a greater extent than ever before. Political advertisements, in the form of 60-second and 30-second commercials, as well as the entreaties of candidates who bought air time to speak directly to constituents, saturated the nation's living rooms. It was estimated that $50 million was spent to produce this media blitz and purchase local TV air time. In larger states this meant that approximately sixty cents of every campaign dollar was invested in television promotion. Candidates took their lead from President Nixon regarding the effectiveness of the medium. As this season began, Nixon had made more TV appearances, in the form of press conferences and speeches to the nation, than any of his predecessors in the same amount of time.

This was also a year of snowballing social protest, and the networks touted their own kind of awareness. As the new season approached, they introduced these youth-oriented promotional themes: "We're putting it all together on CBS," "Let's get together on ABC," and "It's happening on NBC." Series with "relevant" themes debuted on all the networks. Stories focusing attention on drug abuse appeared on "Headmaster" (CBS), starring Andy Griffith; the subject of venereal disease was tackled on "The Interns" (CBS), with Broderick Crawford and Mike Farrell; and free legal advice to the poor was given on "The Storefront Lawyers" (CBS), with Robert Foxworth and Gerald S. O'Loughlin.

Other programs with relevancy were "The Psychiatrist" (NBC), starring Roy Thinnes and Luther Adler; "The Young Lawyers" (ABC), with Lee J. Cobb and Zalman King; and "The Senator" (NBC), starring Hal Holbrook. But such relevant shows did not acquire much of an audience, and all of them were off the air at season's end.

Meanwhile, the U.S. government became responsible for some relevancy of its own when it imposed two important changes on the television industry. The first was that Congress, after much debate, enacted a ban on all cigarette advertising on TV. No longer would commercials showing people happily puffing away ever be seen. This was the result of the link between cigarettes and cancer found in the mid-sixties. As the largest source of revenue for the networks, this ban, naturally, affected profits. The second change was that starting the following season, the networks were required to subtract thirty minutes from their three and a half hours of prime-time scheduling. This was imposed to create a better balance of revenue between themselves and their local affiliates.

Now for a look at this season's successes.

Flip Wilson, a young black performer already familiar to viewers, began hosting his own comedy variety series on NBC. He became an overnight sensation in "The Flip Wilson Show," which ranked second this season as well as next. This was a level of popularity never before reached by a black entertainer. Wilson based much of his comedy on his adeptness with several outrageous characters, including Geraldine Jones, a sassy chatterbox and liberated woman who was always exclaiming, "What you see is what you get!"; Reverend LeRoy, pastor of the Church of What's Happening Now; Freddie Johnson, Wilson's Everyman; and Danny Danger, a private detective. After four seasons the show went off the air, but Wilson continued to appear from time to time on comedy specials.

Dennis Weaver starred in "McCloud" (NBC) as Sam McCloud, a contemporary deputy marshal from New Mexico on assignment at Manhattan's 27th Police Precinct to learn sophisticated crime-fighting techniques. It was a long assignment, lasting seven years. This season the show was an hour segment of the short-lived "Four-in-One" series. The next year it expanded to 90 minutes and became one of the rotating shows on "The NBC Mystery Movie," first seen on Wednesday nights and then on Sundays. Others in the cast (they all stayed the entire run) were J. D. Cannon as Police Chief Peter B. Clifford; Terry Carter (the future Colonel Tigh on "Battlestar Galactica") as Sgt. Joe Broadhurst; and Diana Muldaur as Chris Coughlin, McCloud's girlfriend.

The situation comedy "The Partridge Family" (ABC) was about five children and a widowed mother who lived at 698 Sycamore Road, San Pueblo, California. What made the show out of the ordinary for the genre was that it was about rock'n'roll and the clan's show-business experiences (they became very popular in real life). For the next few years, the Partridges joined the Brady Bunch as two of America's most popular TV families. Shirley Jones, David Cassidy, Susan Dey, Danny Bonaduce, Jeremy Gelbwaks, Suzanne Crough, and Dave Madden were featured.

ABC made a bold move by negotiating an $8 million-per-year deal for the rights to telecast pro football games on Monday nights during the season. Previously, games had not been played regularly on anything but weekends. But the gamble paid off, and "Monday Night Football" has since become a fixture on the network's fall schedule each year. The premiere game was between the New York Jets and the Cleveland Browns. Keith Jackson, Howard Cosell, and Don Meredith were the original trio of commentators to handle the play-by-play. Frank Gifford replaced Jackson the next season.

"The Odd Couple" was a situation comedy based on Neil Simon's 1965 Broadway play, which three years later was made into a movie, before coming to ABC this season. The men forming this couple were a meticulous photographer and a messy *New York Herald* sportswriter who were both divorced and sharing apartment 1102 at 1049 Park Avenue, Manhattan. The opening of each episode concluded with the question, "Can two divorced men share an apartment without driving each other crazy?'' Viewers each week came to the decision that the answer must be ''no.'' Tony Randall was Felix Unger, the well-organized, compulsively clean half of the couple; Jack Klugman was the disorganized Oscar Madison. Interestingly, both Randall and Klugman appeared at different times in the road show company of the Broadway play: Randall played opposite Mickey Rooney and Klugman appeared with Art Carney. Other regulars in the series were Al Molinaro as Murray the cop; Garry Walberg as poker pal Speed (later he teamed with Klugman on ''Quincy''); and Larry Gelman (Dr. Bernie Tupperman on ''The Bob Newhart Show'' and Max Popkin in ''Needles and Pins'') as Vinnie, another poker pal. After five seasons the series entered syndication, where its following has grown.

Two other situation comedies debuted that were not only popular but were landmarks in quality programming. Mary Tyler Moore (Laura Petrie on ''The Dick Van Dyke Show'') became Mary Richards, a single, thirtyish career woman, on ''The Mary Tyler Moore Show.'' This program was an example of excellent adult comedy rarely matched in a weekly TV series. Mary epitomized the new woman of the new decade—ambitious, self-reliant, interested in romance but not desperate for marriage. She was warm, loving, and vulnerable, in short, a very real person. And this was why so many people enjoyed spending part of their Saturday nights with her during her seven years on CBS. The episodes often took place at Mary's office, the newsroom of station WJM-TV in Minneapolis. The other frequent setting was her small apartment at 119 North Weatherly.

Mary was surrounded by an excellent cast of characters: Lou Grant, her boss, played by Edward Asner (who later had his own ''Lou Grant'' series); Ted Baxter, the pompous news anchorman, played by Ted Knight (later to star in ''Too Close for Comfort''); Murray Slaughter, the head newswriter, played by Gavin MacLeod (later Capt. Merrill Stubing of ''The Love Boat''); Rhoda Morgenstern, Mary's upstairs neighbor and closest friend, played by Valerie Harper, who went on to star in the show's first spinoff, ''Rhoda''; and Phyllis Lindstrom, Mary's landlady, played by Cloris Leachman, who also went on to star in a spinoff, ''Phyllis.'' Other regulars later in the series were Sue Ann Nivens (Betty White) and Georgette Franklin Baxter (Georgia Engel). The series was still going strong when it left the network. To this day it is still entertaining fans in syndication.

On Tuesday evening, January 12, 1971, at 9:30 P.M. on CBS, without any advance publicity, a situation comedy series was quietly introduced that would change the course of TV comedy. ''All in the Family,'' based on the British comedy series ''Till Death Do Us Part,'' was created by Norman Lear and Bud Yorkin. The original pilot for the series was titled ''Those Were the Days'' and was shown to ABC—which did not like it. It took three years before Lear and Yorkin got a network commitment. But once they did, it was evident to all of America that this show was different. Why? Because the show opened new paths for comedy. Stories dealt with bigotry, prejudice, abortion, birth control, homosexuality, vasectomy, and other previously taboo subjects. Derogatory references to ethnic groups also became part of the ongoing dialogue, references such as Spic (Puerto Rican), Hebe (Jew), Spade (black), and Chink (Chinese). And for the first time audiences even heard the flushing of a toilet! Never before in a sitcom had there been any evidence of anyone going to the bathroom.

And who was the catalyst of all that this original series was? Archie Bunker. Played by Carroll O'Connor (a relatively unknown character actor), he was a lower-middle-class loading-dock foreman who lived at 704 Houser Street, in Queens, New York. Edith, played by Jean Stapleton (also relatively unknown), was Archie's wife, a dim-witted but sincere, loving, and honest person. Living with them were their daughter, Gloria, played by Sally Struthers, and her husband, Mike Stivic, played by Rob Reiner (son of Carl Reiner). Over the years many characters appeared in the series, and all but Archie left.

As the eighties began, the show's title changed to ''Archie Bunker's Place'' because he left his job and opened his own business, a local bar he bought from a friend. ''All in the Family'' became the No. 1 show on television in its first full season and remained in that position for five consecutive years. Thereafter, it was usually among the top 15 programs except for a much lower ranking during the 1982–83 season. This resulted in CBS canceling the show.

And as the season concluded, veteran entertainer Red Skelton, after 18 seasons, would say ''God bless'' to his weekly audience for the last time.

THE YOUNG REBELS: September 20, 1970–January 3, 1971, ABC. Rick Ely and Lou Gossett

BAREFOOT IN THE PARK: September 24, 1970–January 14, 1971, ABC. Scoey Mitchill and Tracy Reed

THE SMITH FAMILY: January 20, 1971–January 5, 1972, ABC. Henry Fonda (Chad Smith)

MATT LINCOLN: September 24, 1970–January 14, 1971, ABC. Vince Edwards (Matt Lincoln)

THE ODD COUPLE: Jack Klugman

THE ODD COUPLE: September 24, 1970–July 4, 1975, ABC. Tony Randall and Jack Klugman

NIGHT GALLERY: December 16, 1970–January 14, 1973, NBC. Rod Serling (host)

THE ODD COUPLE: Tony Randall and Jack Klugman

ALIAS SMITH AND JONES: January 21, 1971–January 13, 1973, ABC. Peter Duel (Smith) and Ben Murphy (Jones)

ALL IN THE FAMILY: Jean Stapleton, Sally Struthers, Rob Reiner, and Carroll O'Connor

ALL IN THE FAMILY: January 12, 1971–September 16, 1979, CBS. Jean Stapleton and Carroll O'Connor

ALL IN THE FAMILY: Jean Stapleton and Carroll O'Connor

ALL IN THE FAMILY: Carroll O'Connor and Sally Struthers (Gloria's wedding)

ALL IN THE FAMILY: Jean Stapleton and Carroll O'Connor

THE FLIP WILSON SHOW: September 17, 1970–June 27, 1974, NBC. Flip Wilson and Joe Namath (guest)

THE FLIP WILSON SHOW: Flip Wilson

THE INTERNS: September 18, 1970–September 10, 1971, CBS. Hal Frederick, Sandra Smith, Steve Brooks, Mike Farrell, and Christopher Stone

HEADMASTER: September 18, 1970–January 1, 1971, CBS. Andy Griffith

NANCY: September 17, 1970–January 7, 1971, NBC. Celeste Holm, John Fink, and Renne Jarrett (Nancy Smith)

MAKE ROOM FOR GRANDDADDY: September 23, 1970–September 2, 1971, ABC. Danny Thomas, Michael Hughes, Sherry Jackson, Marjorie Lord, and Hans Conried

THE MARY TYLER MOORE SHOW: September 19, 1970–September 3, 1977, CBS. Mary Tyler Moore and Edward Asner

THE PARTRIDGE FAMILY: September 25, 1970–August 31, 1974, ABC. *(Front)* David Cassidy, Shirley Jones, Susan Dey; *(back)* Brian Forster, Danny Bonaduce, Suzanne Crough

THE SONNY AND CHER COMEDY HOUR: August 1, 1971–May 29, 1974, CBS. Cher Bono and Sonny Bono (co-hosts)

THE MARY TYLER MOORE SHOW: Georgia Engle, Ted Knight, and Mary Tyler Moore

THE MARY TYLER MOORE SHOW: Mary Tyler Moore (Mary Richards)

SAN FRANCISCO INTERNATIONAL: October 28, 1970–August 25, 1971, NBC. Lloyd Bridges

THE MARY TYLER MOORE SHOW: *(Bottom)* Valerie Harper, Mary Tyler Moore, Cloris Leachman; *(top)* Ted Knight, Edward Asner, Gavin MacLeod

THE MARY TYLER MOORE SHOW: Mary Tyler Moore and Ted Knight

McCLOUD: September 16, 1970–August 28, 1977, NBC. Dennis Weaver (Sam McCloud)

ARNIE: September 19, 1970–September 9, 1972, CBS. Herschel Bernardi (Arnie Nuvo) and Roger Bowen

THE TIM CONWAY COMEDY HOUR: September 20, 1970–December 13, 1970, CBS. Danny Thomas (guest) and Tim Conway (host)

THE SILENT FORCE: September 21, 1970–January 11, 1971, ABC. Ed Nelson

THE SILENT FORCE: Ed Nelson, Perry Rodriguez, and Linda Day George

THE NEW ANDY GRIFFITH SHOW: January 8, 1971–May 21, 1971, CBS. Andy Griffith and Lee Meriwether

1971-72

Prime-time network television was notably different this year. The first reason was that the Federal Communications Commission (FCC) had ruled that the networks would be limited to three hours per night to present their programming fare (in addition to their traditional 30 minutes of news)—between 7:00 P.M. and 11:00 P.M. The half-hour relinquished, called "access time," was to be given back to the local affiliates. The FCC did not, however, specify which hours within the time frame were to be used. It was assumed that the traditional 7:00–7:30 P.M. weekday time slot for the news would remain. So this meant the networks would have to choose between 7:30 to 10:30 or 8:00 to 11:00. While this may not have seemed like much of a programming change, the effects in fact could be far reaching. If the earlier period was selected, the networks would place more emphasis on delivering shows oriented toward children. This would result in independent producers developing more adult material to fill the late-night access slot, from 10:30–11:00. Conversely, if the 8:00–11:00 period was selected, networks would lose the half-hour (7:30–8:00) of children's time and the local stations could fill it with more readily available material such as game shows, old network series in syndication, and new shows that had been turned down by the networks.

There was quite a bit of bandying about by ABC, CBS, and NBC before the season's start concerning an agreement on a uniform prime-time period. While each network had the choice of selecting its own hours within the FCC framework, it was understood that different prime-time hours for different networks could mean even more competition than already existed. After fully examining the situation, they agreed it would be in their best interest for prime time to be uniformly set from 8:00 to 11:00 P.M.

The second reason prime time looked different this season was that many old favorites were missing from the network lineups: "The Ed Sullivan Show" was

gone after 23 years; "Lassie," after 17 years; "Lawrence Welk," 16 years; the town of Mayberry, North Carolina, 11 years (eight seasons as part of "The Andy Griffith Show" and three as "Mayberry R.F.D."); "The Virginian" (and its recent title, "The Men from Shiloh"), 9 years; "The Beverly Hillbillies," 9 years; Jim Nabors as "Gomer Pyle" and as a variety show host, 7 years; "Green Acres," 6 years; "Hogan's Heroes," 6 years; "The Kraft Music Hall," 4 years; and "The High Chaparral," 4 years.

As a replacement, viewers would see six Hollywood stars make their weekly television debuts: Jimmy Stewart as an anthropologist in the sitcom "The Jimmy Stewart Show"; Shirley MacLaine as a photographer in the comedy series "Shirley's World"; Anthony Quinn as a city mayor in the hour-long dramatic series "The Man and the City"; George Kennedy as a Catholic priest in the 60-minute drama "Sarge"; Glenn Ford as a sheriff in "Cade's County"; and Rock Hudson as a police commissioner in the drama "McMillan and Wife." All but the last failed to survive the season.

Over all, few programs would do well enough to return next year, and only the following six had enough success to run at least three seasons.

Last year the creative team of Norman Lear and Bud Yorkin had introduced their first situation-comedy series, "All in the Family." This year they introduced viewers to the biggest new hit of the season, "Sanford and Son," which, like "Family," was also based on a British series ("Steptoe and Son"). "Sanford and Son" starred veteran comedian Redd Foxx as Fred Sanford and Demond Wilson as his son, Lamont, both junk dealers. Fred was sixty-five and cantankerous, and he refused to retire; Lamont was thirty-four and wanted to get out of the junk business for something better. Their business (and residence) was at 9114 South Central, in Los Angeles, and members of this season's cast included Slappy White as Melvin, Don Bexley as Bubba, and Lynn Hamilton as Donna Harris. The show

was an immediate hit, placing 6th this season. In the succeeding three years it did even better, ranking 2nd or 3rd. The series was on for five years on NBC and was responsible for two short-lived spinoffs; "Grady" in 1975 and "The Sanford Arms" in 1977. It can still be seen today in syndication.

"The NBC Mystery Movie" was a successful trio of dramatic series. "McCloud," which premiered last season, was joined this season by two other shows that were to have long runs. Peter Falk starred as "Columbo" (he did not have a first name), a lieutenant in the Central Homicide Division of the Los Angeles Police Department. Each episode opened with viewers witnessing a dastardly crime, usually a murder. Then onto the scene came Columbo to unravel the evil deed through a meticulous investigation of every shred of evidence as he matched wits with his sophisticated adversaries. But the fun in all this was that his working procedure was totally opposite the appearance he projected: Columbo acted like a bumbler, dressed in a dirty old trench coat, and drove a beat-up old car. All this was a ploy to give the culprit a false sense of security. The lieutenant always got his man during the seven years he was on the network.

Rock Hudson, in his first TV role, starred as San Francisco Police Commissioner Stewart McMillan, a polished, urbane individual who was dedicated to his profession, in "McMillan and Wife." Susan St. James co-starred as his effervescent wife, Sally, who was always getting herself involved in his cases. Others in the original cast were Nancy Walker as Mildred, the McMillan's maid, and John Schuck (later of "Holmes and Yoyo") as the commissioner's aide, Sgt. Charles Enright. McMillan solved cases on NBC for six years.

Frank Cannon's appearance set him apart from TV's traditional private eyes. He was heavyset (he really loved high-caloric culinary delights), balding, and older than most in this group, quite a change from what television audiences were accustomed to. Veteran actor William Conrad played Cannon, and while viewers may not have recognized him, they were probably familiar with his voice. Earlier, he had been the narrator of "The Fugitive" and "The Invaders," and a cartoon voice on "Rocky and His Friends." Earlier still, Conrad was the voice of Marshal Dillon on "Gunsmoke"—the radio series. "Cannon" ran a total of 96 episodes in the five years it was on CBS.

"The New Dick Van Dyke Show," like the original, was created by Carl Reiner. Van Dyke was one of CBS's big stars during the sixties and the network was anxious to have him back in another sitcom. This new series was on for three seasons and went through two formats. The first, lasting two years, had Van Dyke playing Dick Preston, a talk-show host in Phoenix, Arizona. For the final year, the scene switched to Hollywood, where Preston became an actor on a soap opera. Throughout, his TV family remained intact, with Hope Lange (formerly of "The Ghost and Mrs. Muir") as his wife, Jenny, and Angela Powell as his daughter, Annie.

Finally, "Owen Marshall, Counselor at Law" was an hour-long dramatic show starring Arthur Hill in the title role. Marshall was a widower with a twelve-year-old daughter, Melissa, played by Christine Matchett. With a practice in Santa Barbara, California, Marshall was a very warm, soft-spoken, considerate, and compassionate attorney, unlike other more flamboyant, outspoken lawyers on TV at the time. Others in the cast included Lee Majors (who after two seasons left to achieve stardom in "The Six Million Dollar Man") as his associate, Jess Brandon, and Joan Darling as Frieda Krause, his secretary/assistant. ABC aired 69 episodes during the program's three years.

THE GOOD LIFE: September 18, 1971–January 8, 1972, NBC. Larry Hagman and Donna Mills

THE MAN AND THE CITY: September 15, 1971–January 5, 1972, ABC. Anthony Quinn

THE CHICAGO TEDDY BEARS: September 17, 1971–December 17, 1971, CBS. John Banner and Dean Jones

THE CHICAGO TEDDY BEARS: Sarah Fankboner (guest) and Art Metrano

THE PARTNERS: September 18, 1971–September 8, 1972, NBC. Rupert Crosse and Don Adams

THE ABC COMEDY HOUR: January 12, 1972–April 5, 1972, ABC. (Back) George Kirby; (front) Fred Travalena, Frank Gorshin, Raymond Burr (guest), Rich Little, Joe Baker, and Marilyn Michaels

OWEN MARSHALL, COUNSELOR AT LAW: September 16, 1971–August 24, 1974, ABC. *(Front)* Christine Matchett, Arthur Hill (Owen Marshall), Joan Darling; *(back)* Reni Santoni, Lee Majors

COLUMBO: September 15, 1971–September 1, 1978, NBC. Peter Falk (Lieutenant Columbo)

THE JIMMY STEWART SHOW: September 19, 1971–August 27, 1972, NBC. Jonathan Daly, Jimmy Stewart, Julie Adams, Ellen Geer

COLUMBO: Peter Falk and Robert Conrad (guest)

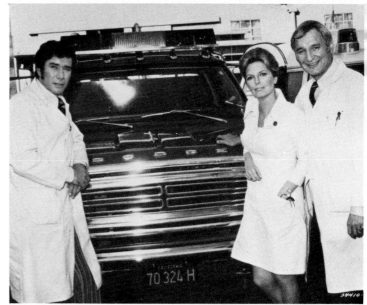

EMERGENCY!: January 22, 1972–September 3, 1977, NBC. Kevin Tighe and Randolph Mantooth

EMERGENCY!: Robert Fuller, Julie London, and Bobby Troup

SANFORD AND SON: Redd Foxx and Demond Wilson

SANFORD AND SON: January 14, 1972–September 2, 1977, NBC. Demond Wilson and Redd Foxx (Fred Sanford)

SANFORD AND SON: Redd Foxx and LaWanda Page

ANNON: September 14, 1971–September 19, 1976, CBS. William Conrad (Frank Cannon)

CANNON: Leslie Charleson (guest) and William Conrad

THE DON RICKLES SHOW: January 14, 1972–May 26, 1972, CBS. Joyce Van Patten, Louise Sorel, and Don Rickles

ARGE: George Kennedy and Ricardo ontalban (guest)

DEPARTMENT S: 1971, syndicated. Peter Wyngarde, Joel Fablani, and Rosemary Nichols

ARGE: September 21, 1971–January 11, 1972, NBC. George Kennedy (Patrick "Sarge" avanaugh) and Sally Shockley

LONGSTREET: September 16, 1971–August 10, 1972, ABC. James Franciscus (Michael Longstreet) and Pax

McMILLAN AND WIFE: September 29, 1971–August 21, 1977, NBC. Susan St. James and Rock Hudson (Stewart McMillan)

McMILLAN AND WIFE: Rock Hudson and Nancy Walker

O'HARA, UNITED STATES TREASURY: September 17, 1971–September 8, 1972, CBS. David Janssen (Jim O'Hara)

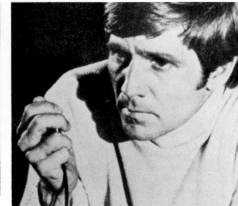

THE SIXTH SENSE: January 15, 1972–December 30, 1972, ABC. Gary Collins

McMILLAN AND WIFE: Susan St. James and Rock Hudson

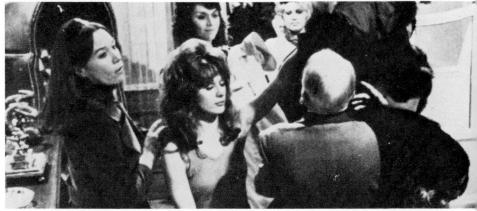

SHIRLEY'S WORLD: September 14, 1971–January 5, 1972, ABC. Shirley MacLaine *(left)* (Shirley Logan)

1972-73

The nation and the world encountered both triumph and tragedy during the period that went from late last season to approximately the midpoint of the new TV year.

In this national-election year, as the major political parties geared up for their quadrennial conventions, Alabama Gov. George C. Wallace, who had become a viable candidate, was seriously wounded in an assassination attempt. Television brought into America's living rooms a vivid reminder of four years earlier, when another presidential candidate—Robert Kennedy—was killed at the hands of an assassin. At the summer conventions, the networks provided their usual extensive coverage of these Republican and Democratic happenings, which this time were less eventful than those of the previous decade.

President Nixon, accompanied by television cameras and the top network newsmen—CBS's Walter Cronkite, NBC's John Chancellor, and ABC's Howard K. Smith—made two historic journeys this year. The first was to inscrutable China to meet with its leaders. The trip was planned with a meticulous efficiency that enabled Nixon to land in Peking during prime-time hours and be seen, live, in the United States via satellite. The coverage of his travels gave Americans their first opportunity to see this sheltered and largely unknown land. Then, on his return home, the president, who knew very well how to maximize the use of TV, stopped off for a few hours in Anchorage, Alaska, so that his arrival in Washington, D.C., would again take place live on prime-time television.

Nixon's second trip was to the Soviet Union to meet with its leaders and sign a nuclear-arms-limitation treaty. As the first American president to visit Moscow, he again shrewdly made maximum use of television throughout the trip.

Just before the new season, Munich, West Germany, hosted the Summer Olympics. ABC's "Wide World of Sports" team, headed by Jim McKay and Howard Cosell, was there to cover this world event for American television.

But the proceedings were completely disrupted when tragedy struck: a group of Arab terrorists invaded the Olympic Village, killed two Israeli athletes, and seized nine members of Israel's Olympic team. The ABC sports team became an on-the-spot news team to cover this calamity, which ultimately resulted in the death of 11 Israelies and 4 terrorists in a shoot-out with West German police and soldiers at the Munich airport.

In the November election, Nixon won, as expected, in a landslide over George McGovern. This resulted in relatively easy election-night coverage for the networks. The only noticeable change to viewers was David Brinkley in the NBC anchor booth without Chet Huntley.

Within several weeks, another president was in the news. Harry Truman, America's first televised chief executive, died on December 27, 1972. And a few weeks later, the Vietnam Peace Agreement was signed and the nation's current chief executive joined millions of other Americans to watch the ceremonies from Paris on television.

By this season, color had really caught on. For the first time color-set sales exceeded those of black and white, and 52 percent of American households were now watching color TV. Television over all was more than ever a part of daily life. The average amount of time per day spent watching the medium now exceeded six hours, also for the first time.

What caused this viewing increase was the novelty of color and the better quality of programming, particularly in the sitcom category. In the last two seasons, some of the best comedies in history had debuted: "All in the Family," "The Mary Tyler Moore Show," "The Odd Couple," and "Sanford and Son." Three of the shows that made up this year's fare were just as impressive: "Maude," "The Bob Newhart Show," and "M*A*S*H." Another show that might have been part of this group was "Bridget Loves Bernie," starring Meredith Baxter and David Birney. It was an ethnic comedy that ended up the

season in fifth place in the ratings but was canceled because this series about the married life of a Jewish boy and an Irish Catholic girl created somewhat of a furor among religious groups, primarily Jewish, regarding the series' "condoning" interfaith marriages. Interestingly enough, Birney and Baxter did get married in real life.

"Maude" was the first spinoff from the current No. 1 "All in the Family." This was another of Norman Lear's breakthrough shows dealing with sex, birth control, unwanted pregnancy, menopause, abortion, death, etc., in the funny, intelligent way viewers had come to expect from a Lear series. Maude Findlay, played by Beatrice Arthur (an accomplished stage and film actress), first appeared in "Family" as Edith Bunker's cousin. She was highly opinionated, liberal, and loud, a match for her bigoted cousin-in-law, Archie. "Maude" immediately became a top show (ranked fourth) and was among the highest-rated programs in its first four seasons. She lived with her fourth husband, Walter, played by Bill Macy (a relatively unknown actor in films), and her divorced daughter, Carol, played by Adrienne Barbeau. Others in the cast were Conrad Bain (later Phillip Drummond in "Diff'rent Strokes") as next-door neighbor Dr. Arthur Harmon; Rue McClanahan as Arthur's wife, Vivian, and Maude's best friend; and Esther Rolle as Florida Evans, the Findlays' maid. The series ran six seasons on CBS.

Comedian Bob Newhart's second time around in television was a big success. He played psychologist Bob Hartley on "The Bob Newhart Show." Suzanne Pleshette was his wife, Emily, a third-grade schoolteacher; Bill Daily was the Hartleys' divorced neighbor and friend, Howard Borden, an airline navigator; and Peter Bonerz was another friend, orthodontist Jerry Robinson, who shared the same office floor and receptionist, Carol Kester Bondurant (Marcia Wallace), with Bob. During the show's early years it was among the top 20 programs. In total, it ran for six seasons on

CBS. Today it can be seen in syndication.

The 4077th Mobile Army Surgical Hospital in Korea during the Korean War was the setting for "M*A*S*H," an antiwar comedy series based on the 1970 hit movie, and earlier novel, of the same name. The show started quietly this season, managing to rank in the top 50, but a change of day and time elevated it to the No. 4 spot next season and it remained a top-10 program thereafter. The series had a very large cast over the years, and only three characters were with the show throughout its entire run: Capt. Benjamin Franklin "Hawkeye" Pierce (Alan Alda), Maj. Margaret "Hot Lips" Houlihan (Loretta Swit), and Father Mulcahy (first George Morgan and then William Christopher). With irreverence and humor, "M*A*S*H" looked at war as no other show ever had before, and its success lasted more than three times longer than the war it depicted. There were 251 episodes in the 11 years it was on CBS, the last of which was the highest-rated series episode in TV history. Today it is just as popular as ever in syndication.

Six dramatic series debuted this season that had viewers tuning in for years.

Buddy Ebsen began a long run as a soft-spoken private detective in "Barnaby Jones." This was quite a departure for the veteran actor who, for many years, had been hillbilly millionaire Jed Clampett on "The Beverly Hillbillies." The departure point for the series was that Jones, who had his own detective agency, had retired and turned the business over to his son. While investigating a case, his son was killed, and Jones came out of retirement to find his murderer. Jones's daughter-in-law, Betty, played by Lee Meriwether, became his assistant and helped him run the Los Angeles agency. Barnaby Jones tracked down many a criminal during his seven years on CBS.

ABC introduced two California-based police series. "The Streets of San Francisco" starred Karl Malden and Michael Douglas as the streetwise veteran detective, Lt. Mike Stone, and his young, college-educated partner, Assistant Inspector Steve Keller. The team worked the streets for five years. "The Rookies" was a little different than most shows of this genre. The emphasis here was on the trials and tribulations of the early years on the police force. Featured were Gerald S. O'Loughlin as Lt. Ed Ryker, the commanding officer who helped mold rookie cops into effective police officers. Georg Stanford Brown, Michael Ontkean, and Sam Melville played the orig-

inal "Rookies"—Terry Webster, Willie Gillis, and Mike Danko. The series lasted four years, with 68 episodes produced.

Jefferson County, Virginia, during the Depression years, was where Earl Hamner, Jr., writer and storyteller, grew up. His experiences in a close-knit, loving family were the basis for "The Waltons." This large-cast show featured Ralph Waite as John Walton; Michael Learned as Olivia Walton; Will Geer as Grandpa Zeb, John's father; Ellen Corby as Grandma Esther, John's mother; and Richard Thomas as John Boy, whose budding career as a writer gave the series its narrative story line. There were six other children in the large Walton family: Judy Norton was Mary Ellen, David W. Harper was Jim-Bob, Jon Walmsley was Jason, Mary Elizabeth McDonough was Erin, Eric Scott was Ben, and Kami Cotler was Elizabeth. No one at the network thought this family drama would catch on so fast, but it did almost immediately. The series was in the top 20 in its first five seasons and ran almost nine years on CBS. The program's success spawned several family-drama series in this decade: "Apple's Way," "The Family Holvak," "The Fitzpatricks," "Little House on the Prairie," "Eight Is Enough," and "The New Land."

"Emergency!" (starting its first full season) was the story of a team of paramedics who worked out of Squad 51 in the Los Angeles County Fire Department. Created by Jack Webb and produced in a straightforward dramatic style, it featured Kevin Tighe as paramedic Roy DeSoto and Randolph Mantooth as paramedic John Gage. Also featured were Robert Fuller as Dr. Kelly Brackett, Julie London as Nurse Dixie

McCall, and Bobby Troup as Dr. Joe Early. This season and the next it was positioned opposite TV's No. 1 show and did relatively well, placing among the top 35 programs. The series was on NBC for five years before going into syndication with the title "Emergency One."

"Kung Fu" was a unique Western that was seen on ABC for three years. Its lead character was a monk born in China, raised in the Shaolin Temple, and trained in the martial arts. He was in the American West in the 1870s because he had fled his homeland after killing a member of the Chinese royal family. While searching for his long-lost brother, he was pursued by Chinese agents and American bounty hunters. The series centered on his experiences fighting injustice wherever he found it while continually on the run. David Carradine played the lead character, Kwai Chang Caine.

INVASION: UFO: 1972, syndicated. Ed Bishop

THE SANDY DUNCAN SHOW: September 17, 1972–December 31, 1972, CBS. Sandy Duncan

HERE WE GO AGAIN: January 20, 1973–June 23, 1973, ABC. Nina Talbot

TEMPERATURES RISING: September 12, 1972–August 29, 1974, ABC. James Whitmore, Nancy Fox, Joan Van Ark, Reva Rose, and Cleavon Little

BRIDGET LOVES BERNIE: September 16, 1972–September 8, 1973, CBS. David Birney (Bernie) and Meredith Baxter (Bridget)

TEMPERATURES RISING: Alice Ghostley and Cleavon Little

THE PAUL LYNDE SHOW: September 13, 1972–September 8, 1973, ABC. Paul Lynde and Elizabeth Allen

THE STREETS OF SAN FRANCISCO: September 16, 1972–June 23, 1977, ABC. Michael Douglas and Karl Malden

MAUDE: September 12, 1972–April 29, 1978, CBS. Beatrice Arthur (Maude) and Bill Macy

MAUDE: Bill Macy, Beatrice Arthur, Conrad Bain, and Rue McClanahan

MAUDE: Beatrice Arthur and Esther Rolle

MAUDE: Bill Macy, Beatrice Arthur, and Adrienne Barbeau

MAUDE: Beatrice Arthur and Rue McClanahan

MAUDE: Hermione Baddeley and J. Patrick O'Malley

GHOST STORY: September 15, 1972–December 22, 1972, NBC. Sebastian Cabot (host)

HEC RAMSEY: October 8, 1972–August 25, 1974, NBC. Richard Boone (Hec Ramsey), Susan Keener (guest), and Harry Morgan

ANNA AND THE KING: September 17, 1972–December 31, 1972, CBS. Lisa Lu (Yul Brynner was the king and Samantha Eggar was Anna)

SEARCH: September 12, 1972–August 29, 1973, NBC. Hugh O'Brian

ABC WIDE WORLD OF ENTERTAINMENT: January 8, 1973–January 10, 1976, ABC. Pat Paulsen (guest)

M*A*S*H: Wayne Rogers

M*A*S*H: Alan Alda

M*A*S*H: Mike Farrell

M*A*S*H: Gary Burghoff

M*A*S*H: Harry Morgan

M*A*S*H: David Ogden Stiers

M*A*S*H: September 17, 1972–February 28, 1983, CBS. Loretta Swit, Alan Alda, Wayne Rogers, McLean Stevenson, Larry Linville, and Gary Burghoff (early cast)

THE PROTECTORS: 1972–74, syndicated. Robert Vaughn, Nyree Dawn Porter, and Tony Anholt

M*A*S*H: *(First row)* Larry Linville, Harry Morgan, Gary Burghoff; *(second row)* Loretta Swit, Alan Alda, Mike Farrell; *(third row)* Jamie Farr, William Christopher (later cast)

M*A*S*H: Loretta Swit and Jamie Farr

THE DELPHI BUREAU: October 5, 1972–September 1, 1973, ABC. Laurence Luckinbill and Robin Strasser (guest)

M*A*S*H: Gary Burghoff and McLean Stevenson

M*A*S*H: Loretta Swit and Larry Linville

THE JULIE ANDREWS SHOW: September 13, 1972–April 28, 1973, ABC. Julie Andrews (hostess)

A TOUCH OF GRACE: January 20, 1973–June 16, 1973, ABC. *(Seated)* Shirley Booth (Grace Simpson) and Marion Mercer; *(standing)* J. Patrick O'Malley and Wayne Berlinger

THE NEW BILL COSBY SHOW: September 11, 1972–May 7, 1973, CBS. Don Knotts (guest) and Bill Cosby

THE LITTLE PEOPLE (THE BRIAN KEITH SHOW): September 15, 1972–August 30, 1974, NBC. Brian Keith, Shelley Fabares, and unknown actor

THE NEW BILL COSBY SHOW: Bill Cosby and Mark Spitz (guest)

BARNABY JONES: January 28, 1973–September 4, 1980, CBS. Buddy Ebsen (Barnaby Jones)

BARNABY JONES: Jill Martin (guest) and Lee Meriwether

THE ROOKIES: September 11, 1972–June 29, 1976, ABC. *(Seated)* Gerald S. O'Loughlin; *(standing)* Michael Ontkean, Sam Melville, and Georg Stanford Brown

BARNABY JONES: Buddy Ebsen and Lee Meriwether

THE WALTONS: September 14, 1972–August 13, 1981, CBS. Michael Learned and Ralph Waite

THE WALTONS: *(Bottom)* Michael Learned; *(top)* Richard Thomas, Will Geer, Ellen Corby

THE CORNER BAR: June 21, 1972–September 7, 1973, ABC. Bill Fiore, Anne Meara, Gene Roche, Shimen Ruskin, and J.J. Barry

LOVE THY NEIGHBOR: June 15, 1973–September 19, 1973, ABC. Joyce Bulifant and Ron Masak

THE ADVENTURER: 1972, syndicated. Catherine Schell (guest) and Gene Barry

THE BOB NEWHART SHOW: September 16, 1972–August 26, 1978, CBS. Marcia Wallace, Bob Newhart, Peter Bonerz, Suzanne Pleshette, and Bill Daily

THE BOB NEWHART SHOW: Marcia Wallace and Bob Newhart

THE BOB NEWHART SHOW: Peter Bonerz, Tom Poston (guest), and Bob Newhart

THE BOB NEWHART SHOW: Jack Riley and unknown actor

ESCAPE: February 11, 1973–April 1, 1973, NBC. Cameron Mitchell and Marion Ross in "Lost"

KUNG FU: October 14, 1972–June 28, 1975, ABC. Keye Luke and David Carradine

KUNG FU: David Carradine

1973-74

On June 17, 1972, five men were arrested for breaking into the Democratic National Headquarters in the Watergate office building in Washington, D.C. This incident was dismissed by a White House spokesman as nothing more than a "third-rate burglary attempt." And when George McGovern attempted to make it an issue during the presidential campaign, it was called a political ploy by a candidate who had no chance of winning at the polls. But two newspaper reporters from the *Washington Post*, Bob Woodward and Carl Bernstein, had been doggedly uncovering bits and pieces of facts that did suggest a tie between the break-in and the White House. And by late 1972, television became actively involved when CBS News began its own investigation. Its efforts enhanced the *Post*'s disclosures and resulted in a two-part report on the evening news with Walter Cronkite. The combined effort of the two news organizations culminated in the biggest TV event of 1973. For 11 weeks television brought the Senate Watergate hearings to a national viewing audience.

Almost 300 hours of rotating coverage (each day one network would take its turn telecasting the hearings) was provided by the networks. The combined estimated cost to them was $10 million in lost advertising and air-time revenue. On the plus side, audience surveys indicated that 85 percent of the nation's households watched all or part of at least one day's proceedings.

As in the celebrated Army-McCarthy hearings of almost two decades earlier, interest was low initially. But the constant exposure bred increased familiarity with the personalities and issues involved, and attention heightened and viewing increased. The hearings also helped the networks fill a programming void that existed before the start of this season. Because of a strike by television writers in the spring, new material, such as unsold series pilots, was not available for summer viewing.

Additionally, by the time this work shutdown ended in June, the new fall schedule was already affected. As a result, the networks had no choice but to gradually introduce the season over a period of a month; new shows and returning programs were aired as they became available. This was a throwback to more than a decade earlier, when fall lineups were last unveiled in a similar manner.

Filling the gap during this period were news programs, specials, and even old series. It was nearly November before the season had settled in and all the new entries had aired. It turned out, though, to be a poor year for new programming: only a handful of shows would survive the season. But of these, five not only survived, they enjoyed good runs.

Two in this group were police shows. The last new series of the fall schedule to premiere wound up first in the ratings among the group. "Kojak," starring Telly Savalas as Police Lt. Theo Kojak, had its genesis in a 1973 made-for-television movie, "The Marcus-Nelson Murders." Kojak worked out of the run-down Manhattan South Precinct, where his friend and associate Frank McNeil, played by Dan Frazer, was the commanding officer. The lieutenant had a loyal group working for him: Det. Bobby Crocker (Kevin Dobson); Det. Stavros (George Savalas, Telly's real-life brother); Det. Rizzo (Vince Conti); and Det. Saperstein (Mark Russell). The series, which presented a realistic look at police work, had a five-year run on CBS, then went into syndication.

The other police series was simply titled "Police Story." It was a quality anthology series that gave an even truer view of law enforcement. This was so because of the efforts of its creator, Joseph Wambaugh, a former Los Angeles police officer and the author of best-selling police novels including "The New Centurions." There were no regular cast members in the series, which would spin off two other police shows: "Police Woman" and "Joe Forrester." NBC aired the series for four years.

Two others in this group were situation comedies. With all of the interesting characters in the new wave of early-seventies sitcoms, it was inevitable that a spinoff from one show would in turn spin off one of its own. "Good Times" was the first example, having descended from "All in the Family" by way of "Maude." It was Maude's maid, Florida Evans, played by Esther Rolle, who got her own series. The story was set in Chicago and concerned itself with Florida, her husband, James, played by John Amos, who was never steadily employed, and their three children. The Evanses were a low-income black family trying hard to make ends meet and hoping to build a future from their apartment in the ghetto. The children were: James Jr. (J. J.), the jive-talking oldest son who used the catchword "Dyn-O-Mite!" (Jimmie Walker); Thelma, the teenage daughter (BernNadette Stanis); and Michael, the youngest (Ralph Carter). Jimmie Walker caught on quickly with viewers and became a much-sought-after personality for TV appearances and commercials. The series ran for five seasons on CBS before going into syndication.

For more than nine years (as of this writing) on Tuesday nights at 8:00 P.M., ABC viewers have welcomed into their homes a song that begins: "Sunday, Monday, Happy Days . . . Tuesday, Wednesday, Happy Days . . . " This is the theme of "Happy Days," a very successful sitcom about teenage life, and beyond, in the fifties. The program debuted after a film about the era, *American Graffiti* featuring Ron Howard, was enthusiastically received by audiences in 1973. However, the series was based on a skit titled "Love and the Happy Day" that appeared on "Love, American Style" (ABC) in 1972, starring Ron Howard as Richie Cunningham and Anson Williams as Potsie Weber. Both Howard and Williams repeated their roles for the series. Others in this large-cast show are: Henry Winkler as Arthur "Fonzie" Fonzarelli, Richie's "cool" friend; Tom Bosley as Howard Cunningham, Richie's father; Marion Ross as Marion Cunningham, his mother; Donny Most as Ralph Malph, another friend;

Erin Moran as Joanie Cunningham, Richie's kid sister; Pat Morita (as Arnold) then Al Molinaro (as Alfred Delvecchio) as the owner of Arnold's, the local hangout; and Scott Baio as Chachi Arcola, Fonzie's young cousin. Today, "Happy Days" continues to be one of the highest-rated programs on TV.

The final solid success this year was the fantasy adventure series "The Six Million Dollar Man," which was based on *Cyborg*, a novel by Martin Caidin. This show about an American astronaut with a superhuman body starred Lee Majors as Col. Steve Austin. During a training mission, Austin was severely injured and was rebuilt using futuristic cybernetic medical science, at a cost of $6 million to the government. He was equipped with two bionic legs, a bionic arm, and a bionic eye, all of which made him much more capable than any normal human being. Austin was employed by the Office of Scientific Information (OSI), a government agency, and given an assortment of treacherous assignments. The show was initially introduced as a monthly feature. By midseason it had become a weekly series. Others in the cast were Richard Anderson as Oscar Goldman, Austin's boss, and first Alan Oppenheimer then Martin E. Brooks as Dr. Rudy Wells, OSI's aeromedical surgeon. The series ran for five seasons on ABC before going into syndication.

TOMA: October 6, 1973–September 6, 1974, ABC. Tony Musante, Simon Oakland, and Susan Strasberg

TOMA: Tony Musante (David Toma)

APPLE'S WAY: February 10, 1974–January 12, 1975, CBS. Muffin, Ronny Cox (George Apple), Patti Cohoon, and Bijoux

BOB AND CAROL AND TED AND ALICE: September 26, 1973–November 7, 1973, ABC. (Clockwise) Robert Urich (Bob), Ann Archer (Carol), Anita Gillette (Alice), and David Spielberg (Ted)

CHASE: September 11, 1973–August 28, 1974, NBC. James McEachin (guest) and Mitchell Ryan (Capt. Chase Reddick)

DIANA: September 10, 1973–January 7, 1974, NBC. Diana Rigg (Diana Smythe)

THE NEW PERRY MASON: September 16, 1973–January 27, 1974, CBS. Monte Markham (Perry Mason)

THE NEW PERRY MASON: Albert Stratton

KOJAK: October 24, 1973–April 15, 1978, CBS. Telly Savalas (Lt. Theo Kojak)

KOJAK: Dan Frazer, George Savalas, and Kevin Dobson

TENAFLY: October 10, 1973–August 6, 1974, NBC. Ramon Bieri (guest) and James McEachin (Harry Tenafly)

TONY ORLANDO AND DAWN: July 3, 1974–December 26, 1976, CBS. Tony Orlando, Dawn (Joyce Vincent Wilson and Telma Hopkins)

HAWKINS: Jimmy Stewart

TONY ORLANDO AND DAWN: Dawn (Joyce Vincent Wilson and Telma Hopkins) with Tony Orlando

HAWKINS: October 2, 1973–September 3, 1974, CBS. Jimmy Stewart (Billy Jim Hawkins)

273

THE SIX MILLION DOLLAR MAN: Lee Majors and Richard Anderson

THE SIX MILLION DOLLAR MAN: January 18, 1974–March 6, 1978, ABC. Lee Majors

LOVE STORY: October 3, 1973–January 2, 1974, NBC. Kurt Russell and Jan Smithers in an episode

THE MAGICIAN: October 2, 1973–May 20, 1974, NBC. Bill Bixby

POLICE STORY: September 25, 1973–August 23, 1977, NBC. David Groh and Don Meredith in an episode

ADAM'S RIB: September 14, 1973–December 28, 1973, ABC. Ken Howard (Adam Bonner) and Blythe Danner

POLICE STORY: Edward Asner and David Huffman in an episode

SHAFT: October 9, 1973–August 20, 1974, CBS. Richard Roundtree (John Shaft)

HAPPY DAYS: January 15, 1974–present, ABC. *(Front)* Donny Most, Erin Moran, Marion Ross, Ron Howard; *(back)* Henry Winkler, Tom Bosley, Anson Williams (early cast)

HAPPY DAYS: Henry Winkler

HAPPY DAYS: Ron Howard

HAPPY DAYS: Al Molinaro, Scott Baio, Henry Winkler, Ted McGinley, Lynda Goodfriend, Marion Ross, and Tom Bosley (later cast)

LOTSA LUCK: September 10, 1973–May 24, 1974, NBC. *(Foreground)* Dom DeLuise, *(background)* Beverly Sanders, Wynn Irwin, and Kathleen Freeman

CALUCCI'S DEPARTMENT: September 14, 1973–December 28, 1973, CBS. James Coco (Joe Calucci) and Jim Starey (guest)

GOOD TIMES: February 1, 1974–February 1, 1979, CBS. Esther Rolle, Jimmie Walker, and Ralph Carter

GOOD TIMES: Charles Siebert (guest), Esther Rolle, and Jimmie Walker

GOOD TIMES: Esther Rolle and John Amos

NEEDLES AND PINS: September 21, 1973–December 28, 1973, NBC. Deirdre Lenihan and Norman Fell

NEEDLES AND PINS: Deirdre Lenihan and Norman Fell

THE GIRL WITH SOMETHING EXTRA: September 14, 1973–May 24, 1974, NBC. Sally Field

ROLL OUT: October 5, 1973–January 4, 1974, CBS. Stu Gilliam and Hilly Hicks

THE GIRL WITH SOMETHING EXTRA: John Davidson and Sally Field

THE COWBOYS: February 6, 1974–August 14, 1974, ABC. A. Martinez

1974-75

Watergate and Richard Nixon continued to dominate the news all through last season, until just before the start of this TV year. While voices around him were growing more vociferous for his impeachment, the president once again turned to television to appeal directly to the people. In an effort to overcome the negative attitude that was rising against him, he embarked on a national speaking tour, though appearing only before sympathetic audiences, with the networks providing full live coverage.

In one of his most effective speeches, Nixon urged the country to move on to more important business and put Watergate aside. During this speech he displayed notebooks that contained pages of edited transcripts of most of the White House tapes requested by the Senate Watergate committee and the courts. He felt that this action showed his willingness to cooperate with the various ongoing investigations and proved that he had nothing to hide. But while this was a very successful speech initially, its results were diminished once the text of the transcripts was examined. Network reporters covering Watergate scrutinized them, prompting all three networks to air specials featuring the reading of transcript excerpts.

These programs, which resulted in a different interpretation of the facts, greatly damaged the president's image —and former staunch supporters began calling for his resignation. Others continued to call for impeachment, indicating that they felt the president would never heed the call to step down. The House Judiciary committee decided to open its final deliberations on impeachment to television but ruled that first it would hear witnesses behind closed doors. Meanwhile, the president, trying to save his sinking ship of state, traveled to the Middle East and Russia, with TV cameras trailing along. He was met with great fanfare and enthusiastic crowds, particularly in Egypt, Syria, and Israel. From there he went to Moscow. Throughout the trip, Nixon projected the image of a great world leader, while at home his political base crumbled.

Upon his return, the reality of impeachment was evident. The networks responded, as they did a year earlier, by setting up rotating coverage of the Judiciary committee's debate. But on August 8 at 9:00 P.M., Nixon appeared on television to announce his resignation, effective the following day at noon. Adhering to his penchant for television, he wanted cameras there in those final hours, as he bid farewell to staff and friends. When Vice-President Gerald R. Ford was sworn in as the 38th president, he declared that "our long national nightmare is over." The nation, its spirits lifted, would again be moving forward as the networks prepared to open their new fall season.

Helping to keep those spirits up would be four new comedies joining this decade's already successful new-wave sitcoms, which included "All in the Family," "The Mary Tyler Moore Show," "The Odd Couple," "Sanford and Son," "Maude," and "M*A*S*H." This meant that now almost a dozen programs were providing well-written humor and entertainment, and that TV was going through a period of unmatched quality in this genre.

Rhoda Morgenstern originally was an insecure, plumpish brunette living in Minneapolis. She was always looking for a man while continually trying to lose weight. That's when most viewers first met her on "The Mary Tyler Moore Show" in 1970. Now, four years later, she was slim, glamorous, confident, and living in New York—but still single. Valerie Harper starred as both the old and new "Rhoda" in this, the first spinoff from the Moore show. In the early episodes, she met and fell in love with Joe Gerard, played by David Groh, and within weeks of the premiere, they were married in a special hour show that enhanced the series' already-strong ratings. Others featured were Nancy Walker (Rosie, the Bounty commercial spokesperson) as Rhoda's mother, Ida; Harold Gould as her father, Martin; Julie Kavner as her sister, Brenda; and Loren-

zo Music, the series co-producer, as the heard, but never seen, Carlton, the doorman. The show was an immediate hit, ranking sixth this season and eighth next year. After four years on CBS, the series entered syndication.

Ed Brown and Chico Rodriguez were the principal characters in the highest-rated new show of the year, "Chico and the Man." The series starred veteran character actor and vaudevillian Jack Albertson as the cynical and sarcastic garage owner, Ed Brown, and stand-up comic Freddie Prinze, newcomer to television, as the high-spirited young Mexican-American who worked for him. East Los Angeles was the setting for this comedy about these two who were from radically different backgrounds. The show was created by James Komack, who himself was a sitcom performer in "The Courtship of Eddie's Father" and "Hennesey." In the middle of the show's third season, Prinze died at the age of twenty-two, an apparent suicide victim. NBC decided to continue the series incorporating other characters but not replacing Prinze's character. One season after the tragedy, the program was canceled. Freddie Prinze still lives in syndication.

"The Jeffersons" was the second successful spinoff from "All in the Family" (after "Maude"). The Bunkers' former neighbors "fin'ly gotta piece of the pie," according to the show's theme song, when George Jefferson's dry-cleaning business grew into a chain of stores, and they "moved on up" from Queens to the fashionable Upper East Side of Manhattan. But his newly acquired wealth didn't stop George from being the short-tempered, bigoted, pompous know-it-all he had always been. Sherman Hemsley starred as George Jefferson, Isabel Sanford was his wife, Louise, and Mike Evans and then Damon Evans (no relation) played Lionel, their twenty-two-year-old son. Others featured were Franklin Cover and Roxie Roker, as prime-time TV's first interracial married couple; Tom and Helen Willis, the Jeffersons' neighbors; Berlinda Tolbert as Jenny Willis, their daughter; and Zara Cully as Mama Jefferson, George's mother. As of this writing, the series was still on CBS.

No one thought that "Barney Miller," ABC's midseason comedy series, would survive. The show was spawned from a rejected pilot titled "The Life and Times of Captain Barney Miller" that was seen on the ABC summer anthology series "Just for Laughs" in 1974. Captain Miller and his crew of laughable detectives worked out of the 12th Precinct in New York City's Greenwich Village. All the episodes took place in the squad room,so viewers never saw a police car, and in the early years, there was never even a uniformed cop around. Eventually, one officer in uniform was seen regularly. Of the many characters in the show, only four were with the series throughout its run: Barney Miller, played by Hal Linden; Sergeant Wojohowicz (Wojo for short), played by Maxwell Gail; Det. Ron Harris, played by Ron Glass; and Inspector Luger, played by James Gregory. The series fooled everybody: it ran for seven years on the network and will probably run even longer in syndication.

Besides the top-rated "Chico," NBC also came up with a trio of top-15 series this season.

"The Rockford Files" starred James Garner as Jim Rockford, a private detective who was an ex-convict, having been set free when new evidence proved what he had been saying all along. Aiding Jim in his investigations was his father, Joe Rockford, played by Noah Beery. Others in the cast were Joe Santos as Sgt. Dennis Becker of the L.A.P.D. and Stuart Margolin as Angel Martin, Rockford's ex-con friend. The series lasted six years on NBC and then went into syndication with the title "Jim Rockford: Private Investigator."

"Police Woman" had the sexiest looking cop on TV, Sgt. Suzanne "Pepper" Martin. Angie Dickinson starred as Pepper, an undercover policewoman on the Los Angeles force. Working with her on the undercover team were Dets. Pete Royster and Joe Styles, played by Charles Dierkop and Ed Bernard. The team's boss was Lt. Bill Crowley, played by Earl Holliman. The series was a spin-off from another NBC series, "Police Story," and lasted four years on the network before going into syndication.

NBC's answer to the popular CBS family drama, "The Waltons," was "Little House on the Prairie." While the setting was different (the American West in the 1870s), the story line of the trials and tribulations of a loving family was similar.

Laura Ingalls Wilder's "Little House" books were the basis for the series. Michael Landon ("Bonanza's" Little Joe) was the force behind the success of the show. Besides being its star, he was the executive producer and a frequent writer and director for the show. This large-cast drama was one of the network's mainstays for nine seasons.

PLANET OF THE APES: September 13, 1974–December 27, 1974, CBS. Galen (Roddy McDowall)

KAREN: January 30, 1975–June 19, 1975, ABC. Karen Valentine (Karen Angelo)

MOVIN' ON: September 12, 1974–September 14, 1976, NBC. Frank Converse and Claude Akins

KHAN!: February 7, 1975–February 28, 1975, CBS. Khigh Dhiegh (Khan)

THE BOB CRANE SHOW: March 6, 1975–June 19, 1975, NBC. Bob Crane, James Sutorius, and Ronny Graham

THE TEXAS WHEELERS: September 13, 1974–July 24, 1975, ABC. (From lower left) Tony Becker, Mark Hamill, Jack Elam, Karen Oberdiear, and Gary Busey

BARETTA: January 17, 1975–June 1, 1978, ABC. Robert Blake (Tony Baretta)

THE ROCKFORD FILES: Noah Beery and James Garner

BARETTA: Robert Blake and Fred (the pet cockatoo)

HARRY O: September 12, 1974–August 12, 1976, ABC. David Janssen (Harry Orwell)

THE ROCKFORD FILES: September 13, 1974–January 10, 1980, NBC. James Garner (Jim Rockford)

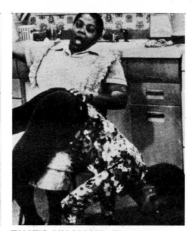

THAT'S MY MAMA: September 4, 1974–December 24, 1975, ABC. Clifton Davis and Theresa Merritt

THAT'S MY MAMA: Theresa Merritt and Clifton Davis

NAKIA: September 21, 1974–December 28, 1974, ABC. Robert Forster (Nakia Parker)

BEACON HILL: August 2, 1975–November 4, 1975, CBS. *(Foreground)* David Rounds, George Rose, Beatrice Straight; *(background)* Richard Ward, Lisa Pelikan, Sydney Swire

BEACON HILL: Stephen Elliott and Paul Rudd

NAKIA: Arthur Kennedy

WE'LL GET BY: March 14, 1975–May 30, 1975, CBS. Jerry Houser, Mitzi Hoag, and Paul Sorvino

WE'LL GET BY: *(Front)* Willie Aames, Mitzi Hoag, Paul Sorvino; *(back)* Jerry Houser, Devon Scott

HOT L BALTIMORE: January 24, 1975–June 13, 1975, ABC. *(Front row)* Robin Wilson and Conchata Ferrell; *(middle row)* Stan Gottlieb, Gloria Leroy, Richard Masur, Al Freeman, Jr., Jeannie Linero; *(back row)* James Cromwell, Lee Bergere, Henry Calvert

LITTLE HOUSE ON THE PRAIRIE: September 11, 1974–March 21, 1983, NBC. *(Seated)* Melissa Gilbert; *(standing)* Lindsay Greenbush, Michael Landon, Karen Grassle, Melissa Sue Anderson (early cast)

LITTLE HOUSE ON THE PRAIRIE: Linwood Boomer and Melissa Sue Anderson (Mary Ingalls's wedding)

PAUL SAND IN FRIENDS AND LOVERS: September 14, 1974–January 4, 1975, CBS. Paul Sand and Andrea Marcovicci (guest)

THE NIGHT STALKER: Darren McGavin

PAUL SAND IN FRIENDS AND LOVERS: Paul Sand

THE NIGHT STALKER: September 13, 1974–August 30, 1975, ABC. Darren McGavin

ALMOST ANYTHING GOES: July 31, 1975–May 9, 1976, ABC. Rosie Grier (participant)

PAPER MOON: September 12, 1974–January 2, 1975, ABC. Jodie Foster and Christopher Connelly

CHICO AND THE MAN: Freddie Prinze (Chico Rodriguez)

CHICO AND THE MAN: *(Front)* Della Reese, Jack Albertson, Raul Garcia; *(back)* Scatman Crothers

GET CHRISTIE LOVE: September 11, 1974–July 18, 1975, ABC. Teresa Graves (Christie Love)

CHICO AND THE MAN: September 13, 1974–July 21, 1978, NBC. Freddie Prinze and Jack Albertson

S.W.A.T.: February 24, 1975–June 29, 1976, ABC. *(Front)* James Coleman, Steve Forrest, Mark Shera; *(back)* Robert Urich, Rod Perry

THE JEFFERSONS: January 18, 1975–present, CBS. *(Front)* Berlinda Tolbert, Isabel Sanford, Mike Evans, Sherman Hemsley, and Zara Cully; *(back)* Paul Benedict, Franklin Cover, and Roxie Roker

THE JEFFERSONS: Berlinda Tolbert, Damon Evans, Isabel Sanford, and Sherman Hemsley

THE MANHUNTER: Dana Elcar (guest) and Ken Howard

BORN FREE: September 9, 1974–December 30, 1974, NBC. James Vickery, Gary Collins, and Diana Muldaur

THE MANHUNTER: September 11, 1974–April 9, 1975, CBS. Ken Howard

BARNEY MILLER: Abe Vigoda and Hal Linden

BARNEY MILLER: Barbara Barrie and Hal Linden (Barney Miller)

BARNEY MILLER: *(Seated)* Ron Glass, Hal Linden; *(standing)* Ron Carey, Maxwell Gail, James Gregory, Steve Landesberg (later cast)

BARNEY MILLER: January 23, 1975–September 9, 1982, ABC. Maxwell Gail, Hal Linden, Ron Glass, Abe Vigoda, and Jack Soo (early cast)

POLICE WOMAN: September 13, 1974–August 30, 1978, NBC. Angie Dickinson

POLICE WOMAN: Angie Dickinson and Earl Holliman

PASSWORD ALL STARS: November 18, 1974–February 21, 1975, ABC. Elizabeth Montgomery (guest) and Allen Ludden (host)

SUNSHINE: March 6, 1975–June 19, 1975, NBC. Cliff DeYoung and Elizabeth Cheshire

LUCAS TANNER: September 11, 1974–August 20, 1975, NBC. David Hartman (Lucas Tanner)

BIG EDDIE: August 23, 1975–November 7, 1975, CBS. Alan Oppenheimer, Sheldon Leonard (Eddie Smith), and Ralph Wilcox

PETROCELLI: September 11, 1974–March 3, 1976, NBC. Barry Newman (Anthony Petrocelli) and Susan Howard

RHODA: Valerie Harper and David Groh (Rhoda's wedding)

RHODA: Nancy Walker and Valerie Harper

RHODA: September 9, 1974–December 9, 1978, CBS. Valerie Harper (Rhoda), Nancy Walker, and Julie Kavner

Before the beginning of the season, television once again gave viewers a front-row seat to a space spectacular: the U.S.-Soviet Apollo/Soyuz linkup. And for the first time ever, the launching, and return, of a Soviet spacecraft was seen in this country live on television. The mission, which involved a number of joint as well as individual experiments, was highlighted by the docking and subsequent face-to-face meeting of the crews while the two crafts were in orbit. For this event to be captured by on-board cameras, the networks spent months working with NASA and the Soviets on the sequence of the mission to allow live coverage during daylight hours. They even went so far as to choreograph the historic handshake between Cmdrs. Thomas Stafford and Aleksei Leonov, so as not to show just their white-suited rear ends.

Back on Earth, the networks began the season with a "family viewing hour." This was a result of a new industry policy that set aside the first hour of prime time, 8:00–9:00 P.M. Eastern Standard Time, for programming suitable for the entire family. The National Association of Broadcasters, after years of pressure by the Federal Communications Commission and parent groups across the country, amended the TV code with a ruling that programs deemed unsuitable for children would start later in the evening. In addition, an on-air warning would have to precede certain shows telecast later in the evening that might be disturbing to a significant part of the adult audience.

Family viewing, however, had no precise definition, and what it meant besides the elimination of excessive sex and violence was left to the industry's judgment. Still, the policy affected numerous programs in development, and several producers and writers challenged it in court. This resulted in a decision that labeled the policy unconstitutional. But the family-viewing rule was not overturned. Instead, the court issued a warning to the government to stay out of program control and urged the networks to work it out themselves. The

family hour became part of the TV environment despite the flaws and contradictions that had surfaced.

The networks were already preparing for the countrywide festivities to commemorate the nation's Bicentennial to be celebrated next Fourth of July. More than a year before the start of this season, CBS had already begun airing its "Bicentennial Minutes." This was a series of one-minute broadcasts appearing every night in prime time, beginning July 4, 1974, and ending on December 31, 1976. Each "Minute" offered a vignette of an occurrence 200 years earlier on that date related to the birth of the nation. Featured were many well-known personalities, including Charlton Heston, Walter Cronkite, Beverly Sills, Paul Newman, Walter Matthau, Kirk Douglas, Alfred Hitchcock, and Milton Berle. The entire series—912 one-minute spots—was sponsored by the Shell Oil Company.

This was to be a landmark season for two of the networks. ABC moved out of its perennial last position in the ratings as its hiring of programming whiz Fred Silverman from CBS began to pay off. For the first time, five of this year's top-10 programs would belong to ABC: "Rich Man, Poor Man" (second), "Laverne and Shirley" (third), "The Bionic Woman" (fifth), "The Six Million Dollar Man" (ninth), and "The ABC Monday Night Movie" (tenth). Another indication of change was that among the top 25, ABC placed more new shows than the other two networks combined. It contributed five, CBS two, and NBC none.

Near the end of the season (June 5), NBC celebrated its 50th anniversary in broadcasting. While it didn't debut any new top-rated programs this season, it did introduce the most innovative comedy show in years, NBC's "Saturday Night Live." This was a live, madcap 90 minutes from 11:30 P.M. to 1:00 A.M. for late-night viewers. The program featured a different guest host each week, as well as "The Not Ready for Prime Time Players," a group of zany comics. The show was an instant hit and represented a

bold leap forward in the art of television comedy.

Now for a look at ABC's five new top-25 shows. The mini-series "Rich Man, Poor Man" was a 12-hour serialized adaptation of Irwin Shaw's best-selling novel. This short-run dramatic show about the fate and fortunes of Rudy Jordache (Peter Strauss) and his brother Tom (Nick Nolte) received 23 Emmy nominations. Its success prompted a 21-part sequel, "Rich Man, Poor Man—Book II," that aired at the start of next season. Although it did well in the ratings, it could not equal the original.

"Laverne and Shirley" was a situation-comedy spinoff from the top-rated "Happy Days." The series took place in the fifties and had the girls, who worked together at the local brewery, living together at 708 Hampton Street in Milwaukee. Penny Marshall was Laverne DeFazio and Cindy Williams was Shirley Feeney in this show that is already in syndication and is getting high ratings. Other leads in the cast included Phil Foster as Frank DeFazio, Laverne's overprotective father; David L. Lander as Andrew "Squiggy" Squiggman; Michael McKean as Lenny Kolowski, the girls' friends and co-workers; and Betty Garrett as Edna Babish, their landlady.

"The Bionic Woman" was a spinoff from another successful ABC series, "The Six Million Dollar Man." Lindsay Wagner starred as Jaime Sommers, who, because of a severe accident, was reconstructed with bionic legs, a bionic right arm, and a bionic right ear, all contributing to her superhuman abilities. Like her friend Steve Austin (the Six Million Dollar Man), she worked for the Office of Scientific Information (OSI), taking on all sorts of dangerous assignments. Other cast members were Richard Anderson as Oscar Goldman, her boss, and Martin E. Brooks as Dr. Rudy Wells, OSI's aeromedical surgeon. At the conclusion of next season, the network dropped the show and NBC picked it up. After one year on its new network, it entered syndication.

"Starsky and Hutch" was an hour-long police series centered around two young undercover cops. Paul Michael Glaser was Dave Starsky and David Soul was his partner, Ken Hutchinson. But although the guys were often working undercover, they couldn't help but be seen when they raced around in their red souped-up Ford. Also in the cast were Bernie Hamilton as Capt. Harold Dobey, their commanding officer, and Antonio Fargas as Huggy Bear, the team's street informant. The show was one of the more violent on the air, but it was toned down—enabling it to run as long as it did, four years, and then go into syndication.

"Welcome Back, Kotter" was a situation comedy about a high-school teacher who, after 10 years, returned to teach at the school from which he graduated. He was assigned to a class made up of academic misfits who referred to themselves as the Sweathogs. Stand-up comic Gabe Kaplan played Gabe Kotter, and Marcia Strassman was his wife, Julie. The Sweathogs were John Travolta (who became a movie star while still on the show) as Vinnie Barbarino, Robert Hegyes as Juan Epstein, Ron Palillo as Arnold Horshack, and Lawrence-Hilton Jacobs as Freddie "Boom Boom" Washington. Also featured was John Sylvester White as the school's vice-principal, Michael Woodman. As an added touch, Kaplan displayed his comic abilities as each episode ended with Kotter telling his wife a joke. During the first two seasons of its five-year run, the series was among the top-20 programs and the series' theme song, by John Sebastian, made the top of the charts in 1976.

CBS's new top shows were the 6th-rated "Phyllis" and the 12th-placed

"One Day at a Time." "Phyllis" was another spinoff from Mary Tyler Moore's show but, in comparison, this sitcom was just a flash in the pan. While the show did very well this season, it went into oblivion by the end of the next season and was canceled. Cloris Leachman played the title role and Lisa Gerritsen played Bess Lindstrom, her teenage daughter.

"One Day at a Time," on the other hand, is still a big hit for the network. This Norman Lear comedy was about a divorced career woman trying to raise her two teenage daughters. The original cast was Bonnie Franklin as Ann Romano, a woman with 17 years of marriage behind her; Mackenzie Phillips as her older daughter, Julie; Valerie Bertinelli as younger daughter Barbara; and Pat Harrington, Jr., as Dwayne Schneider, the macho superintendent of the building they lived in. As of this writing, the series is in its eighth season on the network.

THE GHOST BUSTERS: September 4, 1975–September 4, 1976, CBS. Forrest Tucker, Larry Storch, and Tracy the Gorilla (played by Bob Burns)

JOE FORRESTER: September 9, 1975–August 30, 1976, NBC. Lloyd Bridges (Joe Forrester)

McCOY: October 5, 1975–March 28, 1976, NBC. Tony Curtis (McCoy)

DON ADAMS SCREEN TEST: 1975, syndicated. Contestant, Frank Gorshin (guest), and Don Adams (host)

WHEN THINGS WERE ROTTEN: September 10, 1975–December 24, 1975, ABC. Dick Gautier

WHEN THINGS WERE ROTTEN: *(Foreground)* Richard Dimitri; *(background)* Dick Van Patten, Bernie Kopel, Dick Gautier, Misty Rowe, and David Sabin

FAMILY: March 9, 1976–June 25, 1980, ABC. Meredith Baxter Birney, Gary Frank, James Broderick, Sada Thompson, and Kristy McNichol

STARSKY AND HUTCH: September 10, 1975–August 21, 1979, ABC. David Soul (Ken Hutchinson) and Paul Michael Glaser (Dave Starsky)

MOBILE ONE: September 12, 1975–December 29, 1975, ABC. Unknown actor and Jackie Cooper

STARSKY AND HUTCH: David Soul and Paul Michael Glaser

THE BIONIC WOMAN: Lindsay Wagner

THE GONG SHOW: 1976, syndicated. Chuck Barris (host) and contestant

SARA: February 13, 1976–July 10, 1976, CBS. Brenda Vaccaro (Sara Yarnell)

THE BIONIC WOMAN: January 14, 1976–September 2, 1978, ABC, NBC. Lindsay Wagner

JIGSAW JOHN: February 2, 1976–September 13, 1976, NBC. Jack Warden (John St. John/Jigsaw John) and Charles Ynfante (guest)

IVAN THE TERRIBLE: August 21, 1976–September 18, 1976, CBS. Lou Jacobi (Ivan), Maria Karnilova, and Phil Reeds

LAVERNE AND SHIRLEY: Penny Marshall and Phil Foster

LAVERNE AND SHIRLEY: Penny Marshall and Cindy Williams

LAVERNE AND SHIRLEY: January 27, 1976–May 10, 1983, ABC. *(Foreground)* Cindy Williams (Shirley Feeney), Penny Marshall (Laverne DeFazio); *(background)* Betty Garrett, Eddie Mekka, David Lander, Michael McKean, and Phil Foster

THE PRACTICE: January 30, 1976–January 26, 1977, NBC. *(Front)* Allen Price, Danny Thomas, Damon Ruskin; *(back)* Didi Conn, David Spielberg, Shelley Fabares, Mike Evans, Dena Dietrich

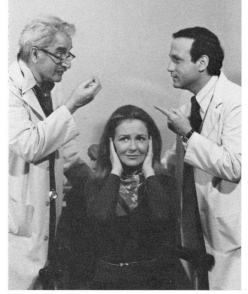

THE PRACTICE: Danny Thomas, Shelley Fabares, and David Spielberg

THE BLUE KNIGHT: December 17, 1975–October 27, 1976, CBS. George Kennedy

FAY: September 4, 1975–October 23, 1975, NBC. Lee Grant (Fay Stuart)

SWISS FAMILY ROBINSON: September 14, 1975–April 11, 1976, ABC. *(Front)* Eric Olsen, Pat Delany, Willie Aames; *(back)* Helen Hunt, Martin Milner

ON THE ROCKS: September 11, 1975–May 17, 1976, ABC. Leonard Stone, Hal Williams, Rick Hurst, Jay Gerber, Bobby Sandler, and *(seated)* José Perez

FAY: Joe Silver and Lee Grant

SWISS FAMILY ROBINSON: Martin Milner and Pat Delany

ON THE ROCKS: José Perez and Bobby Sandler

ONE DAY AT A TIME: December 16, 1975–present, CBS. Chuck McCann, Beverly Sanders, Pat Harrington, Valerie Bertinelli, and Bonnie Franklin

GOOD HEAVENS: February 9, 1976–June 26, 1976, ABC. Season Hubley and Barry Gordon (guests); Carl Reiner starred in this series

MATT HELM: September 20, 1975–January 3, 1976, ABC. Laraine Stephens and Tony Franciosa (Matt Helm)

ONE DAY AT A TIME: *(Front)* Bonnie Franklin; *(back)* MacKenzie Phillips, Valerie Bertinelli

SPACE: 1999: Martin Landau and Barbara Bain

SPACE: 1999: Catherine Schell

ONE DAY AT A TIME: Pat Harrington and Teri Ralston (guest)

SPACE: 1999: 1975–77, syndicated. Martin Landau, Barbara Bain, and Barry Morse

DOCTORS HOSPITAL: September 10, 1975–January 14, 1976, NBC. Stefan Gierasch (guest) and George Peppard

THE MONEYCHANGERS: (Mini-series) December 4–19, 1976, NBC. Anne Baxter and Kirk Douglas

RICH MAN, POOR MAN: (Mini-series) February 1–March 15, 1976, ABC. Susan Blakely and Peter Strauss

RICH MAN, POOR MAN: *(First row)* Van Johnson, Dorothy McGuire, Peter Strauss, Susan Blakely, and Nick Nolte; *(second row)* Edward Asner, Murray Hamilton, Robert Reed, Norman Fell, and Talia Shire; *(third row)* Lynda Day George, Dick Sargent, Kim Darby, Craig Stevens, Dorothy Malone, and George Maharis

PHYLLIS: Mary Tyler Moore (guest) and Cloris Leachman

PHYLLIS: September 8, 1975–August 30, 1977, CBS. Henry Jones, Cloris Leachman (Phyllis), and Robert Alda (guest)

PHYLLIS: Lisa Gerritsen and Cloris Leachman

SWITCH: September 9, 1975–September 3, 1978, CBS. Robert Wagner

SWITCH: Eddie Albert, Robert Wagner, and Sharon Gless

NBC'S SATURDAY NIGHT LIVE: October 11, 1975–present, NBC. *(First row)* Chevy Chase, John Belushi; *(second row)* Jane Curtin, Laraine Newman, Gilda Radner; *(third row)* Bill Murray, Garrett Morris, Dan Aykroyd (original cast)

NBC'S SATURDAY NIGHT LIVE: Joe Piscopo, Robin Duke, Gary Kroeger, Tim Kazurinsky, Brad Hall, Julia Louis-Dreyfus, Mary Gross, Eddie Murphy (later cast)

MOSES THE LAWGIVER: (Mini-series) June 21–August 2, 1975, CBS. Burt Lancaster

KATE McSHANE: September 10, 1975– November 12, 1975, CBS. Sian-Barbara Allen (guest) and Anne Meara (Kate McShane)

THE MONTEFUSCOS: September 4, 1975–October 23, 1975, NBC. Joe Sirola and Naomi Stevens (Tony and Rose Montefusco)

MOSES THE LAWGIVER: Anthony Quayle

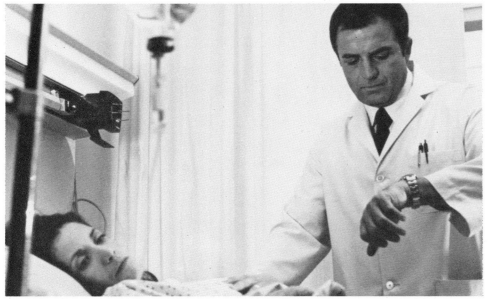

MEDICAL STORY: September 4, 1975–January 8, 1976, NBC. Edith Diaz and Vince Edwards (guests)

WELCOME BACK, KOTTER: September 9, 1975–August 3, 1979, ABC. *(Front row)* Lawrence-Hilton Jacobs, John Travolta; *(middle row)* Gabriel Kaplan, Marcia Strassman; *(back row)* Ron Palillo, John Sylvester White, Robert Hegyes

WELCOME BACK, KOTTER: Robert Hegyes and John Travolta

WELCOME BACK, KOTTER: Gabriel Kaplan (Gabe Kotter)

WELCOME BACK, KOTTER: Marcia Strassman

WELCOME BACK, KOTTER: Ron Palillo, John Travolta, Lawrence-Hilton Jacobs, Robert Hegyes, John Sylvester White, and Gabriel Kaplan

CITY OF ANGELS: February 3, 1976–August 10, 1976, NBC. Wayne Rogers and Diane Ladd (guest)

BERT D'ANGELO/SUPERSTAR: February 21, 1976–July 10, 1976, ABC. Dennis Patrick, Paul Sorvino (Bert D'Angelo), and Robert Pine

BRONK: September 21, 1975–July 18, 1976, CBS. Jack Palance (Lt. Alex Bronkov)

THE FAMILY HOLVAK: September 7, 1975–October 27, 1975, NBC. Julie Harris and Glenn Ford

BARBARY COAST: Doug McClure

BARBARY COAST: William Shatner

POPI: January 20, 1976–August 24, 1976, CBS. Enita Diaz, Hector Elizondo, Anthony Perez, and *(foreground)* Dennis Vazquez

BARBARY COAST: September 8, 1975–January 9, 1976, ABC. William Shatner and Doug McClure

DONNY AND MARIE: January 23, 1976–January 19, 1979, ABC. Marie and Donny Osmond

DONNY AND MARIE: Donny and Marie Osmond

JOE AND SONS: Barry Miller and Richard Castellano

JOE AND SONS: September 9, 1975–January 13, 1976, CBS. Richard Castellano (Joe Vitale)

DOC: September 13, 1975–October 30, 1976, CBS. Elizabeth Wilson and Barnard Hughes ("Doc" Joe Bogert)

1976-77

Television provided the nation with a spectacular day-long 200th birthday party on July 4, 1976. The worldwide coverage, most of it live, roamed from Guam in the Pacific to the Grand Canyon in Arizona to London's River Thames to "Operation Sail" and the Tall Ships in New York Harbor. The president visited Valley Forge, Pennsylvania, and then went on to Philadelphia to recall the first Fourth of July as "the beginning of a continuing adventure . . . unfinished, unfulfilled but still unchallenged as a model of social and political achievement." Following his speech, millions of viewers across the nation watched as the Liberty Bell was softly sounded with a rubber mallet.

This was a day of mammoth exhibitions. The largest was the more than 225 sailing ships, flying 31 flags, that paraded up the Hudson River in New York. There was also a 22-nation fleet of naval units that lined Upper New York Bay and the Hudson for an international review presided over by Vice-President Nelson Rockefeller. Only through television could the entire nation share in this once-in-a-lifetime experience.

This historic occasion was followed, within days, by another history-making event; television screens across the country and the world flashed the first live pictures of the landscape of the planet Mars. America's *Viking I* made the first successful landing on the red planet, as it is known, and transmitted spectacular photographs of a rocky, wind-scarred red desert plain while it began the first direct search for life on another world. The robot spacecraft had completed an 11-month voyage of nearly half a billion miles to bring us these images.

A few weeks later, the Democratic National Convention was held in New York. A relative newcomer to national politics, Jimmy Carter of Georgia, who had been on the campaign trail for 19 months, overwhelmingly received the party's nomination for president. When the Republicans held their national convention in Kansas City, Missouri, in mid-

August, President Ford fought a hard battle with Ronald Reagan for the nomination and narrowly edged him out.

Walter Cronkite, the dean of political anchormen, again headed up CBS's full coverage of these quadrennial happenings. NBC's senior convention anchorman, David Brinkley, was teamed with John Chancellor to fully cover the conventions while ABC offered abbreviated coverage, a nightly digest running about two hours. CBS and NBC always looked at the conventions as an image builder, even though only 30 percent of TV homes tuned in on an average night. And they traditionally spent heavily to bring these events to the electorate. The estimate of the money doled out by the two networks in 1976 to cover the conventions was approximately $10 million each.

In the Ford-Carter campaign, televised debates were employed for the first time in 16 years. It was generally felt that they provided the narrow margin of victory for Carter and sent the first incumbent president to defeat since Herbert Hoover.

Another narrow victory had already taken place when ABC barely edged out CBS for first place in the cumulative ratings for the entire previous season. ABC demonstrated its newfound programming strength, particularly during last year's "second season" and summer period, and it was even anticipated that it would win over CBS by a larger margin than what the final outcome showed. But no matter, for ABC was battling the giant CBS head to head, and was winning.

This was so because it kept coming up with the "right" programs. Of the handful of new shows to make the top 30 this season, ABC led the way with four, including "Charlie's Angels" and "Three's Company," the two highest-rated new programs. CBS had only one, "Alice," which placed 30th, while NBC did not have a single high-rated regular new weekly series. It did have "The Big Event," an umbrella title for assorted movies and specials seen at various

starting times on Sunday nights.

At midseason, ABC, doing things right again, presented one of TV's milestone programs, a mini-series that was the most-watched dramatic show in the history of the medium, "Roots." This 12-hour adaptation—seen for eight consecutive nights—of Alex Haley's novel traced his family's history, beginning in the mid-eighteenth century in Africa. Each of the eight telecasts was among the 15 highest-rated single programs of all time and the concluding episode was seen by more viewers than ever before in TV's history. Heading the enormous cast were LeVar Burton, John Amos, Ben Vereen, Cicely Tyson, Leslie Uggams, Edward Asner, and Robert Reed.

"Charlie's Angels" was the top-rated new show of the season. Charlie was Charles Townsend, owner of a detective agency bearing his name (who was heard but never seen), and the Angels were three very sexy private detectives who worked for him. The original cast consisted of the Angels—Kate Jackson (last seen on "The Rookies") as Sabrina Duncan, Farrah Fawcett-Majors (Wella Balsam's commercial spokesperson) as Jill Monroe, and Jaclyn Smith (Breck shampoo's spokesperson) as Kelly Garrett—and David Doyle as John Bosley, Charlie's assistant, and John Forsythe as the voice of Townsend. The series was among the top 20 shows throughout its five years and the show's theme song by Henry Mancini was among the top hits of 1977. Currently, Charlie and his girls can be seen in syndication.

The second-highest-rated new show, "Three's Company," achieved 11th place in the ratings even though it had a limited run this season. Its success enabled it to become a regular weekly series the next year. The series was about the cohabitating misadventures of two very attractive young women and a young man who shared an apartment in Los Angeles. The original cast was John Ritter as Jack Tripper, Joyce DeWitt as Janet Wood, and Suzanne Somers as Chrissy Snow. The series is still a top-rated program.

The best NBC could do in a series was "Quincy, M.E.," starring Jack Klugman as a Los Angeles County medical examiner. This was a show that at times dealt with contemporary issues such as drug abuse, alcoholism, child abuse, and the plight of the handicapped. Never a top-rated series, it endured seven years on the network and is currently in syndication.

Among some interesting final notes to this season, former President Nixon ended his silence on Watergate and agreed to discuss the issue in a series of interviews with David Frost. He was guaranteed $600,000 and 10 percent of the profits derived from the sale of the four 90-minute telecasts. These programs were shown over a special network of 185 stations. Audience survey estimates revealed that the first show was seen by 45 million viewers, making it the highest-rated news/interview program in history. David O. Selznick's 1939 movie classic, *Gone With the Wind*, was finally released to television this season. NBC paid $5 million for the rights to a single national telecast. It was shown in two parts on successive nights and achieved the highest rating for a movie in history. And CBS was so impressed with the type of programming ABC was developing, it was even willing to take on shows its rival no longer wanted. ABC introduced "The Tony Randall Show" and "Wonder Woman" (starring Lynda Carter) this season but discarded them at the end of the TV year. CBS immediately picked them up for the following season.

HUNTER: February 18, 1977–May 27, 1977, CBS. James Franciscus (James Hunter)

HUNTER: Linda Evans and James Franciscus

SUGAR TIME: August 13, 1977–May 29, 1978, ABC. Didi Carr, Barbi Benton, and Marianne Black

WESTSIDE MEDICAL: March 15, 1977–August 25, 1977, ABC. Ernest Thompson, Linda Carlson, and James Sloyan

SPENCER'S PILOTS: September 17, 1976–November 19, 1976, CBS. Todd Susman and Christopher Stone

COS: September 19, 1976–October 31, 1976, ABC. Bill Cosby (Cos)

THE McLEAN STEVENSON SHOW: December 1, 1976–March 3, 1977, NBC. McLean Stevenson

MOST WANTED: October 16, 1976–April 25, 1977, ABC. Shelly Novack and Robert Stack

GIBBSVILLE: November 11, 1976–December 30, 1976, NBC. Gig Young

CHARLIE'S ANGELS: September 22, 1976–August 19, 1981, ABC. Jaclyn Smith, Farrah Fawcett-Majors, and Kate Jackson (the original Angels)

CHARLIE'S ANGELS: Kate Jackson, Cheryl Ladd (replaced Farrah Fawcett-Majors), and Jaclyn Smith

CHARLIE'S ANGELS: Jaclyn Smith, Shelly Hack (replaced Kate Jackson), and Cheryl Ladd

QUINCY, M.E.: October 3, 1976–March 23, 1983, NBC. Jack Klugman (Quincy)

QUINCY, M.E.: Robert Ito, Joseph Roman, Jack Klugman, and Peter Virgo, Jr. (guest)

QUINCY, M.E.: Jack Klugman and Katherine Justice (guest)

FAMILY FEUD: 1977–present, syndicated. Richard Dawson (host)

MR. T. AND TINA: September 25, 1976–October 30, 1976, ABC. Susan Blanchard (Tina Kelly) and Pat Morita (Taro Takahashi/Mr. T.)

ALICE: Linda Lavin and Beth Howland

THE ANDROS TARGETS: January 31, 1977–July 9, 1977, CBS. James Sutorius (Mike Andros) and Richard Kiley (guest)

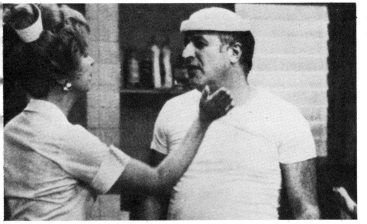

ALICE: Polly Holliday and Vic Tayback

ALICE: Marvin Kaplan, Beth Howland, Polly Holliday, Vic Tayback, and Linda Lavin

ALICE: September 29, 1976–present, CBS. Linda Lavin (Alice), Polly Holliday, and Vic Tayback

THREE'S COMPANY: March 15, 1977–present, ABC. Suzanne Somers, John Ritter, Isabel Wolfe (guest), and Heather Lowe (guest)

THREE'S COMPANY: Joyce DeWitt, John Ritter, and Jenilee Harrison

THREE'S COMPANY: Suzanne Somers, John Ritter, Richard Kline, and unknown actor

THREE'S COMPANY: (Front) Priscilla Barnes, John Ritter, Joyce DeWitt; (back) Richard Kline, Jenilee Harrison, Don Knotts

BLANSKY'S BEAUTIES: February 12, 1977–May 21, 1977, ABC. Nancy Walker (Nancy Blansky) and her "Beauties"

THE BARBARA WALTERS SPECIAL: December 14, 1976–present, ABC. Prime Minister Menachem Begin with Barbara Walters

THE BARBARA WALTERS SPECIAL: Mr. and Mrs. Bob Hope with Barbara Walters

THE BARBARA WALTERS SPECIAL: Vice-President and Mrs. Mondale with Barbara Walters

ALL'S FAIR: September 20, 1976–August 15, 1977, CBS. Richard Crenna and Bernadette Peters

THE LIFE AND TIMES OF GRIZZLY ADAMS: February 9, 1977–July 26, 1978, NBC. Dan Haggerty (James "Grizzly" Adams)

THE MUPPET SHOW: 1976–present, syndicated. Jim Henson and the Muppets

ROOTS: (Mini-series) January 23–30, 1977, ABC. LeVar Burton

ROOTS: Ben Vereen

FUTURE COP: March 5, 1977–August 6, 1977, ABC. John Amos, Michael Shannon, and Ernest Borgnine

ROOTS: Cicely Tyson and Maya Angelou

ROOTS: Lloyd Bridges

C.P.O. SHARKEY: Sosimo Hernandez (guest) and Don Rickles

CODE R: January 21, 1977–June 10, 1977, CBS. Martin Kove, Tom Simcox, Susanne Reed, and James Houghton

C.P.O. SHARKEY: December 1, 1976–July 28, 1978, NBC. Don Rickles (C.P.O. Otto Sharkey)

SIROTA'S COURT: December 1, 1976–April 13, 1977, NBC. *(Foreground)* Fred Willard; *(left)* Kathleen Miller, Owen Bush, Michael Constantine (Matthew J. Sirota), Cynthia Harris, Ted Ross

KINGSTON: CONFIDENTIAL: March 23, 1977–August 10, 1977, NBC. Raymond Burr (R. B. Kingston) and James McEachin (guest)

BUSTING LOOSE: January 17, 1977–November 16, 1977, CBS. Jack Kruschen, Adam Arkin, and Pat Carroll

EIGHT IS ENOUGH: March 15, 1977–August 29, 1981, ABC. Dick Van Patten and family

FANTASTIC JOURNEY: February 3, 1977–
April 13, 1977, NBC. Roddy McDowall

FANTASTIC JOURNEY: Scott Thomas, Ike Eisenmann, Karen Somerville, Susan Howard,
Jared Martin, and Carl Franklin

JESUS OF NAZARETH: (Mini-series) April 3 and 10, 1977, NBC. Robert Powell (Jesus)

HOLMES AND YOYO: September 25, 1976–
December 11, 1976, ABC. Richard B. Shull
(Alexander Holmes) and John Shuck (Gregory
"Yoyo" Yoyonovich)

WHAT'S HAPPENING: August 5, 1976–April
28, 1979, ABC. Haywood Nelson, Fred Berry,
and Ernest Thomas

THE KALLIKAKS: Edie McClurg, David Huddleston, and Bonnie Ebsen

THE KEANE BROTHERS: August 12, 1977–September 2, 1977, CBS. John and Tom Keane

THE KALLIKAKS: August 3, 1977–August 31, 1977, NBC. Bonnie Ebsen and David Huddleston

DOLLY: 1976, syndicated. Dolly Parton (hostess)

WONDER WOMAN: December 18, 1976–September 11, 1979, ABC, CBS. Lynda Carter

BALL FOUR: September 22, 1976–October 27, 1976, CBS. Jim Bouton, Ben Davidson, and Sam Wright

BALL FOUR: Jaime Tirelli, Jim Bouton, Ben Davidson, and Bill McCutcheon

SERPICO: September 24, 1976–January 28, 1977, NBC. David Birney (Frank Serpico)

THE TONY RANDALL SHOW: September 23, 1976–March 25, 1978, ABC, CBS. Tony Randall

THE HARDY BOYS: January 30, 1977–August 26, 1979, ABC. Parker Stevenson (Frank Hardy), Shaun Cassidy (Joe Hardy)

THE TONY RANDALL SHOW: Tony Randall and Brad Savage

MARY HARTMAN, MARY HARTMAN: 1976–77, syndicated. Louise Lasser (Mary Hartman)

LOVES ME, LOVES ME NOT: March 20, 1977–April 27, 1977, CBS. Kenneth Gilman and Susan Dey

LOVES ME, LOVES ME NOT: Susan Dey

LOVES ME, LOVES ME NOT: Kenneth Gilman

THE NANCY WALKER SHOW: September 3, 1976–December 27, 1976, ABC. Nancy Walker and William Daniels

THE NANCY WALKER SHOW: Nancy Walker and Beverly Archer

GONE WITH THE WIND: November 7–8, 1976, NBC (highest-rated movie in TV history). Clark Gable and Vivien Leigh

FISH: February 5, 1977–June 8, 1978, ABC. *(Seated)* Sarah Natoli, Lenny Bari, Abe Vigoda, Florence Stanley, and John Cassisi *(Standing)* Barry Gordon, Todd Bridges, Denise Miller

FISH: Florence Stanley and Abe Vigoda

THE NANCY DREW MYSTERIES: February 6, 1977–July 30, 1978, ABC. Janet Louise Johnson (the second Nancy Drew)

THE NANCY DREW MYSTERIES: George O'Hanlon, Jr., Pamela Sue Martin (the original Nancy Drew), William Schallert, and Jean Rasey

EXECUTIVE SUITE: September 29, 1976–February 11, 1977, CBS. Stephen Elliott, Sharon Acker, Leigh McCloskey, and Mitchell Ryan

SZYSZNYK: August 1, 1977–January 25, 1978, CBS. Susan Lanier, Olivia Cole, Ned Beatty (Nick Szyszynk), and Leonard Barr

1977-78

As this season began, television was completing 30 years of providing full prime-time evening programming. And the industry was doing better than ever. Viewers were watching more than ever—6 hours and 18 minutes a day in the average home, which resulted in higher earnings and profits for the networks and individual stations. The industry as a whole had an income of almost $6 billion last year.

It had long been recognized that television was the most effective communications medium and the strongest social force in the nation. But in recent history the medium played an especially significant part in the life of the country, from the civil-rights movement and the youth revolution of the sixties to changing public opinion against military involvement in Southeast Asia and the retiring of Presidents Johnson and Nixon before their time. Television's influence was far beyond the dreams of its creators, and it gained the support and loyalty never before achieved by any entertainment vehicle. All this in just 30 years.

For most of this time, ABC, the smallest and youngest of the three networks, was perennially far behind its stronger competitors. In the beginning, NBC was the powerhouse; as the sixties began, CBS became dominant and remained there. Now ABC, whose fortunes had changed in recent years, estimated its swing from third to first place was worth around $60 million in profits each year. It overcame its struggle to survive by employing innovative and imaginative programming concepts as well as resourceful economic tactics. Its efforts resulted in having 7 of last season's top 10 shows: "Happy Days," "Laverne and Shirley," "ABC Monday Night Movie," "Charlie's Angels," "The Six Million Dollar Man," "ABC Sunday Night Movie," and "Baretta."

During this TV year, the networks offered approximately 100 prime-time shows (excluding all the prime-time movies) to a receptive audience. Many of these were new, but only nine would

return for a full second season. And four of those have endured and, as of this writing, are still on the air: ABC's "The Love Boat," "Fantasy Island," and "20/20," and CBS's "Dallas." One, NBC's "CHiPS," ran for six seasons, and three others lasted four or more seasons: "Lou Grant" and "The Incredible Hulk" on CBS and "Soap" on ABC. The other show that survived the season, "Carter Country" on ABC, was canceled after the next year.

"The Love Boat," an hour-long situation comedy, was modeled after the early seventies' "Love, American Style," also on ABC. The new series presented several comedy sketches, all romantically inclined, that were interwoven with one another. The old series had been an anthology, the short skits complete and separate from one another. "The Love Boat" became an immediate hit and has been among the top shows since. All the activity took place aboard the cruise ship *Pacific Princess*, with Gavin MacLeod (most recently Murray on "The Mary Tyler Moore Show") as Capt. Merrill Stubing; Bernie Kopell as ship's Dr. Adam Bricker; Fred Grandy as Burl "Gopher" Smith, the purser; Ted Lange as Isaac Washington, the bartender; and Lauren Tewes as Julie McCoy, the social director. The series was noted for the guests it attracted each week: just about anybody who was anybody turned up on the boat, including Milton Berle, Douglas Fairbanks, Jr., and Mary Martin, just to name a few.

As soon as ABC realized the big hit it had with "Love Boat," it quickly developed a similar program, "Fantasy Island," which premiered at midseason. This hour series was set on an island resort where each week the guest character's fantasies came true. There were usually two stories presented and the action shifted back and forth from one fantasy to the other. The only regular cast members were Ricardo Montalban as Mr. Roarke, the owner of Fantasy Island, and Herve Villechaize as Tattoo, his midget-size assistant. Guest stars who had their fantasies come true in-

cluded Joan Collins, Adrienne Barbeau, Carol Linley, Paul Burke, Ron Ely, and Dennis James. From this first season, "Fantasy Island" followed "Love Boat" on Saturday evenings, enabling the network to win the night in the ratings for years.

Late in the season, CBS introduced, in a trial run, a dramatic series about a wealthy Texas oil family. The results were satisfactory and the show was included in next season's fall schedule. "Dallas" took another full season to build an audience, but the network's patience paid off. It became the sixth-rated show and did not stop climbing until it reached the No. 1 position in the 1980–81 season. At the halfway point of the 1982–83 TV year, the series still occupied that lofty place. This nighttime soap opera had legions of fans who on the evening of November 21, 1980, watched the episode titled "Who Shot J. R.?" and made it the highest-rated individual telecast, to that time, in TV's history. The series had a large cast but one character stood out; the scheming J. R. (John Ross) Ewing, the man everyone loved to hate. Larry Hagman (of "I Dream of Jeannie" and "The Good Life") became a superstar playing this villainous character.

"20/20," ABC's answer to CBS's "60 Minutes," debuted late in the season. This news-magazine show began as a weekly, then was seen monthly, and finally returned to weekly status. The first telecast had TV newcomers Harold Hayes and Robert Hughes as co-hosts. Their debut was poorly received and they were quickly replaced by TV veteran Hugh Downs, whose pace and style were better suited to the environment of the show. It improved significantly, and became a news staple for the network.

The California Highway Patrol was the background setting for the police series "CHiPS." The show centered on the daily experiences of two conscientious motorcycle highway patrol officers. The original cast included Larry Wilcox as Ofc. Jonathan Baker, Erik Estrada as Ofc. Frank "Ponch" Poncherello, and

Robert Pine as their commanding officer, Sgt. Joe Getraer. The series built an audience slowly and experienced cast changes, but still managed to run six seasons.

CBS introduced two series that starred veteran TV performers. "Lou Grant," starring Edward Asner, originated as a character on the situation comedy "The Mary Tyler Moore Show," with Asner in the same role. However, when Grant "moved" to Los Angeles to become a newspaper city editor, the new series no longer was a comedy. Instead it was a straight dramatic show that involved itself with many issues of the day. "Lou Grant" was on the network for five years.

"The Incredible Hulk," starring Bill Bixby, was a comic-book adventure series based on two made-for-television movies. Bixby played research scientist David Banner, who was accidentally exposed to gamma radiation that caused a dramatic change in his body chemistry when he became angry. The resulting Hulk, a grotesque creature of incredible strength, was played by Lou Ferrigno, a former Mr. America. The show caught on and ran for almost five years.

"Soap" was a prime-time spoof of afternoon soap operas. The series was labeled adult comedy and dealt with such delicate subjects as adultery, nymphomania, and homosexuality, in addition to race, religion, and organized crime. Some of the topics had been dealt with in earlier sitcoms, but "Soap" went a little further. The show generated such controversy before its debut that it almost did not become a reality. Most of the protests died out after the first few episodes and it went on to become a successful series for ABC, running four seasons. Katherine Helmond and Robert Mandan headed the large cast.

Among other things going on this season, CBS, in September, celebrated its 50th anniversary in broadcasting. After 26 years as an NBC exclusive, baseball's World Series was telecast on ABC. Hereafter, this annually top-rated sporting event would alternate yearly between the two networks. Late in the season, NBC's mini-series "Holocaust" became the most watched entertainment show in the network's history and second-rated behind "Roots."

THE MAN FROM ATLANTIS: September 22, 1977–May 2, 1978, NBC. Belinda J. Montgomery and Patrick Duffy

WE'VE GOT EACH OTHER: October 1, 1977–January 7, 1978, CBS. (Seated) Oliver Clark, Beverly Archer; (standing) Ren Wood, Tom Poston, Joan Van Ark

THE HARVEY KORMAN SHOW: April 4, 1978–August 3, 1978, ABC. Susan Lawrence and Harvey Korman

SAM: March 14, 1978–April 18, 1978, CBS. Sam (Labrador retriever), Len Wayland, and Mark Harmon

JOE AND VALERIE: April 24, 1978–May 10, 1978, NBC. Paul Regina (Joe) and Char Fontane (Valerie)

RICHIE BROCKELMAN, PRIVATE EYE: March 17, 1978–April 14, 1978, NBC. Barbara Bosson and Dennis Dugan (Richie Brockelman)

ROSETTI AND RYAN: September 22–November 10, 1977, NBC. Squire Fridell (Frank Ryan), Julie Cobb (guest), and Tony Roberts (Tony Rosetti)

THE INCREDIBLE HULK: Lou Ferrigno (the Hulk)

THE INCREDIBLE HULK: March 10, 1978–June 2, 1982, CBS. Bill Bixby transforms into the Hulk

THE INCREDIBLE HULK: Bill Bixby

THE BETTY WHITE SHOW: September 12, 1977–January 9, 1978, CBS. John Hillerman, Betty White, and Georgia Engel

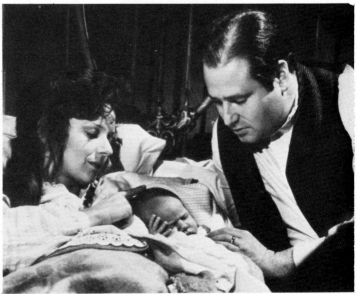

FREE COUNTRY: June 24, 1978–July 22, 1978, ABC. Judy Kahan and Rob Reiner

SANFORD ARMS: September 16, 1977–October 14, 1977, NBC. LaWanda Page and Theodore Wilson

FANTASY ISLAND: Ricardo Montalban with guests Linda Day George and Victor Buono

SANFORD ARMS: Tina Andrews, Theodore Wilson, and John Earl

FANTASY ISLAND: January 28, 1978–present, ABC. Ricardo Montalban and Herve Villechaize

BIG HAWAII: September 21, 1977–November 30, 1977, NBC. John Dehner

EVENING IN BYZANTIUM: (Mini-series) August 1978, syndicated. Eddie Albert and Glenn Ford

BABY, I'M BACK: January 30, 1978–August 12, 1978, CBS. Tony Holmes, Demond Wilson, and Kim Fields

THE SAN PEDRO BEACH BUMS: September 19, 1977–December 19, 1977, ABC. (Seated) Stuart Pankin, John Mark Robinson; (standing) Jeffry Druce, Chris Murney, Darryl McCullough

WHAT REALLY HAPPENED TO THE CLASS OF '65?: December 8, 1977–July 27, 1978, NBC. Kim Cattrall and John Rubinstein

PROJECT U.F.O.: February 19, 1978–January 4, 1979, NBC. William Jordan and Caskey Swaim

CARTER COUNTRY: September 15, 1977–August 23, 1979, ABC. Harry Vernon and Kene Holliday

DALLAS: April 2, 1978–present, CBS. Steve Kanaly, Patrick Duffy, Victoria Principal, Barbara Bel Geddes, Jim Davis, Charlene Tilton, Larry Hagman, Linda Gray

HUSBANDS, WIVES & LOVERS: March 10, 1978–June 30, 1978, CBS. Charles Siebert and Claudette Nevins

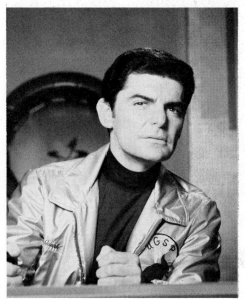

QUARK: February 24, 1978–April 14, 1978, NBC. Richard Benjamin (Adam Quark)

THE ROLLER GIRLS: April 24, 1978–May 10, 1978, NBC. *(Center)* Terry Kiser; *(front)* Rhonda Bates, Marcy Hanson; *(back)* Candy Ann Brown, Joanna Cassidy, Marilyn Tokuda

LOGAN'S RUN: September 16, 1977–January 16, 1978, CBS. Randy Powell, Heather Menzies, Donald Moffat, and George Harrison (Logan)

LUCAN: September 12, 1977–December 4, 1978, ABC. Kevin Brophy (Lucan)

OPERATION PETTICOAT: September 17, 1977–October 26, 1978, ABC. John Astin, Richard Gilliland, Bond Gideon, Dorrie Thomson, Jamie Lee Curtis, and Melinda Naud

CHiPS: September 15, 1977–April 10, 1983, NBC. Larry Wilcox and Erik Estrada

CHiPS: Larry Wilcox and Erik Estrada

THE BASTARD: (Mini-series) May 1978, syndicated. Mark Needy, Eleanor Parker, Andrew Stevens, and Patricia Neal

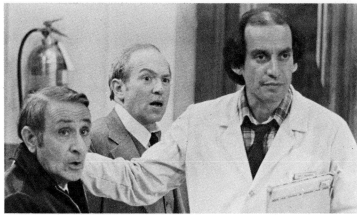

A.E.S. HUDSON STREET: March 23, 1978–April 20, 1978, ABC. Ralph Manza, Stefan Gierasch, and Gregory Sierra

SOAP: September 13, 1977–April 20, 1981, ABC. Katherine Helmond and Robert Guillaume

A.E.S. HUDSON STREET: (Seated) Susan Peretz, Gregory Sierra; (standing) Stefan Gierasch, Bill Cort, Ray Stewart, Allan Miller, Rosana Soto, and Ralph Manza

SOAP: (Seated) Billy Crystal, Cathryn Damon, Katherine Helmond, and Jennifer Salt; (standing) Robert Urich, Ted Wass, Richard Mulligan, Robert Guillaume, Robert Mandan, Jimmy Baio, Diana Canova, and Arthur Peterson

MULLIGAN'S STEW: October 24, 1977–December 13, 1977, NBC. *(Bottom)* Suzanne Crough; *(middle)* Sunshine Lee, Elinor Donahue, Lawrence Pressman, and K.C. Martel; *(top)* Chris Ciampa, Lory Kochheim, Julie Anne Haddock, and Johnny Doran

20/20: Dave Marash, Sylvia Chase, Thomas Hoving, Hugh Downs, and Geraldo Rivera

20/20: June 6, 1978–present, ABC. Hugh Downs (host)

THE FITZPATRICKS: September 5, 1977–January 10, 1978, CBS. *(Clockwise)* Michele Tobin, James Vincent McNichol, Clark Brandon, Bert Kramer, Mari Clare Costello, Derek Wells, and Sean Marshall

LOU GRANT: September 20, 1977–September 13, 1982, CBS. Linda Kelsey, Jack Bannon, and Edward Asner (Lou Grant)

LOU GRANT: Edward Asner, Daryl Anderson, Robert Walden, and Cliff Potts

LOU GRANT: Mason Adams and Nancy Marchand

ON OUR OWN: October 9, 1977–August 20, 1978, CBS. Lynnie Greene, Remark Ramsay (guest), and Bess Armstrong

JAMES AT 15: October 27, 1977–July 27, 1978, NBC. David Hubbard and Lance Kerwin (James Hunter)

ON OUR OWN: (Foreground) Lynnie Greene, Georgann Johnson, Bess Armstrong, Michael Tucci, and Dixie Carter

ON OUR OWN: Dixie Carter and John Christopher Jones

THE REDD FOXX COMEDY HOUR: September 15, 1977–January 26, 1978, ABC. Redd Foxx (host)

THE RETURN OF CAPTAIN NEMO: March 8, 1978–March 29, 1978, CBS. Jose Ferrer (Captain Nemo)

SPACE FORCE: April 28, 1978 (one episode), NBC. Joe Medalis

HAVING BABIES (JULIE FARR, M.D.): March 7, 1978–April 18, 1978, ABC. Beverly Todd, Susan Sullivan (Julie Farr, M.D.), and Mitchell Ryan

THE LOVE BOAT: *(Front)* Lauren Tewes, Gavin MacLeod, Jill Whelan; *(back)* Fred Grandy, Ted Lange, Bernie Kopell

THE LOVE BOAT: September 24, 1977–present, ABC. *(Clockwise from bottom)* Gavin MacLeod, Fred Grandy, Ted Lange, Bernie Kopell, and Lauren Tewes

HOW THE WEST WAS WON: February 12, 1978–April 23, 1979, ABC. James Arness

THE LOVE BOAT: Gavin MacLeod and Les Gerber

HOW THE WEST WAS WON: James Arness

1978-79

Once again, television was present for triumph and tragedy. From the White House lawn, cameras telecast live an event the world thought it would never see. Egypt's President Anwar Sadat and Israel's Prime Minister Menachem Begin signed a treaty ending a state of war that had existed between their countries for 30 years. President Carter also signed the Hebrew, Arabic, and English versions of the Camp David accord as a witness.

From the depths of space, cameras aboard the *Voyager* probe transmitted pictures of Jupiter and its moons. Viewers around the world were awed by these spectacular images of the giant sphere that the craft began taking when it got within 172,500 miles of the planet.

In the tiny country of Guyana, South America, cameras filmed the ambush attack of NBC reporter Don Harris and photographer Robert Brown, who were murdered while covering the Jonestown mass-suicide story.

In the Central American country of Nicaragua, cameras secretly recorded the brutal murder of ABC's Bill Stewart, who was on assignment covering the civil war there. He was ordered to lie face down on the ground by a government soldier who then shot him point-blank in the head.

In programming, this season was one of the most competitive and expensive in years. The networks juggled their schedules continually, causing viewers a great deal of confusion and making it difficult for them to establish regular viewing patterns. At one point during this intensely contested season, the networks each scheduled a blockbuster program on the same night: February 11. ABC premiered the eagerly awaited TV movie about the life of Elvis Presley, with Kurt Russell in the title role. CBS aired part one of a rerun of the movie that had received the highest rating in history, *Gone With the Wind*. And NBC debuted the Academy Award-winning *One Flew Over the Cuckoo's Nest*, starring Jack Nicholson.

ABC scored another impressive feat with "Roots: The Next Generations," a sequel to the original mini-series. This was a seven-night, 12-hour, $18-million production. The series opened in 1882 and traced 88 years in the history of Alex Haley's family, ending with the author himself being portrayed in contemporary times. This sequel did not dominate the ratings as had the original "Roots," but all seven episodes scored high enough to have placed within the week's top 11 programs. Some of the principal performers were Henry Fonda, Richard Thomas, Olivia de Havilland, Harry Morgan, Ruby Dee, Paul Winfield, James Earl Jones, and Marlon Brando—in his first dramatic appearance on television in 30 years.

The networks did best with situation comedies this year. And "Mork and Mindy" was the best of the best, becoming the top-rated new show of the season. The rulers of the planet Ork dispatched one of their own kind, Mork, to study life on Earth. This alien, who looked very human, landed in Boulder, Colorado, and met a young woman who befriended him. Comedian Robin Williams starred as Mork and Pam Dawber co-starred as Mindy. Others in the cast were Conrad Janis as Frederick McConnell, Mindy's father, and Elizabeth Kerr as Cora Hudson, her grandmother. The series was on ABC for four years.

"Diff'rent Strokes" starred Conrad Bain (most recently Dr. Arthur Harmon on "Maude") as millionaire Philip Drummond, who adopted two Harlem orphans who were the sons of his late housekeeper. Gary Coleman and Todd Bridges played the eight-year-old Arnold Jackson and his brother, thirteen-year-old Willis. But it was little Arnold who always stole the show. The series was NBC's top-rated sitcom its first three seasons and continues to do well today.

"The Dukes of Hazzard," an hour-long comedy series set in Hazzard County, Georgia, was about life in the rural South. The simple plots always involved fast cars, beautiful girls, and moonshine whiskey. The central characters were three cousins who always managed to

have a good time despite their constant run-ins with the corrupt local power boss. The original cast included John Schneider as Bo Duke, Tom Wopat as Luke Duke, Catherine Bach as Daisy Duke, Sorrell Brooke as Jefferson Davis "Boss" Hogg, and Denver Pyle as wise Uncle Jesse. The CBS show has been in the top 10 the last three seasons.

The Sunshine Cab Company was the appropriate setting for ABC's "Taxi." The original cast included Judd Hirsch as Alex Rieger, a sensible career cabby; Tony Danza as Tony Banta, a part-time boxer; Jeff Conaway as Bobby Wheeler, an aspiring actor; Marilu Henner as Elaine Nardo, a would-be art dealer; Danny DeVito as Louie DePalma, the cynical dispatcher; and Andy Kaufman as Latka Gravas, the mechanic who couldn't quite master the English language. This season as well as next the series was a top-rated show. In the subsequent two years, its popularity diminished and it was dropped from the network's schedule after its fourth season. Then NBC decided to include it in its lineup and "Taxi" began its fifth season on a new network, only to suffer plummeting ratings and cancellation again. But within a few weeks after their decision was made NBC reconsidered and gave "Taxi" a second chance. "Taxi's" reprieve was not successful and the network canceled the show at the conclusion of the television season.

"WKRP in Cincinnati" was set in a 5,000-watt radio station in Cincinnati, Ohio. The series was about the diverse group of "characters" that made up the staff: Andy Travis (Gary Sandy), the program director; Dr. Johnny Fever (Howard Hesseman), the day DJ; Venus Flytrap (Tim Reid), the night DJ; Arthur Carlson (Gordon Jump), the station manager; Jennifer Marlow (Loni Anderson), the receptionist; Les Nessman (Richard Sanders), the news director; and Herb Tarlek (Frank Bonner), the sales manager. This wacky bunch was seen on CBS four seasons.

In other news of the season, ABC had a gigantic flop with "Battlestar Galactica." This hour-long space-adventure series was introduced in a three-hour telecast at a reported cost of $3 million. The series was one of the most expensive ever made for TV, but its appeal was short-lived and it did not survive the season. A show of a different nature on NBC had a trial run and became part of the fall schedule the next season. The show, "Real People," a human-interest program that is still on the air, has several co-hosts, including Sara Purcell, Fred Willard, John Barbour, Skip Stephenson, and Bill Rafferty. But its real stars were the real-life people it profiled. ABC ended the TV year with the five top-rated shows: "Laverne and Shirley," "Three's Company," "Mork and Mindy," "Happy Days," and "Angie." This was icing on the cake for television's No. 1 network.

PLEASE STAND BY: 1978, syndicated. *(Seated)* Dick Schaal, Elinor Donahue; *(standing)* Stephen Michael Schwartz, Bryan Scott, Darian Mathias

THE MacKENZIES OF PARADISE COVE: March 27, 1979–May 18, 1979, ABC. *(Front)* Randi Kiger, Lori Walsh; *(back)* Sean Marshall, Keith Mitchell, Shawn Stevens

THE WAVERLY WONDERS: September 22, 1978–October 6, 1978, NBC. Joe Namath

SWORD OF JUSTICE: October 7, 1978–August 11,1979, NBC. Dack Rambo and Bert Rosario

TURNABOUT: January 26, 1979–March 30, 1979, NBC. Sharon Gless and John Schuck

THE WHITE SHADOW: November 27,1978–July 22, 1981, CBS. Ken Howard

MRS. COLUMBO: February 26, 1979–September 6, 1979, NBC. Kate Mulgrew (Mrs. Kate Columbo)

REAL PEOPLE: April 18, 1979–present, NBC. *(Clockwise from left)* Sara Purcell, Skip Stephenson, Byron Allen, Bill Rafferty, and John Barbour

WHO'S WATCHING THE KIDS?: September 22, 1978–December 15, 1978, NBC. Jim Belushi and Larry Breeding

FLYING HIGH: September 29, 1978–January 23, 1979, CBS. Kathryn Witt, Pat Klous, and Connie Sellecca

THE BAD NEWS BEARS: March 24, 1979–July 26, 1980, CBS. Jack Warden

THE BAD NEWS BEARS: Jack Warden and the Bears team

WKRP IN CINCINNATI: January 15, 1979–September 20, 1982, CBS. Gordon Jump, Gary Sandy and Howard Hesseman

WKRP IN CINCINNATI: *(First row)* Loni Anderson, Howard Hesseman; *(second row)* Richard Sanders, Gary Sandy, Jan Smithers, Tim Reid; *(third row)* Frank Bonner, Gordon Jump

PAPER CHASE: September 19, 1978–July 17, 1979, CBS. James Stephens and John Houseman

FLATBUSH: February 26, 1979–March 12, 1979, CBS. *(Front)* Randy Stumpf and Vincent Bufano; *(back)* Adrian Zmed, Joseph Cali, Sandy Helberg

WKRP IN CINCINNATI: Gary Sandy and Gordon Jump

THE RUNAWAYS: May 29, 1979–September 4, 1979, NBC. Karen Machon and Alan Feinstein

BILLY: February 26, 1979–April 28, 1979, CBS. Steve Guttenberg (Billy Fisher) and James Gallery

VEGA$: September 20, 1978–October 16, 1981, ABC. Robert Urich

GRANDPA GOES TO WASHINGTON: September 20, 1978–January 16, 1979, NBC. Larry Linville and Jack Albertson

VEGA$: Tony Curtis, Judy Landers, Phyllis Elizabeth Davis, and Robert Urich

MISS WINSLOW AND SON: March 28, 1979–May 2, 1979, CBS. Roscoe Lee Brown, Darleen Carr (Susan Winslow), Elliott Reid, and Sarah Marshall

CENTENNIAL: (Mini-series) October 1, 1978–February 4, 1979, NBC. Robert Conrad

CENTENNIAL: Richard Chamberlain

BATTLESTAR GALACTICA: September 17, 1978–April 29, 1979, ABC. *(Front)* Maren Jensen; *(back)* Dirk Benedict, Richard Hatch, Lorne Greene

THE EDDIE CAPRA MYSTERIES: September 22, 1978–January 12, 1979, NBC. Vincent Baggetta (Eddie Capra)

IKE: (Mini-series) May 3–6, 1979, ABC. Lee Remick and Robert Duvall (Ike)

TAXI: Judd Hirsch and Danny DeVito

TAXI: Tony Danza and Judd Hirsch

THE NEXT STEP BEYOND: 1978, syndicated. Eric Howell and Harry Chambers in an episode

SALVAGE 1: January 29, 1979–November 11, 1979, ABC. Trish Stewart, Joel Higgins, and Andy Griffith

TAXI: September 12, 1978–April 13, 1983, ABC, NBC. *(Front)* Marilu Henner, Jeff Conaway, Danny DeVito; *(back)* Randall Carver, Andy Kaufman, Judd Hirsch, Tony Danza

MORK AND MINDY: September 14, 1978–August 12, 1982, ABC. Pam Dawber (Mindy) and Robin Williams (Mork)

THE ROPERS: March 13, 1979–May 22, 1980, ABC. Norman Fell and Audra Lindley (Stanley and Helen Roper)

CO-ED FEVER: February 4, 1979 (only episode), CBS. Heather Thomas, Alexa Kenin, and Cathryn O'Neil

DIFF'RENT STROKES: November 3, 1978–present, NBC. Gary Coleman, Dody Goodman, and Conrad Bain

MORK AND MINDY: Pam Dawber and Robin Williams

DIFF'RENT STROKES: Todd Bridges and Gary Coleman

DIFF'RENT STROKES: Conrad Bain and Gary Coleman

IN THE BEGINNING: September 20, 1978–November 1, 1978, CBS. Priscilla Lopez and McLean Stevenson

$1.98 BEAUTY SHOW: 1978, syndicated. Rip Taylor (host) and contestants

IN THE BEGINNING: Priscilla Lopez and McLean Stevenson

APPLE PIE: September 23, 1978–October 7, 1978, ABC. *(Front)* Jack Gilford, Dabney Coleman, Rue McClanahan, Caitlin O'Heaney; *(back)* Mike Binder, Dick Libertini

THE DUKES OF HAZZARD: January 26, 1979–present, CBS. James Best, Sorrell Brooke, John Schneider, Tom Wopat, and Catherine Bach

ROOTS: THE NEXT GENERATIONS: (Mini-series) February 18–25, 1979, ABC. Marlon Brando and James Earl Jones

ROOTS: THE NEXT GENERATIONS: Alex Haley (author) and actors playing Haley—James Earl Jones, Damon Evans, and Christoff St. John

STOCKARD CHANNING IN JUST FRIENDS: March 4, 1979–August 11, 1979, CBS. Stockard Channing

STOCKARD CHANNING IN JUST FRIENDS: (Seated) Lou Criscuolo, Stockard Channing, Lawrence Pressman, and Albert Insinnia; (standing) Mimi Kennedy, Gerrit Graham, Sydney Goldsmith

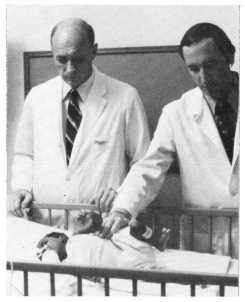

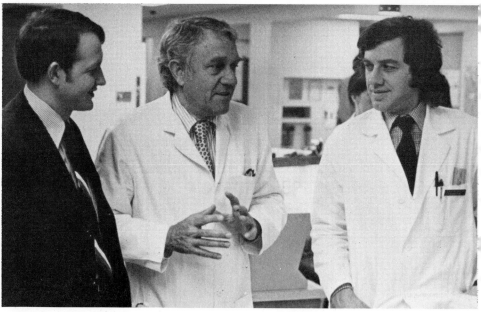

LIFELINE: October 8, 1978–September 6, 1979, NBC. Dr. Paul Ebert and Dr. Kevin Turley

LIFELINE: Dr. Glen Church, Dr. Theodore Kurze, and Dr. Oleg Chikovani

W.E.B.: September 13, 1978–October 5, 1978, NBC. Pamela Bellwood

THE AMERICAN GIRLS: September 23, 1978–November 10, 1978, CBS. Debra Clinger, David Spielberg, and Priscilla Barnes

B.J. AND THE BEAR: (Front) Julie Gregg, Laurette Spang, Carlene Watkins; (center) Spray Rosso, Daryle Ann Lindley, Janet Louise Johnson, Angela Aames, Sonia Manzano; (back) Greg Evigan

W.E.B.: Dana Wynter (guest) and Andrew Prine

B.J. AND THE BEAR: February 10, 1979–September 13, 1980, NBC. Greg Evigan (B.J. McKay) and Claude Akins

MAKIN' IT: February 1, 1979–March 16, 1979, ABC. David Naughton

MAKIN' IT: *(Front)* David Naughton, Denise Miller, and Greg Antonacci; *(back)* Lou Antonio, Ellen Travolta

BROTHERS AND SISTERS: Larry Anderson, Amy Johnston, and Chris Lemon

BROTHERS AND SISTERS: January 21, 1979–April 6, 1979, NBC. William Windom, Mary Crosby, and Jon Cutler

ANGIE: February 8, 1979–October 23, 1980, ABC. *(Front)* Donna Pescow, Tammy Lauren; *(back)* Debralee Scott, Doris Roberts, Robert Hays, Sharon Spelman, Diane Robin

ANGIE: Robert Hays and Donna Pescow (Angie Falco Benson)

BLIND AMBITION: (Mini-series) May 20–23, 1979, CBS. Martin Sheen, Rip Torn, and Lawrence Pressman

THE NEW AVENGERS: September 15, 1978–March 23, 1979, CBS. Patrick MacNee, Joanna Lumley, and Gareth Hunt

DELTA HOUSE: January 18, 1979–April 28, 1979, ABC. *(First row center)* John R. Vernon (Dean Wormer) and the entire Delta House fraternity of Faber College

THE NEW AVENGERS: Gareth Hunt

DELTA HOUSE: Josh Mostel

1979-80

National and international events weren't the only news on television this season. TV made a little "news" of its own.

In national news, the season had just begun when Pope John Paul II arrived in the United States. While millions got a glimpse of the pontiff, many millions more saw him on TV as cameras followed him on his pilgrimage to Boston, New York, Philadelphia, rural Iowa, and Chicago. The pope concluded his visit in Washington, D.C., meeting with President Carter.

In international news, the big story began shortly after John Paul's visit when Jimmy Carter was faced with his gravest crisis. A mob of Moslem "students" took over the U.S. Embassy in Teheran, Iran, and seized more than 60 Americans hostage. All three networks reported every available detail of the hostage crisis (critics claimed the media were manipulated by the so-called students), including their own interviews with the Ayatollah Khomeini, the religious zealot who had overthrown the shah of Iran. At first, the networks presented daily late-night wrap-ups of the crisis, but as it wore on, CBS and NBC pulled back their coverage, presenting nightly summaries only if some dramatic development had occurred.

This then leads to the news TV itself was making. ABC continued to cover the hostage crisis as it had from the start: a 15-minute late-night report each weekday evening for the duration of this bizarre event. It was out of this news story that the network debuted a new concept in news programming—"Nightline," with Ted Koppel, who moderated an in-depth look at a newsworthy occurrence each night.

For the first time, all three networks began the fall season with regularly scheduled prime-time news magazine programs. CBS's "60 Minutes" was the oldest and most popular of the trio. ABC's "20/20" was starting its second full season. And NBC's "Prime Time Sunday" had debuted just before the season began, with Tom Snyder as host.

Two veteran television reporters became news themselves. Howard K. Smith, an ABC news analyst and commentator, resigned after a disagreement over journalistic philosophy. Daniel Schorr, a former CBS news correspondent who was involved in a controversial leak of a congressional report on the CIA, was named senior correspondent for the Cable News Network, a new 24-hour TV news service.

Another cable TV innovation, this time on the Cable Public Affairs Network, provided coverage of the U.S. House of Representatives, whose members, after years of debate over the matter, permitted live telecasts of its sessions.

In sporting news, ABC set an Olympic Games ratings record when 22,050,000 households tuned in to its videotaped replay of the U.S. Hockey Team's victory over the invincible Russians.

Few new entertainment programs achieved enough success to survive the season. But of the six that did, all but one—"Buck Rogers in the 25th Century" (NBC), starring Gil Gerard—are now in their fourth year.

"Benson" was a spinoff from ABC's situation-comedy series "Soap," in which Robert Guillaume, as Benson, was the Tate family's cook. This new ABC series had Benson moving on to become the manager of the large household of the state's governor. Others featured were James Noble as the governor; Inga Swenson as Gretchen Kraus, the housekeeper; and Caroline McWilliams as Marcie Hill, the secretary.

"Trapper John, M.D." was an hour-long medical drama starring Pernell Roberts (formerly Adam Cartwright on "Bonanza") as Dr. John "Trapper" McIntyre, chief surgeon of San Francisco Memorial Hospital. The character had originated on the Korean War hit series "M*A*S*H." In this series, Trapper was seen many years later. Co-starring was Gregory Harrison as Dr. Alonzo "Gonzo" Gates, a young doctor who in many respects was Trapper's younger self. From this season on, the CBS series has been among the top 25 shows each year.

ABC's "Hart to Hart" was an adventure/detective series about a wealthy businessman and his author wife who both enjoyed playing amateur detectives when their busy schedules permitted. Robert Wagner and Stefanie Powers were Jonathan and Jennifer Hart. Also featured was Lionel Stander as Max, their aide.

At midseason, CBS premiered a spin-off from its popular "Dallas" series, "Knots Landing." This continuing drama centered on the lives of Valene and Gary Ewing, outcasts of the Ewing clan. Ted Schackelford and Joan Van Ark starred as the black sheep of the wealthy Texas oil family, living in southern California.

And ABC introduced an hour-long human-interest program late in the TV year—"That's Incredible!" The show profiled unusual people and strange phenomena and was co-hosted by Cathy Lee Crosby, John Davidson, and football's Fran Tarkenton.

Finally, some goings-on on NBC: the network had the distinction of presenting the first entertainment special to be filmed for American television within the People's Republic of China, a three-hour Bob Hope special, "On the Road to China." "The Tonight Show Starring Johnny Carson—The 17th Anniversary Show" was telecast live in prime time. This has since become the way the annual anniversary show has been aired. And the network this season resurrected its corporate trademark, the peacock. Retired in 1975, it was brought back to enhance the new "Proud as a Peacock" promotional campaign the network adopted this year.

RETURN OF THE SAINT: December 21, 1979–August 15, 1980, CBS. Ian Ogilvy

STRUCK BY LIGHTNING: September 19, 1979–October 3, 1979, CBS. Jack Elam

GALACTICA 1980: January 27, 1980–May 4, 1980, ABC. Robyn Douglas, Kent McCord, Lorne Greene, and Barry Van Dyke

ME AND MAXX: March 22, 1980–July 25, 1980, NBC. Joe Santos and Melissa Michaelson (Maxx Davis)

BUCK ROGERS IN THE 25TH CENTURY: September 27, 1979–April 16, 1981, NBC. Erin Gray and Gil Gerard (Buck Rogers)

UNITED STATES: March 11, 1980–April 29, 1980, NBC. Rossie Harris, Beau Bridges, Helen Shaver, and Justin Dana

THE SIX O'CLOCK FOLLIES: April 24, 1980–September 13, 1980, NBC. Larry Fishburne, Arrika Wells, and A. C. Weary

BUCK ROGERS IN THE 25TH CENTURY: *(Foreground)* Erin Gray and Gil Gerard in a twenty-fifth-century city

THE MARY TYLER MOORE HOUR: March 4, 1979–June 6, 1979, CBS. Mary Tyler Moore and Nancy Walker (guest)

NOBODY'S PERFECT: June 26, 1980–August 28, 1980, ABC. (Top) Michael Durrell; (center) Ron Moody; (bottom) Cassie Yates

THE LAZARUS SYNDROME: September 11, 1979–October 9, 1979, ABC. Louis Gossett, Jr.

PARIS: September 29, 1979–January 15, 1980, CBS. James Earl Jones (Woody Paris) and Hank Garrett

THAT'S INCREDIBLE!: March 3, 1980–present, ABC. John Davidson, Cathy Lee Crosby, and Fran Tarkenton (hosts)

THE ASSOCIATES: September 23, 1979–April 17, 1980, ABC. Wilfred Hyde-White, Alley Mills, and Martin Short

SEMI-TOUGH: May 29, 1980–June 19, 1980, ABC. Bruce McGill, Markie Post, and David Hasselhoff

BENSON: September 13, 1979–present, ABC. Robert Guillaume (Benson)

A MAN CALLED SLOANE: September 22, 1979–December 22, 1979, NBC. Robert Conrad (Thomas R. Sloane)

KATE LOVES A MYSTERY: October 18, 1979–December 6, 1979, NBC. Don Stroud and Kate Mulgrew (Kate Callahan)

BENSON: *(Front)* Missy Gold, Robert Guillaume, Ethan Phillips; *(back)* Rene Auberjonois, Inga Swenson, James Noble

THE BAXTERS: 1979–80, syndicated. Anita Gillette and Larry Keith (Nancy and Fred Baxter)

240 ROBERT: September 3, 1979–December 10, 1979, ABC. Mark Harmon, Joanna Cassidy, and John Bennett Perry

FLO: Sudie Bond and Henry Jones

HERE'S BOOMER: March 14, 1980–August 29, 1980, NBC. Johnny (Boomer)

YOUNG MAVERICK: November 28, 1979–January 16, 1980, CBS. Charles Frank (young Ben Maverick), James Garner (Bret Maverick), and Jack Kelly (Bart Maverick)

FLO: Vic Tayback (guest) and Polly Holliday

WHEN THE WHISTLE BLOWS: March 14, 1980–July 27, 1980, ABC. Tim Rossovich, Phillip Brown, Ben Markley, Doug Barr, and Dolph Sweet

FLO: Leo Burmester and Lucy Lee Flippin

FLO: March 24, 1980–July 21, 1981, CBS. Polly Holliday (Florence Jean Castleberry/Flo) and Barbara Babcock (guest)

THE TIM CONWAY SHOW: March 22, 1980–August 31, 1981, CBS. Harvey Korman and Tim Conway (host)

SHIRLEY: October 26, 1979–January 25, 1980, NBC. Shirley Jones (Shirley Miller)

SHIRLEY: Peter Barton and Bret Shryer

OUT OF THE BLUE: September 9, 1979–December 16, 1979, ABC. James Brogan, Olivia Barash, Clark Brandon, and Jason and Shane Keller

SHIRLEY: Shirley Jones, Rosanna Arquette, and Edward Winter (guest)

CALIFORNIA FEVER: September 25, 1979–December 11, 1979, CBS. *(Foreground)* Jimmy McNichol; *(background)* Lorenzo Lamas, Michele Tobin, Marc McClure

OUT OF THE BLUE: Hannah Dean and James Brogan

GOOD TIME GIRLS: Georgia Engel, Lorna Patterson, Annie Potts, and Francine Tacker

GOOD TIME GIRLS: January 22, 1980–August 29, 1980, ABC. *(Bottom)* Annie Potts, Lorna Patterson; *(center)* Georgia Engel, Adrian Zmed, Francine Tacker; *(top)* Merwin Goldsmith, Marcia Lewis, Peter Scolari

THE LAST CONVERTIBLE: (Mini-series) September 24–26, 1979, NBC. Edward Albert and Deborah Raffin

346

A NEW KIND OF FAMILY: September 16, 1979–January 5, 1980, ABC. Gwynne Gilford and Eileen Brennan

A NEW KIND OF FAMILY: *(Front)* O.J. (family dog, Heinz), Rob Lowe, David Hollander; *(back)* Lauri Hendler, Gwynne Gilford, Eileen Brennan, and Connie Ann Hearn

KNOTS LANDING: December 27, 1979–present, CBS. Donna Mills and Ted Schackelford

THE BIG SHOW: March 4, 1980–May 27, 1980, NBC. *(Top)* Graham Chapman, Charlie Hill, Shabba-Doo; *(center)* Mimi Kennedy; *(bottom)* Owen Sullivan

KNOTS LANDING: Donna Mills and John Pleshette

HART TO HART: Jason Evers (guest), Lionel Stander, and Allyn Ann McLearie (guest)

THOSE AMAZING ANIMALS: August 24, 1980–August 23, 1981, ABC. Priscilla Presley, Burgess Meredith, and Jim Stafford

MISADVENTURES OF SHERIFF LOBO: September 18, 1979–September 2, 1980, NBC. Camilla Sparv (guest) and Claude Akins (Sheriff Elroy S. Lobo)

HART TO HART: September 22, 1979–present, ABC. Robert Wagner and Stefanie Powers (Jonathan and Jennifer Hart)

HART TO HART: Robert Wagner and Stefanie Powers

THE MARTIAN CHRONICLES: (Mini-series) January 27–29, 1980, NBC. Rock Hudson and Darren McGavin

ONE IN A MILLION: January 8, 1980–June 23, 1980, ABC. *(Foreground)* Shirley Hemphill; *(background)* Ann Weldon, Keene Curtis, Carl Ballantine, Mel Stewart, and Richard Paul

SANFORD: March 15, 1980–September 10, 1980, NBC. Redd Foxx (Fred Sanford)

STONE: January 14, 1980–March 17, 1980, ABC. Robby Weaver, Dennis Weaver (Sgt. Dan Stone), and Pat Hingle

TRAPPER JOHN, M.D.: September 25, 1979–present, CBS. Charles Siebert, Madge Sinclair, Pernell Roberts (Dr. John "Trapper" McIntyre), Gregory Harrison, Brian Mitchell, and Christopher Norris

TENSPEED AND BROWN SHOE: January 27, 1980–July 11, 1980, ABC. *(Front)* Ben Vereen (E.L. "Tenspeed" Turner) and Jeff Goldblum (Lionel "Brown Shoe" Whitney)

B.A.D. CATS: Steven Hanks, Michelle Pfeiffer, and Asher Brauner

SPEAK UP AMERICA: April 20, 1980–October 10, 1980, NBC. Marjoe Gortner and Rhonda Bates

B.A.D. CATS: January 4, 1980–February 8, 1980, ABC. Asher Brauner, Michelle Pfeiffer, Vic Morrow, Steven Hanks, and Jimmie Walker

THE CHISHOLMS: January 19, 1980–March 15, 1980, CBS. Les Lannom and James Van Patten

THE CHISHOLMS: *(Front)* James Van Patten, Susan Swift, Stacey Nelkin, and Brian Kerwin; *(center)* Ben Murphy; *(back)* Robert Preston, Rosemary Harris

THE FACTS OF LIFE: August 24, 1979–present, NBC. *(Foreground)* Molly Ringwald, Julie Piekarski; *(kneeling)* Mindy Cohn, Kim Fields; *(standing)* Julie Anne Haddock, Lisa Whelchel, Charlotte Rae, John Lawlor, Felice Schachter

PHYL AND MIKHY: May 26, 1980–June 30, 1980, CBS. Murphy Cross (Phyl) and Rick Lohman (Mikhy)

THE LAST RESORT: September 19, 1979–March 17, 1980, CBS. Ray Underwood, Walter Olkewicz, Larry Breeding, and Robert Costanzo

ARCHIE BUNKER'S PLACE: September 23, 1979–April 4, 1983, CBS. *(Seated)* Danielle Brisebois, Carroll O'Connor (Archie Bunker); *(standing)* Jason Wingreen, Martin Balsam, Danny Dayton, Bill Quinn

ARCHIE BUNKER'S PLACE: Carroll O'Connor, Anne Meara, and Martin Balsam

ARCHIE BUNKER'S PLACE: Michael Alldredge (guest), Carroll O'Connor, Martin Balsam, and Mel Bryant

ARCHIE BUNKER'S PLACE: Carroll O'Connor, Alan Melvin, and Martin Balsam

HOUSE CALLS: Richard Stahl, Lynn Redgrave, and Wayne Rogers

HOUSE CALLS: December 17, 1979–September 13, 1982, CBS. Wayne Rogers and David Wayne

 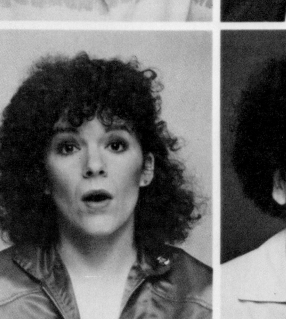 

FRIDAYS: April 11, 1980–October 22, 1982, ABC. *(Top)* Bruce Mahler, Brandis Kemp, John Roarke; *(middle)* Darrow Igus, Melanie Chartoff, Michael Richards; *(bottom)* Mark Blankfield, Maryedith Burrell, Larry David

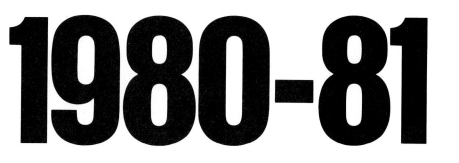

1980-81

Television watchers saw a world of events happen, and one world event that didn't, on the small screen this year (unless they already had giant-screen TV).

Just before the start of the season, they saw the traditional gavel-to-gavel network coverage of the Republican National Convention, which met in Detroit to nominate Ronald Reagan for president and George Bush as his running mate. From New York, they saw the Democrats renominate President Carter and Vice-President Mondale.

Afterward, they saw Carter and Reagan engage in just one debate, a 90-minute exchange that took place in Cleveland. All three networks carried the live event, which achieved a 58.9 percent rating and an 84 percent share of the audience.

Then, following Reagan's election-night victory, they saw him take the oath of office at his festive inauguration and, at the conclusion of his address, saw the American hostages, after 444 days in captivity, arrive at the U.S. Army base in Wiesbaden, West Germany.

Not long afterward, they saw something they had seen before but never wanted to see again. As the president was leaving the Washington, D.C., Hilton Hotel after addressing a labor meeting, news cameras recorded an assassination attempt on him by a lone gunman. Reagan, as well as his press secretary and two law-enforcement officers, was wounded in the burst of shots. Television continually kept the nation informed of the president's condition from the time he entered the hospital until he returned to the White House.

The final event they saw was the mission of the first reusable spacecraft, the space shuttle *Columbia*. Launched from the Kennedy Space Center in Florida, the winged craft orbited the earth 36 times over a period of 54 hours and 22 minutes before landing at Edwards Air Force Base in California the way any conventional plane does. Soon after the *Columbia* re-entered the atmosphere, viewers saw a dramatic live TV picture of

it 73 miles from the landing sight. Then, 13 miles from touchdown, a chase plane with television cameras aboard began transmitting live pictures until it was back on Earth once again. The mission was the first time American astronauts had ventured into space in nearly six years.

The world event viewers didn't get to see occurred before the season's start. NBC had committed a record $100 million to telecast the Summer Olympic Games from Moscow. But the Soviet's invasion of Afghanistan had led to the United States issuing a warning that it would boycott the Games if the U.S.S.R. didn't pull its forces out. The Russians didn't and, after much deliberation, the U.S. Olympic Committee voted in favor of the boycott. This decision was very costly to the network. Besides the money lost in preparation and in advertising revenue, the loss hurt its promotion efforts for the new season.

This season was unlike all others before it because instead of beginning in September it began in November. An actor's strike that began during the summer halted production on all made-for-television movies, most prime-time filmed and taped series, and all theatrical films. The strike was brought about by the Screen Actors Guild (SAG) and the American Federation of Television and Radio Artists (AFTRA), both of which wanted to win for their members a share of the money earned by producers selling the rights to distribute programs on pay-TV systems and on prerecorded video cassettes and disks. It wasn't until late September that the unions reached a tentative settlement with the producers. This was followed by three weeks for ratification by the rank and file and then three or four weeks more before the first new shows were ready to air.

But once the season began, this became a relatively good year for programming. While there were fewer new programs introduced than in recent years, a greater percentage of them returned the following season. Of the

approximately 30 new shows to debut, 10 made it back for a second season.

The NBC shows were: "Flamingo Road," a prime-time soap opera with a Southern setting, starring Howard Duff, Mark Harmon, Morgan Fairchild, and Cristina Raines; the situation comedy "Harper Valley P.T.A.," starring Barbara Eden; the musical variety show "Barbara Mandrell and the Mandrell Sisters"; and the gritty police drama "Hill Street Blues," with an ensemble cast headed by Daniel J. Travanti and Michael Conrad.

ABC shows were "Too Close for Comfort," a sitcom about an overprotective father, starring Ted Knight and Nancy Dussault; "It's a Living," a comedy about five waitresses working in an expensive restaurant, with Susan Sullivan, Ann Jillian, Marian Mercer, Wendy Schaal, Gail Edwards, and Barrie Youngfellow (the title was changed to "Making a Living" next season); "The Greatest American Hero," a fantasy adventure series starring William Katt and Robert Culp; and the torrid prime-time soap opera "Dynasty," with John Forsythe and Linda Evans heading a large cast.

CBS shows were: "Magnum P.I.," a detective series starring Tom Selleck, with John Hillerman; the medical series "Nurse," starring Michael Learned and Robert Reed; and "Private Benjamin," a situation comedy based on the hit movie, with Eileen Brennan, Lorna Patterson, and Hal Williams.

Finally, CBS ended two years of speculation when it named Dan Rather to succeed the retiring Walter Cronkite as the anchorman on "The CBS Evening News." Roger Mudd, a longtime CBS correspondent who for years was assumed to be the heir apparent to "the most trusted personality in America," then switched to NBC to co-anchor its evening newscast. After 29 years as CBS's chief anchor for special events and 19 years as anchorman for the nightly news, Cronkite concluded his final broadcast in this way: "For almost two decades we have been meeting like this in the evening and I'll miss that. But those who have made anything of this departure have made too much. This is but a transition, a passing of the time. Old anchormen, you see, don't fade away. They just keep coming back for more. And that's the way it is, Friday, March 6, 1981. I'll be away on assignment and Dan Rather will be sitting in for the next few years. Good night.''

PETER AND PAUL: (Mini-series) April 12 and 14, 1981, CBS. Raymond Burr

THE TWO OF US: April 6, 1981–August 10, 1982, CBS. Peter Cook and Mimi Kennedy

THE BRADY BRIDES (BRADY GIRLS): February 6, 1981–April 17, 1981, NBC. Maureen McCormick and Eve Plumb

CONCRETE COWBOYS: February 7, 1981–March 21, 1981, CBS. Geoffrey Scott and Jerry Reed

WALKING TALL: January 17, 1981–June 13, 1981, NBC. Bo Svenson

PARK PLACE: Harold Gould

BOSOM BUDDIES: November 27, 1980–August 12, 1982, ABC. Tom Hanks and Peter Scolari

PARK PLACE: April 9, 1981–April 30, 1981, CBS. Harold Gould, David Clennon, and Mary Elaine Monti

PRIVATE BENJAMIN: Eileen Brennan and Lorna Patterson (Private Judy Benjamin)

PRIVATE BENJAMIN: April 6, 1981–January 25, 1983, CBS. Lorna Patterson, William Daniels, and Barbara Barrie

LADIES MAN: October 27, 1980–February 21, 1981, CBS. *(Front)* Betty Kennedy, Allison Argo; *(center)* Simone Griffeth, Natasha Ryan, Lawrence Pressman, Louise Sorel; *(back)* Karen Morrow

NUMBER 96: December 10, 1980–January 2, 1981, NBC. Number 96 cast

BARBARA MANDRELL AND THE MANDRELL SISTERS: November 18, 1980–June 26, 1982, NBC. Phyllis Diller (guest), Irlene Mandrell, and Barbara Mandrell (hostess)

TOO CLOSE FOR COMFORT: November 11, 1980–April 7, 1983, ABC. Nancy Dussault and Ted Knight

FLAMINGO ROAD: January 6, 1981–July 20, 1982, NBC. Morgan Fairchild

TOO CLOSE FOR COMFORT: Nancy Dussault, Rebecca Holden (guest), and Ted Knight

TOO CLOSE FOR COMFORT: Lydia Cornell and Ted Knight

FLAMINGO ROAD: Howard Duff and Alice Hirson

PALMERSTOWN: March 20, 1980–June 9, 1981, CBS. Jermain H. Johnson, Jonelle Allen, Bill Duke, and Star-Shemah Bobatoon

FLAMINGO ROAD: Mark Harmon and Cristina Raines

SECRETS OF MIDLAND HEIGHTS: December 6, 1980–January 24, 1981, CBS. Robert Hogan (top), Stephan Manley and Daniel Zippi

SECRETS OF MIDLAND HEIGHTS: Mark Pinter and Jordan Christopher

MAGNUM P.I.: December 11, 1980–present, CBS. Tom Selleck (Thomas Magnum) and John Hillerman

NURSE: April 2, 1981–August 17, 1982, CBS. Michael Learned

NURSE: Robert Reed

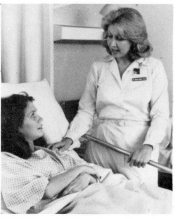

NURSE: Ann Kerry (guest) and Michael Learned

FOUL PLAY: January 26, 1981–August 23, 1981, NBC. Barry Bostwick and Deborah Raffin

ENOS: November 5, 1980–September 19, 1981, CBS. Samuel E. Wright, John Dehner, and Sonny Shroyer (Enos Strate)

NERO WOLFE: January 16, 1981–August 25, 1981, NBC. Lee Horsley, Delta Burke, and William Conrad (Nero Wolfe)

ENOS: Fran Ryan and John Dehner

LOBO: December 30, 1980–August 24, 1981, NBC. Ellen Bry (guest), Brian Kerwin, Mills Watson, and Claude Akins (Sheriff Elroy S. Lobo)

DYNASTY: John Forsythe, Al Corley, and Bo Hopkins

RIKER: March 14, 1981–April 11, 1981, CBS. Josh Taylor (Frank Riker)

WALTER CRONKITE—Last appearance on the CBS Evening News, March 6, 1981.

DYNASTY: Linda Evans and John Forsythe

DYNASTY: January 12, 1981–present, ABC. *(Front)* Heather Locklear, Linda Evans, John Forsythe, Joan Collins, and Pamela Sue Martin; *(back)* Al Corley, Lee Bergere, John James

HILL STREET BLUES: January 15, 1981–present, NBC. Michael Conrad and Daniel J. Travanti

HILL STREET BLUES: Veronica Hamel and Daniel J. Travanti

HILL STREET BLUES: Barbara Bosson and Joe Spano

CRASH ISLAND: April 11, 1981 (one telecast), NBC. Meadowlark Lemon and Greg Mullavey

QUICK AND QUIET: August 18, 1981 (one telecast), CBS. William Windom and Rick Lohman

SHOGUN: (Mini-series) September 15–19, 1980, NBC. Richard Chamberlain

SHOGUN: Toshiro Mifune

362

HARPER VALLEY P.T.A.: Mills Watson and Joyce Bulifant (guest)

HARPER VALLEY P.T.A.: January 16, 1981–August 14, 1982, NBC. *(Seated center)* Barbara Eden surrounded by cast

FREEBIE AND THE BEAN: December 6, 1980–January 24, 1981, CBS. Hector Elizondo (Sgt. Dan "The Bean" Delgado) and Tom Mason (Sgt. Tim "Freebie" Walker)

TWO THE HARD WAY: August 18, 1981 (one telecast), CBS. Fred McCarren, Lyle Waggoner, and Eugene Roche

IT'S A LIVING (MAKING A LIVING): October 30, 1980–September 10, 1982, ABC. Ann Jillian, Barrie Youngfellow, Gail Edwards, Wendy Schaal, and Susan Sullivan

BREAKING AWAY: November 29, 1980–July 6, 1981, ABC. Shaun Cassidy, Barbara Barrie, Vincent Gardenia, and the Breaking Away team

MASADA: (Mini-series) April 5–8, 1981, ABC. Peter Strauss and Peter O'Toole

MASADA: Christopher Biggins, David Warner, and Clive Francis

MASADA: Peter Strauss, Giulia Pagano, and David Block

THE GREATEST AMERICAN HERO: March 18, 1981–February 3, 1983, ABC. William Katt and E. J. Peaker

I'M A BIG GIRL NOW: October 31, 1980–July 24, 1981, ABC. (Front) Danny Thomas, Rory King, Diana Canova; (back) Sheree North, Michael Durrell, Deborah Baltzell, Martin Short

1981-82

Strikes by unions whose members provide entertainment for television affected viewers again. Before this TV year, the major-league baseball season came to an abrupt halt when the franchise owners and the players failed to agree on a matter related to the free-agent system. Approximately one third of the season was lost before players and owners reached a compromise on the free-agent compensation issue and the boys of summer returned.

Then, for a second straight year, the television season was delayed by a strike in Hollywood. Members of the Writers Guild of America struck for 13 weeks over monies derived from the new TV technologies. The strike was settled in July, with a four-year contract that for the first time gave writers a share of producer revenues from the fast-growing pay-TV and home-video markets.

There were two spectacular news events that had viewers flocking to their sets. The first was enjoyed by hundreds of millions of people in more than 70 countries as they watched Charles, prince of Wales, heir to the British throne, marry Lady Diana Frances Spencer in an elaborately staged ceremony in Saint Paul's Cathedral in London. Television brought to the world the full pomp and pageantry that is Britain with this symbol of the continuity of the monarchy and thus, the nation itself.

The second occurred shortly before the new season commenced. *Voyager II*, an unmanned U.S. spacecraft, transmitted the first ever close-up photographs of the ringed planet Saturn back to Earth. At approximately 63,000 miles from the cloud top that covers the planet, the craft's cameras and instruments became operational and the incredibly spectacular sight of the giant gaseous planet heartened earthbound scientists and awed viewers. *Voyager II* then continued on to Uranus, which it is expected to reach—and transmit pictures from—in 1986.

The writers' strike, which delayed the opening of the season, resulted in the networks introducing their new shows as they became available, some beginning as late as January. In preparing for the new TV year, the networks canceled almost two dozen series that failed to maintain consistently good ratings and announced plans to bring in approximately the same number to replace them. A distinguishing feature of the new shows was a reduced emphasis on sex. There was a general feeling that this resulted from a threatened boycott of sponsors' products by the Coalition for Better Television in protest against sex, violence, and profanity. Another feeling was that TV was merely responding, as it always did, to shifts in its audience's mood. Caught up in this atmosphere was the cancellation of two popular series that were representative of the type of programming in question, "Charlie's Angels" and "Vega$."

CBS, attempting to read the public's pulse, offered "Mr. Merlin," a situation comedy about a reincarnated sorcerer; a transplanted "Walt Disney," the longtime hour anthology; "Simon and Simon," about a pair of private eyes who were brothers; "Jessica Novak," about a TV news reporter; "Falcon Crest," a continuing drama about a contemporary family with vast California vineyard holdings; and "Shannon," a drama about a widowed detective raising his ten-year-old son.

ABC debuted "Code Red," about the trials and tribulations of a big-city fire battalion chief; "The Fall Guy," about a Hollywood stuntman; "Today's FBI," a police series; "Strike Force," a series about a big-city special police unit; "King's Crossing," a continuing drama; and "Open All Night," a sitcom about the owner of a 24-hour food market.

NBC's new entries relied in many cases on long-established stars: Tony Randall in "Love, Sidney," a situation comedy about a gay commercial artist; James Arness in "McClain's Law," about an ex-cop who rejoins the force; and James Garner in "Bret Maverick," the role he made famous in the late fifties. Other new series were "Father Murphy," a spinoff from "Little House on

the Prairie"; "Lewis and Clark," a sitcom about a New Yorker who owns a country-music club in Texas; "Gimme a Break," a sitcom about a housekeeper for a widowed police captain and his children; and "Chicago Story," an hour-long dramatic series.

Those were the programs that aired during the first part of this season. There were, of course, other shows that debuted in the traditional "second season" of the TV year. But of all the new entries, 12 survived and were on next year's fall lineups.

The CBS shows were: "Walt Disney," which was on the network for the first time (Disney began on ABC in 1954, moved to NBC in 1961, and in 1981 found itself on CBS—moving from its customary Sunday-night slot to Saturday night); "Simon and Simon," starring Jameson Parker and Gerald McRaney; "Falcon Crest," whose large cast was headed by Jane Wyman and Robert Foxworth; and "Cagney and Lacey," (second season), about two policewomen, starring Meg Foster, then Sharon Gless, and Tyne Daly.

New shows that succeeded on ABC were: "The Fall Guy," starring Lee Majors; "T. J. Hooker" (second season), a police series starring William Shatner; "9 to 5" (second season), an office sitcom with Rita Moreno, Valerie Curtin, Rachel Dennison, Jean Marsh, and Jeffrey Tambor; and "Joanie Loves Chachi" (second season), a situation comedy featuring Scott Baio and Erin Moran.

NBC's returnees were: "Father Murphy," starring former Los Angeles Ram football star and sportscaster Merlin Olsen; "Love, Sidney"; "Gimme a Break," starring Nell Carter and Dolph Sweet; and "Fame" (second season), featuring Debbie Allen repeating her movie role.

An interesting note to the concluding chapter of this book: David Brinkley, a legendary figure in television journalism, surprised many industry insiders by announcing he would leave NBC after 38 years (on radio and TV) with the network. Like Walter Cronkite's retirement the previous season, Brinkley's departure from the network signaled the end of an era for NBC. Soon after his announcement, he revealed he would join ABC.

MR. MERLIN: October 7, 1981–September 15, 1982, CBS. Clark Brandon and Barnard Hughes (Max Merlin)

STRIKE FORCE: November 13, 1981–September 24, 1982, ABC. Richard Romanus, Michael Goodwin, Robert Stack, Trisha Noble, and Dorian Harewood

ONE OF THE BOYS: Olympia Duckakis and Mickey Rooney

ONE OF THE BOYS: January 23, 1982–August 20, 1982, NBC. Mickey Rooney

9 TO 5: March 25, 1982–present, ABC. Rachel Dennison, Valerie Curtin, Jeffrey Tambor, and Rita Moreno

FAME: January 7, 1982–April 7, 1983, NBC. *(Foreground)* Debbie Allen

CAGNEY & LACEY: March 25, 1982–March 28, 1983, CBS. Tyne Daly (Mary Beth Lacey) and Meg Foster (Chris Cagney)

FATHER MURPHY: November 3, 1981–December 28, 1982, NBC. Katherine Cannon and Merlin Olsen (John Michael Murphy/ Father Murphy) at Father Murphy's wedding

LOVE, SIDNEY: October 28, 1981–April 11, 1983, NBC. Tony Randall (Sidney Shorr) and Betty White

FATHER MURPHY: Merlin Olsen, Katherine Cannon, and Douglas V. Fowley

SHANNON: November 11, 1981–March 31, 1982, CBS. Kevin Dobson (Jack Shannon) and Charlie Fields

FALCON CREST: December 4, 1981–present, CBS. *(Seated)* Jane Wyman and Abby Dalton; *(standing, first row)* Robert Foxworth, Susan Sullivan, Margaret Ladd, and Lorenzo Lamas; *(standing, second row)* Billy Moses, Jamie Rose, Chao-Li Chi, and Nick Ramus

REPORT TO MURPHY: April 5, 1982–May 31, 1982, CBS. Michael Keaton (Murphy) and Simone Griffeth (guest)

REPORT TO MURPHY: Michael Keaton and Donnelly Rhodes

MAGGIE: October 24, 1981–May 21, 1982, ABC. *(Seated)* Robert Kiger, James Hampton; *(standing)* Miriam Flynn (Maggie Weston), Garin Bougie

BEST OF THE WEST: September 10, 1981–August 23, 1982, ABC. Tom Ewell, Joel Higgins, Carlene Watkins, Christopher Lloyd, and Leonard Frey

MAGGIE: Fay Hauser, Marcia Rodd, and Miriam Flynn

FALCON CREST: Robert Foxworth and Jane Wyman

THE PHOENIX: March 19, 1982–September 15, 1982, ABC. Richard Lynch and E. G. Marshall

THE PHOENIX: Shelley Smith and Judson Scott

SIMON AND SIMON: November 24, 1981–present, CBS. Jameson Parker (A. J. Simon), Gerald McRaney (Rick Simon), and Kenneth Mars

BAKER'S DOZEN: March 17, 1982–June 30, 1982, CBS. *(Front)* Cindy Weintraub, Thomas Quinn; *(middle)* Alan Weeks, Ron Silver; *(back)* Doris Belack (Captain Baker), Sam McMurray, John DelRegno

Q.E.D.: March 23, 1982–April 27, 1982, CBS. Sarah Berger (guest), A. C. Weary, and Sam Waterston

McCLAIN'S LAW: November 20, 1981–August 24, 1982, NBC. James Arness (Jim McClain)

POLICE SQUAD: March 4, 1982–March 25, 1982, ABC. Alan North and Leslie Nielsen

MARCO POLO: (mini-series) May 16–19, 1982, NBC. Ken Marshall (Marco Polo) and Ying Ruocheng

MARCO POLO: Ying Ruocheng

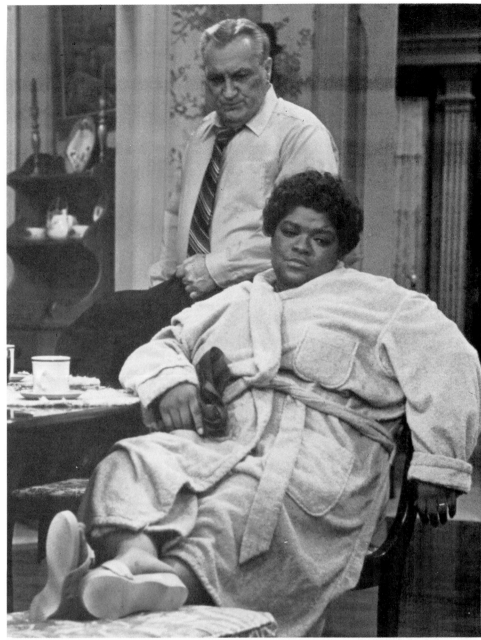

GIMME A BREAK: October 29, 1981–present, NBC. Nell Carter and Dolph Sweet

OPEN ALL NIGHT: November 28, 1981–March 5, 1982, ABC. Susan Tyrrell, George Dzunda, and Sam Whipple *(top)*

OPEN ALL NIGHT: Susan Tyrrell, Sam Whipple, Mary Jackson, and Art Kassul

JESSICA NOVAK: November 5, 1981–December 3, 1981, CBS. Helen Shaver (Jessica Novak), Andrew Rubin, and Eric Kilpatrick

KINGS CROSSING: January 16, 1982–February 27, 1982, ABC. Bradford Dillman and Mary Frann

LEWIS AND CLARK: October 29, 1981–July 30, 1982, NBC. *(First row)* Wendy Holcombe, David Hollander, Amy Linker; *(middle row)* Mike McManus, Gabe Kaplan (Stewart Lewis), Ilene Graff, Guich Koock (Roscoe Clark); *(back row)* Clifton James, Aaron Fletcher

TEACHERS ONLY: April 14, 1982–April 9, 1983, NBC. Norman Bartold, Lynn Redgrave, and Norman Fell

T. J. HOOKER: March 13, 1982–present, ABC. William Shatner (T. J. Hooker) and Adrian Zmed

CHICAGO STORY: March 6, 1982–August 27, 1982, NBC. *(Front)* Kristoffer Tabori, Maud Adams, Vincent Baggetta, and Molly Cheek; *(back)* Daniel Hugh Kelly, Dennis Franz, Richard Lawson, and Craig T. Nelson

DARKROOM: November 27, 1981–July 8, 1982, ABC. James Coburn (host)

DARKROOM: Robert Webber in an episode

NO SOAP RADIO: April 15, 1982–May 6, 1982, ABC. Steve Guttenburg

INSIDE AMERICA: April 4, 1982–April 25, 1982, ABC. Shawn Weatherly, Dick Clark (host), and Lynn Swann

TODAY'S F.B.I.: Carol Potter and Mike Connors

JOANIE LOVES CHACHI: March 23, 1982–December 16, 1982, ABC. Scott Baio (Chachi) and Erin Moran (Joanie)

TODAY'S F.B.I.: October 25, 1981–August 14, 1982, ABC. Mike Connors

THE FALL GUY: October 28, 1981–present, ABC. Lee Majors and Doug Barr

CODE RED: November 1, 1981–September 2, 1982, ABC. Lorne Greene

MAKING THE GRADE: April 5, 1982–May 10, 1982, CBS. Steven Peterman and Krista Errickson (guest)

CODE RED: Lorne Greene

379